NEW WOMEN'S WRITING FROM ISRAEL

NEW WOMEN'S WRITING
FROM ISRAEL

Edited by Risa Domb

VALLENTINE MITCHELL
LONDON • PORTLAND, OR.

Published in Great Britain by
VALLENTINE MITCHELL
Newbury House, 900 Eastern Avenue,
Ilford, Essex IG2 7HH, England

and in the United States of America by
VALLENTINE MITCHELL
c/o ISBS, 5804 N.E. Hassalo Street,
Portland, Oregon 97213-3644

Copyright © 1996 Institute for the Translation
of Hebrew Literature, Israel

British Library Cataloguing in Publication Data

New women's writing from Israel
    1. Short stories, Hebrew – 20th century – Women authors –
    Translations into English 2. Short stories, English – 20th
    century – Women authors – Translated from Herbrew
    I. Domb, Risa
    892.4'3'01'089287 [FS]

    ISBN 0-85303-307-2 (cloth)
    ISBN 0-85303-308-0 (paper)

Library of Congress Cataloging-in-Publication Data

New women's writing from Israel / edited by Risa Domb.
        p.   cm.
    Translations from Hebrew.
    ISBN 0-85303-307-2. — ISBN 0-85303-308-0 (pbk.)
    1. Short stories, Israeli—Translations into English. 2. Short
stories, Israeli—Women authors. I. Domb, Risa.
PJ5059.E8N49 1996
892.4'301089287—dc20   96-21338
                                                          CIP

Typeset by Vitaset, Paddock Wood, Kent
Printed in Great Britain by Bookcraft (Bath) Ltd

For
Miriam and Chimen Abramsky,
my teachers, mentors and closest friends
From Risa

Contents

Introduction

by RISA DOMB

A N ANTHOLOGY is a personal choice of a collection of literary works, and this anthology of short stories is no exception. Whilst I attempted to choose stories which are representative of contemporary Israeli women's writing, ultimately it is my personal taste which has dictated the stories to be included. Furthermore, my selection sometimes reflects not only my own affinity with the texts, but that of the translators'. Taking this into account, inevitably injustice has been done to some writers whose work has not been included. No doubt another anthology will put this bias right.[1]

I must state from the outset that my reasons for compiling an anthology of women's writing are not politically orientated. I am not at all convinced that in the pursuit of a purely literary study, one should isolate one group of writers on the basis of their gender. However, I regard the emergence of women's writing in Israel as a special case. Male-orientated national concerns have preoccupied modern Hebrew writing since its beginning, and it is the departure from this tradition which has brought about a shift of marginal characters to the central stage in Israeli fiction today. This opened the doors to an unparalleled influx of women writers who realized that they could now participate in writing. Although they broke new ground, most of their writing is not revolutionary, angry, intense, or committed to change, like other feminist literature. But, to my mind, by no means of lesser importance, is their poetic achievement of pushing the frontiers of what can be written about. Often their protagonists are women, struggling to expose the illusion embedded in the romantic

1

myth, attempting to create a more authentic female voice. The majority of these authors are of the new generation of women novelists that have emerged in the last few decades. Their achievement is remarkable, especially when seen in the context of the development of Hebrew literature. I would therefore like to place them within the historical framework of the development of Hebrew literature. For the convenience of English readers, I refer as much as possible to translated works, even though as a result the picture presented might be somewhat stilted.

Israeli literature is part of a continuous literary corpus, called Modern Hebrew literature, which extends beyond fixed geographical boundaries. Modern Hebrew literature emerged not in Israel but in Europe over two hundred years ago, at the time when Jewish life began to come out of its seclusion and reach out for Western culture. It was then that Modern Hebrew literature, along with European Humanism, shifted its vision from God to man and became secular, giving rise to the movement of Jewish Enlightenment (1781–1871).[2] This movement began in Prussia as a rationalist movement and by the middle of the nineteenth century had assumed a romantic-nationalist aspect, as the major Jewish cultural centres shifted from western to eastern Europe.[3] The wave of pogroms that struck Russian Jewry in the 1880s undermined the realization of the ideal of Jewish emancipation in Europe and indirectly initiated the Zionist movement. This brought about yet another geographical shift. The different waves of Jewish immigrants finally moved the Hebrew cultural centre from Europe to the Holy Land, or Palestine as it was then called. It is only since 1948, with the establishment of the State of Israel, that 'Israeli literature' came into being. Because of this unique history any discussion of women's writing has to take into consideration the two geographical centres: Europe, and Palestine which subsequently became Israel.

In these centres, women writers were scarce. During the whole period of Enlightenment, Rachel Morpurgo (1790–1871) published one volume of mediocre poems, and was the exception in Modern Hebrew literature.[4] Jewish tradition was partly responsible for this situation, since it had opposed the education of women. Hebrew was taught only to young men, as it was used for religious and ritual purposes in which women had no part. Hebrew, which has been used by Jews ever since Biblical times, over a period of some 3000 years, was adopted as the means of creating the new enlightened Jewish culture in Europe. Thereby Jews established a new relationship with modern culture as well as with the Jewish past.[5]

Women, however, could not participate in the new literary activity. Hebrew poetry drew from biblical and liturgical sources, which were not familiar to the majority of women. Jewish women in Europe could give vent to their poetic talents either in Yiddish, their spoken language, or in Russian, but not in Hebrew.[6] In the early 1920s, Fradel Stock and Zilla Drapkin wrote erotic poems in Yiddish, but when it came to writing in Hebrew there was a poetic as well as a linguistic obstacle.[7] Whilst Yiddish writing did not insist on the national element as a required poetic norm, Hebrew poetry did. Professor D. Miron convincingly claims that because of this prevailing poetic norm at the turn of the century, women's Hebrew writing, and women's poetry in particular, could not be accommodated.[8] There were no women writing poetry during this period of time. The leading male poets, H.N. Bialik (1873–1934) and S. Tchernichovsky (1875–1943), established the ideological dictum which insisted on the symbiosis of the collective experience with the private, of the myth of the nation with the myth of the individual. Since women did not take part in the initial stages of the Hebrew revival, they could not respond to these poetic demands. Only when the poetics of Bialik's generation was challenged by the new generation of writers of the 1920s, did women's poetry come to its own.

The development of women's prose writing was different from that of poetry for several reasons. At the turn of the century, Hebrew prose was more open to autobiographical and confessional writing than poetry was. Women were able to contribute to this genre, as they could incorporate the full range of their experience. In addition, their horizons and experiences were further extended as they began to assume a full part in the Jewish national revival in Palestine. Significantly, these women writers

3

were married to public figures and were exposed to people and events which shaped the new society. They had all received a secular education in Europe, and were as ideologically committed as their male counterparts. They were just as eager to describe the new pioneering life and to propagate further immigration to the homeland as their male counterparts. A further reason which might have facilitated women's participation in prose writing was put forward by Y. Berlowitz.[9] She suggested that, to a certain extent, it was due to the efforts of Ben-Yehuda[10] who attempted to transform what he regarded to be the cold, rational literature of the Diaspora into a more sensuous and emotional literature in Palestine. Believing that women are more emotional than men, he appealed to them for their help and opened the pages of the leading literary magazines, of which he was one of the most influential editors. He encouraged women to write, including his wife Hemda Ben-Yehuda (1873–1951), whose sentimental stories describe with great pathos the important role of women in raising the future generation in the homeland. Unlike her optimistic stories, Nehama Puhachevsky (1869–1934) portrayed the disillusioned pioneers and described their hardship, especially that of the Oriental and Yemenite communities in the new settlements. Yita Yelin (1868–1943) gave a detailed picture of the everyday life of a Jewish family in Jerusalem, and like other contemporary women writers, focused on her immediate surroundings. Their writing was not revolutionary, but rather followed contemporary male writing. They shared a common feature with their male counterparts in their aim to express their love of the country.

A similar theme dominated most of women's poetry written in the period subsequent to the First World War, when the prevailing literary norms of Bialik's generation were challenged and personal, lyrical poetry was allowed to flourish. This was one of the reasons why at that juncture, women Hebrew writers could participate and unlike their European counterparts, found their niche in poetry more than in prose. The outstanding woman poet of that period was Rachel[11] (1890–1931), whose poetry can be seen as an uninterrupted hymn to the Land of Israel. This does not necessarily stand in contrast with Miron's suggestion that her

4

poems are 'typically feminine' and that 'they are lyrical, short, emotional, intellectually unpretentious and they deal with subjects such as loneliness, illness, death.'[12] In her poetry Rachel paved the way for a galaxy of women writers. Elisheva[13] (1888–1949) who, like Rachel, started her literary career in Russian, wrote romantic, sentimental poetry in Hebrew, and in her prose dwelt mainly on the themes of alienation and love. By contrast to the conservative poetics of these two writers, the poetry of Esther Raab (1894–1981), the only native poet at that time, was radical. In her poetry she expressed unrestrained desires, and used the cruel landscape of Palestine as a suitable background for expressing her social rebelliousness and the anarchy of her emotional state. This was also reflected in her uncontrolled, unrhymed verse, and in her deliberately 'incorrect' syntax.[14] Yocheved Bat-Miriam (1901–1980) was just as radical in her poetry. Whilst the themes of her poetry were traditional, such as yearning for childhood innocence, love for a person or a landscape, fear of death and alienation, she managed to assimilate the techniques of contemporary Russian poets, first of the Symbolists and then of the Futurists. This created a tension between her idiom and her Jewish piety, which made her verse difficult, and it often defies the critic.[15] Leah Goldberg (1911–1970), as well as Anda Pinkerfeld-Amir, wrote verse for children, but she is best known for her modernist poetry. In line with contemporary European modernist poetry, she often expressed the poet's inner struggle during the act of writing, and the difficulties in overcoming this inherently artificial medium. Leah Goldberg was active in the field of literary criticism and translation, especially from Russian, and was in search of revolutionary techniques. She experimented with prose as well as drama. Her play 'Ba'alat Ha'armon' ('The Castle Owner') introduced the difficult theme of the Holocaust to women's writing. Modern Hebrew drama was slow to develop. This was partially because traditional Judaism opposed performing arts, but mainly because in its early stages there were only few Hebrew-speakers who could participate as an audience.

None of these women poets spoke in the first person plural as did some of their male counterparts. They wrote out of personal experience without attempting to represent it as the collective experience. They paved the way for the future generation of contemporary women poets. Dahlia Ravikovitch (b. 1936) was established as one of Israel's leading younger poets when her first book of poems appeared in 1959. Her verse conveys a strong feeling of disorientation and loss, and a complaint about the injustice that the poet finds in existence itself. Invariably, this injustice is expressed as a strong feminist protest against a suppressive society.

Ravikovitch's rebelliousness stands in contrast with the traditional and religious world of Zelda (1914–1984). She is the only contemporary woman poet who was orthodox, and who possessed the inner security of a religious person. These two poets, different though they are, were not provocative in their writing and cannot be defined as 'feminist' writers. They did not strive to differentiate themselves from male writing, but rather to complement it. This poetic stance has changed with the appearance of poets such as Dalia Hertz, Hamutal Bar-Yosef, Hedva Harehavi, Rachel Halfi, Agi Mishol, Maya Bejerano, Sigalit Davidowitz, and Leah Ayalon. Although they do not overtly call for sexual equality, they expose erotic feelings and emotions which are exclusively feminine, and which their predecessors were inhibited to express. The revolutionary poet who paved the way for the poets of the 1980s was Yonah Wallach (1944–1985). She dared to present a provocative woman with blatant sexuality and expressed a wounded and rejected female soul which turned towards madness and mystery.[16]

As shown above, women poets enjoyed a fairly uninterrupted span of creativity ever since lyrical and personal poetry became acceptable within the poetics of the canon. However, due to cultural and historical circumstances, the development of women prose writers was intermittent. Devorah Baron (1887–1956) stands out as an exception, as she links the early beginnings of women's writing at the turn of the century with its subsequent development. Although some of her stories are situated in Palestine, she invariably returned to the small town in Eastern Europe and portrays the difficult burden of orthodox Jewish womanhood in a restrained realistic style.[17] It should be noted that Baron's preoccupation with recapturing the vanished Jewish world was not entirely out of line with mainstream Hebrew fiction, which sought to reflect the collective experience of the community.

The experience of war was naturally the main theme which occupied the literature of the first generation of Hebrew writers in the newly established Israel, the writers of the War of Independence of the 1940s and early 1950s. Still feeling the responsibility to help shape their society, they glorified heroism and comradeship. It has been suggested that women could not reflect any of this in their writing, as it was outside their personal experience. Be this as it may, their writing was peripheral to the central experience of the country. It was only with the next generation of writers, the generation of 'The New Wave'[18] writers of the 1960s and 1970s, that women's prose writing found its niche. These writers reacted against their predecessors and strove away from regionality towards universalism, and from reflecting the problems of the community to reflecting those of the individual. They sought to free themselves from the influence of the Russian literary tradition. This had been a major influence in Hebrew literature ever since it had flourished in Russia. When the Zionist dream came into being, the hitherto shared communal values began to shake. Instead of the native Israeli hero fighting for freedom, marginal and displaced characters began to occupy Israeli fiction. All the stories in this anthology are from this period on.

Amalia Kahana-Carmon (b. 1930), whose first book was published in 1966, is the most prominent female fiction writer of the New Wave as well as of this one. One of her stories is included in this anthology. She is a prose poet whose phrases are often rhymed and the rhythm of the unique syntax, the short, cut, sentences contribute to the musical quality of her writing. The language is rich in metaphors, and she often uses unusual biblical words, esoteric expressions, and elevated style. In so doing, the author draws attention to the medium she is using, and sharpens the reader's ability to accept the magic of the fictional world from which it is is created. Much of her work, such as the story included in the anthology, concerns ordinary human beings who seek and find a mystic moment of revelation in their everyday lives, only to lose it again. The pluralistic expansion of Hebrew letters enabled the novelist Noami Fraenkel (b. 1920) to incorporate new immigrants in her prose. These remants of the Holocaust are the complete antithesis of the model of the native Israeli hero who occupied Israeli fiction for over a decade. The protagonist of the story included in the anthology by Sh. Hareven (b. 1931) is a survivor who was left with the unbearable memories of her experiences during the Holocaust. She joins the gallery of Hareven's other lonely Jerusalemite characters of anti-heroes. It is worth mentioning Hareven's collection of essays on social and cutural issues in her book 'Tismonet Dolcinea' ('Dolcinea Syndrom', 1981). They are an important contribution to the field of this declining literary genre. Significantly, as well as Hareven's story, three other stories in this anthology portray different aspects of the Holocaust experience. Ruth Almog's (b. 1936) protagonist reflects the effects of the trauma not only on the first generation of survivors, but on the second generation. Like most of Almog's characters, she is a passive woman who, like the seven women in her book 'Nashim' ('Women'), cannot find an expression for their intense femininity and eroticism. The protagonist in her novel 'Shorshei 'Avir' ('Roots of Light', 1987), who did have the courage to search for it, failed even in finding an alternative. Leah Aini and Nava Semel, of a younger generation of writers, reflect the undercurrent of tension between the older generation of survivors and the younger generation, raised in Israel. On reflection, it seems to me that there is no discernible difference in the portrayal of this subject between male and female writers.

Yehudit Hendel (b. 1926), in her novel 'Rehov Hamadregot' ('The Street of Steps', 1955), wrote about social and cultural clashes, tensions and misunderstanding arising when Eastern and Western Jews meet in their homeland. This uncomfortable facet of Israeli society was not often reflected in fiction previously. In her more recent book of short stories, 'Kesef Katan' ('Small Change', 1988), Hendel reveals an hostility to men, well illustrated in her story in the anthology. Shulamit Lapid (b. 1934) took an even more blatantly feminist stance in her novels and short stories, as the story included demonstrates. H. Bat-Shahar (a pseudonym) belongs to the writers whose main works came to the fore in the 1990s, and who mark a new direction in Israeli women's writing. Together with Haya Esther and Mira Magen they mark an interesting new phenomenon – the entry of practicing orthodox Jews into mainstream Israeli Literature. Savyon Liebrecht, Nurit Zarchi and Orly Castel-Bloom express an overt female declaration of identity, eroticism, repressed sexual urges, and social and cultural protestations in their works. Haya Esther (a pseudonym) is the only writer in this anthology to portray the life of Israeli women within the confines of strict Jewish orthodoxy.

From this brief survey we can see that the change in the mainstream Israeli experience has meant a greater openness in literature, and a pluralism of voices has emerged, incorporating those of women writers. As a result, the writers could at last abandon their traditional place in Hebrew literature and assume their rightful role in its development. There are several questions that can be asked when reading these stories: Do women write differently from men as a result of biological differences? Women have different bodies and different physical experiences, but do these differences produce a distinctively gendered discourse? It is true that women have written within the constraints of patriarchy and followed the generic conventions of an essentially male culture for generations. Women sometimes write like men and men can write like women. Is it therefore possible to show that women's writing is gendered in some way? These questions are currently in the forefront of literary debate, and I hope that the examination of the following stories will help towards answering at least some of them. Above all, it is hoped that this anthology will introduce the English reader to the wider reaches of Israeli fiction.

NOTES

1. To the best of my knowledge, there have been only two other anthologies in English of Israeli women's writing: Ribcage: Israeli Women's Writing, ed. Carol Diament and Lily Rattok, Hasassah, New York, 1994, and Stories from Women Writers of Israel, Star, New Delhi, 1995. The only other two

anthologies are in Hebrew: *Sippurei Nashim Bnot Ha'aliah Harishona* (*Stories of Women of the First Aliah*), ed. Y. Berlowitz, Tarmil, Tel Aviv, 1984, and *Hakol Ha'acher-Sipporet Nashim Ivrit* (*The Other Voice: Women's Fiction in Hebrew*), ed. L. Ratok, Hasifriah Hahadasha, Hakibbutz Hameuchad, Tel Aviv, 1994.

2. See Simon Halkin, *Modern Hebrew Literature From the Enlightenment to the Birth of the State of Israel: Trends and Values*, Shocken Books, New York, 1974.

3. See the introduction to T. Carmi, *The Penguin Book of Hebrew Verse*, 1981.

4. See E. Silberschlag, *From Renaissance to Renaissance II*, 1977, pp.157–76.

5. See R. Alter, *Modern Hebrew Literature*, 1975.

6. For more on this see the introduction to *Gender and Text in Modern Hebrew and Yiddish Literature*, ed. Naomi B. Sokoloff, Anne Lapidus Lerner, Anita Norich, Jewish Theological Seminary of America, New York and Jerusalem, 1992.

7. For more on Zilla Drapkin see Janet Hadda's article in *Gender and Text in Modern Hebrew and Yiddish Literature*, op. cit., p.93–112.

8. See Dan Miron, *'Imahot meyasdot, 'ahyot horgot, 'al shtey hathalot bashira ha'eretsyiraelit hamodernit* (*Founding Mothers, Stepsisters*), Hakibbutz Hameuched, 1991 (Heb.).

9. See Yaffa Berlowitz, *Sippurei Nashim Bnot Ha'aliyah Harishona*, op. cit.

10. Ben-Yehuda is the compiler of the first Hebrew Dictionary and is regarded as the initiator of the use of Hebrew as a spoken language.

11. Pseudonym for Rachel Bluwstein.

12. Op. cit.

13. Pseudonym for Elisaveta Ivanovan Zirkowa.

14. For more on Raab's poetry see the article by Anne Lapidus Lerner in *Gender and Text in Modern Hebrew and Yiddish Literature*, op. cit., pp.17–38.

15. See A. Band, in *The Modern Hebrew Poem Itself*, Shocken Books, New York, 1974. For more on the poetry of Bat-Miriam see the article by Ilana Pardes in *Gender and Text in Modern Hebrew and Yiddish Literature*, op. cit., pp.39–63.

16. See the critic Ariel Hirschfield in *Modern Hebrew Literature*, op. cit., pp.20–23.

17. See, for example, her book *The Thorny Path and Other Stories*, Israel Universities Press, 1969, and *Hebrew Short Stories, An Anthology*, selected by S.Y. Penueli and A. Ukhmani, Institute for the Translation of Hebrew Literature, 1965, Volume One, pp.169–181.

18. As it was termed by the leading Israeli scholar Gershon Shaked.

1

Until the Entire Guard has Passed

by LEAH AINI

FROM TIME to time he couldn't resist leaning over the rail of the balcony to peer at the path leading to his house. He still had some twenty minutes to wait, and the men didn't usually arrive early, although Dr Mashiah, the dentist, was capable of popping up suddenly a quarter of an hour before the rest, eager as ever, his hat crumpled in his hands.

He smiled to himself nervously, and turned to inspect the living room once more. The two heavy armchairs had been moved against the wall, and the round table brought into the middle of the room, where the imitation-crystal hanging lamp cast a slight shadow on the navel of the room. A woollen army blanket, old but freshly laundered, was spread on the table meticulously. In the centre, a new pack of cards stood to attention together with writing paper and a fountain pen carefully filled with ink. On the footstool stood the old fan, poised and ready to rattle the air. He glanced at the blanket once again and then left the rail and hurried to the sideboard. His gaze darted among the ornaments until he found what he was looking for. He placed a polished glass ashtray on the table and then returned to the balcony, swallowing his excitement.

Passers-by walked down the street with hands clasped behind their backs, and children scampered among them. They sauntered down the street and back again. The intense heat of the Sabbath eve was still exhibiting lavish signs of dying, and most of the men were clad only in white vests and shorts. The children jumped about barefoot. Old women sat on rickety chairs outside their houses, flapping in vain at the fetid, steamy air with flowery sweat-soaked handkerchiefs.

His wife came in and he turned again to inspect the room. Sophie, who was in the final months of her pregnancy, dragged the four tall chairs to the table and smoothed the blanket from time to time. He didn't rush to help her. Instead, he leaned his elbows against the blazing rail and watched her with concern. Now she had only one house-dress left – all the others were too small and stifled her stomach. He glanced at her belly, which stood out before her like a strange hill teeming with life, and a tiny thrill of delight ran about at the base of his spine, like an animal with multiple slender legs. They had been married about three years, but had decided not to have the child until they were properly established in the little carpentry workshop. And indeed, only when the old women who spent the summer days glued to the walls of their houses began to greet the meticulous and prompt carpenter and his delicate wife, hurrying to take him his meals even in the broiling midday heat – it was only then that Sophie had wanted to conceive, and he willingly consented. But the peak of social acceptance was when Baruch the upholsterer, to whom he sometimes brought furniture frames for covering, suggested that he become the fourth hand in the traditional card game, which was an established routine among several groups of players in the southern neighbourhood. He remembered how his fingernail reddened with excitement on the frame of the bare chair, and he couldn't help wiping away his sweat with the back of a hand powdered with itchy sawdust.

He was already sufficiently versed in the ways of the neighbourhood to know that the upholsterer's group, which should really be called the dentist's group, was the oldest and most respected. After Dario, the old porter at the electrical appliances shop, succumbed to a fatal heart attack – there had been much gossip as to who would be the fourth hand. The other member of the club was Samson the butcher, owner not only of his big shop with its modern and sophisticated cold-storage facilities, and the empty lot near the school, but also of the grocery store attached to the shop, which was leased to the tiny shopkeeper. Baruch the upholsterer was also known for spending his spare time repairing vehicles that had been written off as wrecks. With admirable determination, he often worked wonders, sending some rusty and wheezing old banger, bought with the limited savings of a soldier, racing down the road like a wild colt, with hooves flailing and nostrils steaming.

But presiding over the club was none other than Dr Mashiah, the widower dentist, who lived above his little surgery and was widely respected for his gentle hands and modest fees. In particular, he earned the gratitude of mothers, because at the start of the school year he would lecture the school children on proper brushing and deficient nutrition. Not only that, but afterwards he would examine the mouths of the urchins free of charge.

Now Levi rubbed his calloused hands with pleasure, and smoothed down his light shirt. Sohpie had gone to work in the kitchen and he again turned his back on the room, scanning the street anxiously. Suddenly, a great fear crept, like a chilling blast of wind, onto his face, stiffening his sprouting stubble. The heat was unbearable, but that wasn't the problem. The game, which took place every Sabbath at the home of one of the players, was to be held for the first time in his house, and he wondered how he would manage to get past 11 o'clock. Usually the game finished at midnight, since all were early risers, but the critical time could be expected to come an hour before this, and suddenly he was no longer confident of the fortune that had seemed to smile on him till now.

Light taps on the door roused him, and he hurried to the entrance, greeting the old dentist with evident pleasure. Gradually the others appeared, scrubbed and perfumed and wearing neat white shirts, rubbing their broad hands together in keen anticipation, as if scenting a victorious run of cards. Sophie came in too, wearily smiling, moving ponderously, to greet the guests and to pour cold water with lemon slices into glasses. Her neck flushed at the compliments of the men on seeing her full stomach, infused with new life, and she made an effort not to spill water on the tray in her delight, hurrying away to hide in the kitchen.

13

The host pressed the button of the fan which hummed softly, and they all took their places round the table. The cards were distributed at first with slow deliberation, and then with growing momentum from round to round. The dentist, who loved to sing to himself, soon began humming softly while he deftly sorted his cards, and the butcher, though used to the distracting crooning, tried to set his fleshy face in a frown.

Levi smiled thinly and swivelled, in the intervals between his turns, to write down the names of the participants in the order they were sitting. From time to time he stared at his hand, at the accordion of cards alternately opening and closing, his heart singing the fourth verse. For two and a half hours the game proceeded smoothly, as the small sums of money piled up alternately in front of the host and the butcher. The dentist, who was used to losing because he was a poor player, didn't seem unduly perturbed, and he continued with his soft humming, although the upholsterer was visibly tense during the deal, and was often enraged at the sight of a desirable card tossed casually to one of the others. At around 10 o'clock Sophie appeared again, bearing a silver-plated tray which exuded the smell of fresh baking, went away and returned with slices of moist cucumber, hard-boiled eggs freckled with paprika, and red cubes of sweet watermelon. As one, the four men threw their cards on the table, moved their chairs back in anticipation, and hastily set about the food. Levi glanced at his wife with satisfaction, seeing her sinking gently into one of the armchairs, her hands clasped contentedly around her stomach, revelling in Dr Mashiah's sighs. The dentist was licking his thin and oily fingers like a child, before seizing another helping of juicy watermelon.

'Well done, Sophie!' The plump butcher was complimenting her now, sugary saliva running down his solid chin, his eyes moist with desire.

Only Baruch the upholsterer was bolting his food, as if eager to return to the table as quickly as possible and recoup his losses.

When the refreshments had been consumed, Levi helped his wife rise from the armchair, a line of worry etched between his eyes. Sophie ignored his look and approached with hands clasped to gather the dishes. When she returned for the third time – now with cups of fragrant coffee on a little tray which had muddy pools gathering at its edges – she was already fingering the tightly stretched button on her belly, and her movements were jerky.

'Perhaps you should go and rest, you look very tired!' suggested Dr Mashiah, and she responded to his kindly eyes with awkward gratitude. 'Yes, you should go and lie down,' said Levi, a cautious threat in his voice. Then he glanced knowingly at the rectangular clock on the sideboard, expecting his wife, in extreme nervousness, to follow suit.

A soft pallor spread over Sophie's face, and her lips were clenched. Now she thrust her hands into the big pockets of her smock, stretching the tight cloth across her belly, which seemed to have swelled appreciably in the last hour. She shrugged her shoulders, in vain ignoring the penetrating looks of her husband, until she blurted a hasty 'Goodnight' and all but fled from the room. The butcher, whose turn it was to deal, gathered the cards towards him very slowly, his worried eyes still preoccupied with the strange disappearance of the hostess. As he began shuffling the pack, he turned cautiously to the dentist, whose delicate fingers were tapping smoothly on the blanket.

'Maybe her time has come?' he asked hesitantly, with a meaningful glance at the carpenter.

The dentist shook his head, smiled, and gathered up his cards eagerly. Impatient to start the game and annoyed by the interruption, the upholsterer urged the carpenter, who was still a little stunned, to make up his mind and throw down a card.

'Come on! Come on! Let's get back to the game!' he urged, and Levi, startled, threw down one of his cards without even noticing its value.

He wiped away his sweat and looked fearfully at the butcher, but the latter was already ordering his cards, arranging his best sets, as usual, in the upper storey, and, looking pleased with himself, he turned to seize the card thrown down for him in telling haste.

'What's true is true. A poker face you don't have …' the dentist teased, enjoying the sight of the butcher's childish face, while humming melodiously.

15

The butcher's hairy eyebrows rose for a moment in disdain, then he angrily ignored the words.

Levi took his eyes from them, but while still debating whether to peer at the clock again or to throw down another card distractedly, he was forestalled by the first hand-clap, sharp and loud. He swallowed his saliva and froze in midthrow, even though it wasn't his turn. A series of loud and harsh hand-claps came rolling down in the wake of the first: a repetitive, staccato avalanche, assaulting the ears of the players. Trembling, he discarded a red queen, and peered at the others, startled.

For the moment they weren't troubled by it, with the exception of Baruch the upholsterer, who moved uncomfortably in his chair, his lips pursed. After a few minutes he couldn't restrain himself and he cried, 'That's your crazy neighbour, right? Damn it! You can't even play a quiet game of cards round here!'

'What crazy neighbour?' hummed the dentist in amusement.

The upholsterer threw down his superfluous card angrily and explained, 'My wife told me. The deaf old woman who lives upstairs, who hardly ever goes out. Three times a day she claps her hands for half an hour – without stopping! I don't understand how you can live here!' he uttered resentfully, the newly drawn card conciliating his voice a little.

Levi struggled with his vocal chords, until he heard his metallic mumble creeping out somehow – 'You get used to it ...' and then glanced sideways at the butcher, seeing the green number under the thick hair of his arm, lit up for a moment in the light of the lamp as he reached to snatch up the card thrown down for him. Taking courage he added, 'It's because of the Germans. That's what she told someone ... told me.' He didn't know where his voice was coming from, but his lips continued to form the words. 'The convent where she hid during the war was close to the SS head-quarters. Every time the guard on patrol passed near the place, the nuns taught the frightened children to clap their hands until the entire guard had passed ...' he whispered, flushed with shame. He looked again at the butcher, desperate for his understanding, but he only lifted dull eyes to the lamp, shrugged his powerful shoulders and said dismissively: 'Nobody came out in one piece.'

He hurriedly lowered his eyes in time, making an effort to decide which of his cards to throw down, but not one of his cards matched the others. For a moment he stared at the jumbled sets, and then closed the coloured fan, as if by doing so he could stop his ears as well.

The dentist hummed sadly and laid a short set of clubs on the table. 'It isn't so bad,' he said. 'I have a patient, an Auschwitz survivor, who's completely round the bend.' He launched into a lengthy story, but Levi could hear only the beating of his heart, pursuing in vain the tempo of the hand-claps, as stiff and as rhythmic as boots thudding on a parade ground. The upholsterer, whose luck had improved somewhat, waved aside the distraction impatiently, again urging the others to concentrate on the game.

Gradually the clapping subsided and faded, as it had begun – out of nothing. The clock ticked on to midnight, and the dentist rose from his chair, stretching gracefully, despite the considerable sum he had lost. The upholsterer, gratified by his victory, was still poring over the score. When he found that the butcher was in fact the overall winner, he glowered, but began to share out the profits fairly. Now they all rose and went out to the balcony. The butcher stuffed the banknotes into his pocket with obvious impatience, and hung back a little from the others. The heat had subsided now, but the air was still humid and leaden, barely stirred by the lazy, intermittent gusts of wind rising from the sea. The dentist tried to take a few deep breaths, but the experiment only elicited a sour grimace from the upholsterer, who was wiping the sweat from the nape of his neck with a handkerchief.

At last the guests began to take their leave of the host, and the last to shake his rather tense hand was the dentist. His handshake was soft and consoling, like a woman's and his eyes were kind.

'Tell Sophie that we enjoyed the meal very much, and many thanks. Next week – at my house, don't forget,' he warned, taking his pale blue hat from the hook and softly closing the door behind him.

Levi's polite smile disappeared at once. Slowly he shuffled towards the living room, seeing the heap of cards on the table, the blanket which had slipped slightly, and the ashtray, black with watermelon pips. The coffee cups were encrusted with muddy grounds, and the lamp glared tastelessly. He switched off the light and the fan, and stepped dejectedly to the kitchen. Like an automaton he took two ice-cubes from the freezer, found the little kitchen towel, wrapped the ice in the soft material, and turned to the bedroom.

Sophie was sprawled on the bed, her pallor melted into cold sweat, her hands hanging limp at her sides. Her large belly towered above her, concealing most of her neck from him. He approached the bed, trying in vain to dispel the wave of nausea that had assailed him, and turned over his wife's hands.

Sophie let him do this, as if she were a doll. The palms of her hands were red and hot, her flesh tingling like roasted meat. He enclosed a dripping ice-cube in each of her tormented fists, and wrapped them both in the towel. Then he moved away from her and sat on the end of his bed, his back turned to her. From behind him he heard the whisper of the ice in her hands, and the rasping of the towel in turns.

Sophie's voice was hoarse.

'Did they say anything?'

Long minutes passed before he found an answer, deep in his seared throat:

'What do you think ...' he began harshly. Then he withdrew a little, trying to sound casual as he added, 'They talked about the neighbour. I think they believe it ...'

Sophie didn't answer, and he knew from the sound of her frantic breathing that tears were streaming down her cheeks. Still he didn't turn round.

'I've asked you before,' she began again in turmoil, 'I've asked you before to tie me up, bind my hands with rope, with steel wire ... at least when there are people here ...'

He uttered a scornful sigh and half-turned towards her. 'And what will you do instead? Beat your head against the wall?' His shoulders rose and fell wearily. 'No, we've discussed it before. You're better off clapping your hands, that way at least you're not doing yourself any harm, they can think what they like ...' Sophie began to wail like an abandoned cub, the towel making its way from her chilled hands to her wet face.

'Stop it! Stop it, that's enough!' he pleaded in despair.

'But it was so, so important to you ... to be the fourth hand and ...' she choked.

'I don't give a damn,' he snorted, but his eyes were wandering.

'And what's going to happen, what's going to happen when the baby is born,' she panted, gasping for breath. 'How will he sleep? I'm a mad woman, a mad mother. I'd be better off dead!' She was groaning now, harried by spasms of weeping.

He rose stiffly, wrenched the damp towel from her face, and then, without any intending to, his hand shot out like an arrow and slapped her cheek.

Sophie's head slumped forward at once, lifeless, but a powerful shudder racked her stomach, and then her weeping resumed, soft and moaning.

'Quiet now, be quiet.'

He straightened her trembling legs, raising the light blanket from her dominant, over-weening belly, which was all-consuming.

Sophie curled up in the bed, her hands limp on her chest, her breathing still irregular.

'Go to sleep. That's enough for today. We'll sort it out,' he concluded angrily.

He returned to his bed and continued sitting with his back to her for some time, until he realized she was asleep. He turned cautiously, and began to undress.

When he slipped into bed, he momentarily clutched her hand, soft as a cotton-wool cloud, intending to put it to his mouth. But he changed his mind, and the hand sank back sleepily and powerlessly onto the bed. He laid his aching head on the pillow, listening to her faint breathing. A yellow moon shone at the window, and by its light he could see the mighty belly, teeming with life. Suddenly it seemed to him he could hear the breathing of the embryo too, tiny and rapid. He smiled to himself, remembering what Dr Mashiah had told him once.

'At this stage,' the dentist had told him, 'he's already smiling and frowning – even sucking a thumb! There's no doubt,' he

19

concluded pleasantly, 'he's going to be a fine, healthy boy!'

A thrill of thin pleasure tickled him, its thousand feet wandering along his spine. Calmly he closed his eyes, slowly dreaming of his baby, and he is already as he himself was in his infancy. Plump and soft-haired, laughter rolling from his mouth, with two pearly teeth blocking a pink and greedy tongue. Sophie, close by him, distracted and sweating, clapping her hands to death. Fear reigns in her face, in the stamping black boots and the claws of the Alsatians. But look at the child, he too is clapping a soft, unsteady hand against its partner, clumsily, without coordination, and starting to dance around in his new white shoes. His mother is very far from him, but he – his tongue hanging from his mouth in a bold and spirited laugh, his head giddy and spinning – and for a long time he turns and turns, clapping and clapping, until the entire guard has passed.

Translated by Philip Simpson

2

A Good Spot

by RUTH ALMOG

I

IT COULD be said of Tzila Kasten that there were two things in her life: her son Urinko and her balalaika.

As for her husband, Arnold Tanzmann, the ties between them were like the tangles in a head of very curly hair: if you leave it uncombed for more than a few days, the only answer is to cut it off.

Tzila Kasten had known some famous people: Marcal Rubin, the composer who had succeeded in getting to Mexico; Broch the novelist, who had fled to the States. There were women too: Milna Yoshinka, who did not escape (Tzila only found this out many years afterwards) and Gertrude Kraus, who, like Tzila, had come to Palestine. Tzila had had the privilege of appearing with Gertrude once (though not in the capital city), but even so, she had never had quite the necessary courage, and her hair remained long, curly and full of tangles until the day she died.

From the moment Urinko was born, Tzila was convinced there was nobody like him in the whole world. But Tanzmann said the child cried too much, so Tzila would lull the child in her arms for hours or whole nights at a time. Tanzmann did not allow this: his book on the rearing of children stated quite clearly it was not to be permitted, but he himself slept the deep sleep of the innocent, waking, like them, at a prescribed hour every morning, so Tzila was able to manage.

When Tanzmann complained, Tzila would say: 'Perhaps he's just hungry.' But Tanzmann replied that his book said a baby should only be fed small portions at regular intervals, and that was the end of the matter.

'Then perhaps I don't have enough milk,' Tzila would say. But Tanzmann explained that the author of the book, a famous German pediatrician, wrote that if a woman could suckle for ten minutes at a time this was a clear indication she had sufficient milk, and that any overfeeding could have dangerous consequences.

Tanzmann had found the book in a second-hand bookshop. It stocked largely German titles, since the refugees from Germany, Austria and Czechoslovakia had arrived in Palestine penniless but with trunks full of books. This had certainly been the case with Elsa, whom Tzila had once made a special journey to Jerusalem to visit, and got such a shock when she saw her that she rushed straight out again to find the nearest grocer's.

Sometimes Tzila would gather together all the things scattered inside her like the fragments of shrapnel in the body of their neighbour Mr. Zahor. Apparently the doctors had used a magnet to take the pieces out, and in winter the pain was particularly acute, overshadowing his face like darkness on the fringes of the sunset. It was at such times that Tzila would permit herself to confide to Tanzmann that there was nobody like Urinko in the whole world. But Tanzmann refused to be swayed, and his reply was always: 'He's a crybaby, that's all. He yowls all night like a randy cat.'

Tanzmann's voice was like sheets of metal clashing together. Sometimes Tzila would pluck up the courage to go on and whisper, 'Perhaps he's just hungry. Perhaps I don't have enough milk.' Tanzmann's replies to this would come in a voice composed only of the echo of iron striking iron: a harsh, grating screech which made the ears ring unpleasantly. His exact words would be: 'I've already told you once what I think. In any case, obedience is the most important lesson in life, that's what my book on education (he had purchased it in the same shop) says, and if we don't start as we mean to go on there'll be a little outlaw in the house, just like Tzila Kasten was when I took her off the street to marry her. And perhaps I was wrong to do it.'

Tzila did not take this seriously. For Tanzmann, practically everyone was an outlaw, especially people who played or sang in the street or in cafés, as she had indeed once done. This meant that Elsa was an outlaw too, of course, and Tanzmann was of the opinion that God had chosen to punish her by taking away her son.

'But,' whispered Tzila – people had already forgotten how strong and resonant her voice had once been – 'he had consumption.'

'And who gave it to him?' shouted Tanzmann. 'Not God? Well?'

Which was why when Tzila went to visit Elsa she kept it a secret from Tanzmann and said instead that she was going to buy new strings for her balalaika. Tanzmann could not object to this; the contract drawn up for them by Dr. Uichselbaum the registrar contained a specific clause regarding the balalaika, and Tanzmann was an 'honourable man' who 'kept his promises', as he was fond of saying. Indeed, signing the contract had been his idea in the first place.

Tzila was a tiny woman with a round, flattish face like an Eskimo's. The skin was stretched tight over her cheekbones, as thin and pink as the skin of a peach, but because it was also as fine as the net canopy which protected Urinko from mosquitos and flies it was possible, from close up, to decipher the network of bluish, fragile veins which ran beneath it. She had a little red nose like a cherry and her china-blue eyes shone and twinkled. She was cheerful by nature, and it came as no surprise that her great love was music; when Tanzmann was not at home she would put the baby on the rug in the main room and play record after record on her gramophone until her arm ached from turning the handle.

She became very plump after having the baby, and since her movements remained quick and agile she resembled nothing so much as a ball rolling itself along. It was obvious she could not return to work as a dancer, but this was of no importance; firstly, because she was more of a singer, and secondly because Tanzmann's contract contained a specific clause covering this situation.

At the beginning, Tanzmann called her Tzila, as did her friends. Thereafter he took to calling her Cecilia, and she would cringe when they heard him.

Tanzmann was not tall, but standing next to Tzila he looked like one of those young trees which get planted at the entrance to courtyards: they have smooth trunks and their leaves are cut into spheres and other shapes. He gave this impression largely because of his hair, which sprouted smoothly and profusely in all directions, with no parting. He wore a black hairnet in bed; if he forgot to do so, his whole head would look like a crowded pincushion in the morning.

He had hollows where his cheeks should have been, and gazed unforgivingly out at the world from shadowed hollows. His sharp features bore a permanent expression of defiance, and his red lips, swelling out below a moustache which was so fine it looked as though it had been drawn on with charcoal, stood in such stark contrast to the rest of his emaciated features that they rendered them dubious.

Initially, Tzila called him 'Fuchsi', or 'my fox'. 'Not just because you look a bit like one,' she explained, 'but because you managed to catch the silly goose.' 'But it's not completely right, is it,' she would continue, 'because you haven't gobbled her up.'

'Not yet,' replied Tanzmann, laughing. 'Not quite yet.'

For all that, she continued to call him Fuchsi for some time, because another of her friends, a cousin of Stefan's who now lived in Haifa up on the Carmel, was also called Arnold; and to set him in contrast to her friend Leo, with whom she had once been head over heels in love, and whose muse had not deserted him.

Ah, Leo! He had married a beautiful, fashionable woman, who had brought such hats, such silk dresses, with her to Tel Aviv. Tzila's heart wept, and remained in pieces for some time afterwards, right up to when Urinko was born. Leo's wife would sit in the café on the promenade where Tzila was working on the very same evenings Tanzmann would go there for a game of chess. From the moment Tzila came out onto the little stage, she fixed her gaze on the woman as she sang the plaintive gypsy love-songs. This might have been the reason she finally decided to sign Tanzmann's contract.

Tanzmann was an expert tanner. He had a small factory on the outskirts of the city and would go to work on his bicycle every morning. Once Tzila was left alone, she would feed Urinko every time he cried. The doctor had said that at his age – he was five months now – he could begin to take cow's milk or even solids provided they were thoroughly heated first. Perhaps this was the reason he cried at night.

One day Tanzmann returned unexpectedly early, apparently because of a headache; he had a tendency to suffer from migraines. He found his wife sitting on the armchair in the main room with Urinko in her lap, feeding him thick white liquid.

Tanzmann checked the time and announced, 'It's bad enough you haven't waited long enough between feedings, what do you think you're doing giving him something that looks like porridge?'

Tzila, startled, made no reply.

Tanzmann took the child from her and put him back in his cot in the small room. Urinko immediately began to cry. Tanzmann picked him up and bounced him up and down, shouting, 'Quiet! Quiet!' But the child was screaming.

'If you don't stop, I'll ...!' bellowed Tanzmann, and shook the child to and fro. But it was hopeless. Tanzmann choked back his anger, put him down, and returned to the main room. Tzila was still in the armchair.

'Look what you've done now, you outlaw,' hissed Tanzmann, and bent over her. An ugly, blue blotch appeared on her left cheek. She gripped the arms of the chair and did not move.

'Do you think this is why I took you off the streets? Is this the thanks I get?'

He bent over her again and the blue blotch became still uglier.

Tanzmann went off to shower. It was a very hot day (which perhaps explained the headache) and he stank of sweat and animal skins.

The sound of the rushing water almost obliterated the baby's cries. Tzila got up, picked up her balalaika and went outside. She sat in the yard on a little stool and played until evening came; the summer sun took a long time to set. The neighbours heard her plucking the strings and remarked, 'How well she plays.' But her voice was hardly audible.

When the sun finally set she went inside and prepared a salad and two omelettes, sliced some black bread and put a bottle of cold water on the table. She called Tanzmann and they sat opposite each other eating in silence. When Tzila looked at her watch, Tanzmann said, 'You've already fed him once, so you can't feed him again now. That's your punishment.' A sneering smile appeared on his lips as he closed them over the end of the sentence.

As was to be expected, that night Tzila lulled her son in her arms. Her breasts had swollen, and the milk had hardened into little crusts around her nipples, but she dared not feed him, not even when she heard Tanzmann snoring. She dozed during the moments the bitter pain receded, but for much of the night her thoughts roamed in her head like travellers lost in the desert. She imagined, for example, that she had sold herself like that brother of Jacob's – what was his name? – just for a bowl of soup. She also considered the meaning of the lies. But this she did not think was so dreadful; she had been an actress, a singer, she was used to it. All the world's a stage, she thought, all actors. So what? Not so terrible. No. But the other matter was more of a problem, the one which forced people to turn the world into a stage. Ah, well, she thought, it can't be helped. There's nothing I can do. The deep desolation of this thought washed over her and almost engulfed her, and she prayed that Urinko would be as free as a bird.

II

And so Urinko grew up between the soft, plump arms of Tzila Kasten who sang him songs by Schubert, and the coarse hands of Tanzmann which bore an ineradicable smell of tanned leather not yet turned into shoes and wallets.

When Urinko was five years old, Tzila brought him a harmonica, which he quickly learned to play so well that he enchanted anyone who heard him. Sometimes Tzila would smile and say to him, 'Suppose we were to go out on the main street and find ourselves a good spot? We could play, and I could sing, too, and we could make a little money and run away to another country, because we can, you know. The war is over, Arnold has gone, Leo goes to Vienna every summer now ... '

The first time she said this, Urinko asked what a 'good spot' was, and she explained it was a spot in the thick of things with lots of passers-by. The second time, Urinko asked, 'Why?' Tzila hesitated before replying, and Urinko said, 'Mutti, when I'm a big boy I'll work with skins and I'll have a big factory and I'll make wallets and shoes from snakes and crocodiles, and I'll make lots of money and I'll take you around the world like Mr. Fogg and his servant, what was he called, Mutti?'

Tzila had forgotten the servant's name. 'But you're such a good musician,' she said.

'I like the smell of the skins,' replied Urinko.

But for the moment he played the harmonica, and took apart and rebuilt all sorts of things. Despite Tzila's insistence that he read lots of books because the books her friends like Franz, Arnold, Leo and even Elsa had written naturally contained all there was to know about culture, Urinko preferred to repair things; and when a neighbour's watch, or radio, or gramophone, or even fridge stopped working, Urinko would be called in, which meant he spent his days running from house to house.

When Urinko went out on his repairs, Tanzmann (if he happened to be at home) would say to him, 'I hope you're not doing it for nothing. That's exploitation, it's not right.'

Urinko had a specific way of working. First he would dismantle the object, observe its structure and make a sketch. Then he would rebuild it, and always, the broken part would miraculously begin to work again. The neighbours were impressed, and sometimes Tzila would permit herself to tell Tanzmann that Urinko was a genius, an Einstein even. Tanzmann was dismissive: 'He's a little outlaw, just like you.' He said this because Urinko was not a good student; his teachers complained that he was disruptive, and that he bullied and threw stones.

More than once a windscreen had been broken and Tanzmann had been forced to pay for the damage. Once Urinko had even broken another child's wrist. The case went to the juvenile court and Tanzmann was fined; but Urinko paid too, in another way.

So it was that Tzila would still whisper to him that perhaps it was time to find a good spot somewhere 'so that you'll never have to have a long face ever again'.

But Urinko refused. He maintained that he liked the smell of skins and that he intended to begin work as soon as he finished his army service.

'But you'll finish high school first?' begged Tzila, and Urinko promised her that he would.

The neighbours said the boy had golden hands but that the rest of him was uncivilized, offensive and downright dangerous, and they refused to let their children be his friends. Once Urinko's voice broke his shoulders broadened and his arms thickened like treetrunks. Nobody dared fight with him now, and he spent the breaks between lessons alone. Even his father had begun to hesitate before touching him.

In his two final years of school he changed; he stopped playing the harmonica and doing repairs. Instead he buried himself in his studies, particularly in mathematics, and in his free time he played chess against himself. Sometimes he would play a game with Tanzmann, or go to the café on the promenade to watch the masters. Once, he challenged the best of them to a game and checkmated him in seven moves, to the general astonishment of everyone. But he never went back after that.

It had now become clear to Tanzmann that he would have to sell his factory, and he grumbled to Tzila: 'If that outlaw thinks I'm paying for him to go to university, he's got another think coming.'

'A college then,' suggested Tzila.

'College or university, Jerusalem or Haifa, I'm still not paying.'

Tzila smiled and said: 'Then perhaps it's time for me to go and find myself a good spot again.'

Tanzmann looked out at her from creases of shadow and said, 'We signed a contract, remember? Promises are made to be kept. But do you know something? I don't care. You can both go, you and him. He was born an outlaw and he'll stay an outlaw, and so are you, and there's nothing to be done about it.'

Tzila took her balalaika out into the yard. She sat on the little stool and played. The neighbours heard her plucking the strings, but her voice was hardly audible. 'She's playing again,' they remarked to each other.

Urinko did not hear her; he was no longer at home. By now he was taking apart tanks and spending odd spells in prison. When the news came one day that Urinko had been wounded, Tzila made the long trip to the military hospital at Sarafend to be with him. She took her balalaika with her and found that the hospital was a good spot; the soldiers said she had a marvellous voice. Before she had left, Tanzmann had said to her, 'He used to be a little outlaw, now he's a big outlaw.' But Tzila's voice rang through the hospital ward like silver bells.

Urinko spent a long time in hospital, and then he was sent to a convalescent home, from which he moved to Haifa to work in the docks. He never came back home. 'You see?' said Tanzmann to Tzila. 'I told you so.'

Urinko worked hard and saved his money. He supplemented his scholarship by working as an official mourner, watching the body at night and on the weekends. Sitting at his post on Friday nights he could see lighted windows where people sat at tables covered in white cloths, with candles in candlesticks. The tables were festive, beautifully set.

Urinko graduated with distinction. Tanzmann announced, 'I'm not going. That suit I brought from Germany which you filled with mothballs is too tight.'

'How do you know if you haven't tried it on?' murmured Tzila, and Tanzmann bellowed back, 'Why do you have to argue over every little thing?'

Tzila went alone. After the ceremony, she and Urinko went for a walk; he pointed out the place where he worked and said, 'Do you see? That's my good spot.' Then he took her by taxi to the park where he used to sit and study, but the park was closed. Tzila spent the night in a hotel and they left Haifa together the following day, she to return home and he to go south to work in the oil drills.

One day Tzila received a letter from Urinko which said:

'Dear Mother, I'm going to Australia. I've found a good job there, also in the oil business. If I get rich I will send you a ticket.

I'm sure there are a lot of good spots in Melbourne. Yours, Urinko.'

'He's gone to Australia,' said Tzila to Tanzmann, who had not asked.

'I'm not surprised,' said Tanzmann, 'it started out as a prison colony, didn't it?'

'You'll see,' said Tzila, 'he'll be a millionaire one day.' But her voice was dead.

As the years went by, Tzila became thin again. Her Eskimo cheeks became even flatter, like planes of sand etched into lines by the desert wind. Every so often a letter would come, and the neighbours would say: 'Listen to her singing. What a voice she has, it's just like bells.'

The first letter said:

'Congratulate me, I have married a millionaire, and now I am rich. I work hard for her father. But I'm happy.'

'Congratulate me, I have a son. We have called him Uriel. I am rich and working hard. But I'm happy.'

'They're short, his letters, aren't they?' said Tanzmann.

'Of course they're short,' said Tzila, 'since when did outlaws write novels?'

Tanzmann looked out at her from shadowed hollows. His hollow cheeks showed no movement, but it could be seen that a little hump was forming on his back.

Another year went by and another letter came. It said:

'Congratulate me. I have a daughter. We've called her Aliza. I am rich. I'm working harder than ever since my father-in-law died. Now I run the whole business. But I'm happy.'

This time Tanzmann did not complain that Urinko's letters were short; he got up from the armchair, went to the kitchen, took a bottle of water from the fridge, poured a glassful and drank. The water filled the hollows for a moment. Tzila came in after him: 'What's the matter with you? Stand up straight.'

'Keep your advice to yourself!' roared Tanzmann.

These three letters were the only ones Tzila ever received from Urinko, despite the fact that she wrote to Melbourne once a fort-night. Sometimes, as she sat opposite Tanzmann in the evenings knitting a sweater for Uriel or for Aliza – a bigger sweater every year – the vague thought of how many good spots there must be in Melbourne would make its way into her head. But when she looked up at Tanzmann and his hump, the thought would dissolve into the notes of some song or other. Then she would pick up her balalaika and play until Tanzmann complained, 'That's enough for today.'

III

The years passed, and Tzila, who had once looked so like a ball rolling itself along, became a matchstick with a silver head. Her hair was as long and curly as ever, and just as full of tangles, but she never cut it. Tanzmann sold his factory and retired. He kept a stock of tanned leather at home and would sometimes sew a wallet or a satchel which Tzila would post to Melbourne together with the latest sweater she had knitted. Sometimes he would repair things; he liked taking them apart and putting them back together. If he found an old radio thrown away in the street he would bring it home, and he once even hired the dustman to drag back an old fridge for him.

'That's dangerous,' said Tzila. 'I've read about children falling into them and getting trapped. They die.'

'There aren't any children left around here,' replied Tanzmann.

While he tinkered, Tzila would play, but the neighbours could hardly hear her now since the area had become so noisy. Buses and lorries filled the street. So even though Tzila sang loudly, nobody told her now what a marvellous voice she had.

One day she received a letter from Aliza. She knew immediately that it was not Urinko's writing, and had worked out who had written the letter before she even opened the envelope. Aliza wrote:

'Dear Grandma, I am writing to tell you my father has disappeared. He told us one day he was going to America on business, he left, and we have not heard from him since. That was almost two years ago. Do you know where he could be? I miss him very much. If you know anything, please write. Yours, Aliza.'

'I told you so,' said Tanzmann. 'I always knew he was an outlaw who couldn't keep his promises.'

Tzila wrote back at once: 'Dear Aliza, I don't know anything. For years I have written to you every fortnight and you have never written back. However, if you do hear anything about Urinko I would be grateful if you would write and let me know immediately.'

Aliza did write from time to time after that, but it was always the same letter: Urinko had not come home and nobody knew where he was.

Tzila had become an old, sad woman, and Tanzmann had become a hunchback, and they were cold in winter. 'We can afford a little luxury now, Cecilia,' said Tanzmann, and bought an electric blanket.

They say it was the blanket that did it. Who can tell? They were two old people sleeping the sleep of the innocent, and they felt nothing.

The neighbours smelled the smoke and summoned the fire brigade, but Tzila and Tanzmann had become cinders long before they succeeded in putting out the fire. Of the balalaika Tzila appeared to be holding in her charred hands only the strings remained, twisted like broken springs.

The neighbours approached the Australian Embassy, but the family informed them that they had not the faintest idea as to where Urinko might be found. The clerk explained to them that the granddaughter had suggested looking for him in one of the hippy colonies on the West Coast, though her mother's private investigator had reported, among other things, that the case was hopeless and that he would never come back. The report said: 'I traced the subject to San Francisco, where he is making a living busking; he plays the harmonica. Everything points to him being a member of a cult though there is no hard evidence to this effect; such cults are extremely suspicious of strangers and cannot be investigated.'

Thus Tzila's prayers were answered, if she had only known.

The neighbours made a collection to bury them side by side along with the strings of the balalaika. They even paid for a tombstone, upon which was inscribed: 'Here lies Tzila (Cecilia) Kasten, singer and musician, and Arnold (Fuchsi) Tanzmann, tanner, who kept his promises.'

Translated by Deborah Silver

3

Among the Geranium Pots

by HANNAH BAT-SHAHAR

EMBRACING THE blue, that was what it felt like. The great, pure pure expanse of colour. Concentrating on it as on a painting by Rothko, in order to compose her peace of mind.

An early, unexpected spring. The slender branches of the Persian lilac were already covered with tender buds. The starlings had already scattered from the dense, dusty cypresses. And Dafna, her daughter, on her way to school. Taller, with the little satchel on her shoulder. Her legs which had grown longer, light sandals on her feet. It seemed like only the evening before, the exhibition of her dolls on the fence, trying to attract the attention of the children in the street. Shabby, crippled dolls, wrapped in rags. As if they were on sale. And the grey evening descending on them. And the crows circling in the air above them, screeching from the cypress trees, as if they had discovered carcasses here.

Never mind, the child's amusing herself, said her mother. Lying in the rocking chair, forgiving and appeased. Bring me the tartan rug, Felina. And Felina hobbled on her ailing legs along the cool, curving railing of the balcony. The pain in her back and the laborious gait. It would never go away, it was chronic. Hard to accept, she was still a young woman, after all. And now this new idea too – Mother's or Dafna's – of decorating the balcony with geraniums, setting the pots out along the railing. I'll paint it and call the painting: My Balcony. Something cluttered, rusty tins, a dense, tangled growth, half of it withered. The roots exposed. As if it had been uprooted from the courtyard of her memory – Morduch's and Mary's and mute Sarah's courtyard. But Mother and Dafna came back from the shop laden with beautiful, round clay pots. Do you think that Raoul will like them, asked Mother. But what did it matter if he liked them. In any case he wouldn't take any notice of them. The old argument between them. All Mother could think about lately was Raoul. Their only important guest. Suddenly she was so crazy about him. His white double chin. The self-satisfied expression on his face. But he's got kind eyes, she would say, look at his eyes. With a kind of tender enthusiasm. He's changed since he returned from abroad. Life over there, alone in a foreign country, has changed him. And you never quarrelled. The divorce, you have to admit, was your idea. A caprice. I never understood it and I never will. And I still think that it was out of the kindness of his heart that he agreed to give you a divorce, mistaken, forgiving kind-heartedness. And perhaps cowardice, too.

Mother of course couldn't imagine the shameful feeling of revulsion. The kind that had overcome Felina last night, in her dream, when she felt the four hairy puppies that suddenly burst out of her father's room writhing between her legs. And even now she holds onto the railing in a panic, seeing the dogs come running out of the open balcony door, falling over each other like dirty balls of wool, tumbling on the wooden bench. Afterwards they begin to bark, first threateningly and then gaily, at the street.

A fine morning. The downstairs neighbour peeps at her. She wraps her robe more tightly round her. Where have the starlings disappeared to. Raoul promised to send workmen to fix the disintegrating fence. The neighbour nods in agreement. Mother is happy too. She offered Raoul the yeast cake strewn with sesame seeds. She always serves him on the dainty flowered plates. Raoul probably remembers them from the days when he used to come to visit Felina's father on business. She, a young girl, would offer him the laden tray. He would follow her hand with his eyes as it transferred the plates and cups to the table. Cautiously his eyes would climb to her arm and her face. And once, unthinkingly, she had touched his hand as she set the cup before him, and he recoiled as if he had been burned.

That fence is falling apart, last night Raoul leant on the railings next to her. His solid presence. His broad hand signalling, throwing a large, rapid shadow over the garden. In her long hostess gown, with her hair loose on her shoulders, was she still beautiful in his eyes. The starlings fill the cypresses at night. The old lamp over the building entrance lights the rose garden path. Yesterday Dafna found a lizard in a crack in the fence, she tells him. He shudders slightly, as if in disgust. With the lizard or with Dafna. Was he still suspicious. As when she was in the hospital after giving birth. Looking at the little cot with cold eyes. He did everything that had to be done conscientiously. He even brought a photographer. Insisting that the two-day-old baby be photographed. Pretending to be happy in his fatherhood. And constantly, urgently questioning the nurse: Who does she resemble. Not me or Felina. So dark. And those strange, thick eyebrows. Felina's heart fell. And there were days when the suspicion grew inside her: She's not mine. They made a mistake in the hospital, they mixed up the babies. A mistake, it's all a mistake.

The crippled dolls on the fence. Dafna's strange. After all, she isn't a baby any more. Raoul is entitled to interfere in her education. To criticize the two women, especially Felina. They spoil her, encourage her strangeness. The ugly dogs, the broken dolls, the uprooted plants. A big pile of empty plant pots on the balcony. A kind of fragile clay wall, dark in the night light. The children gathered in the street below, to laugh at Dafna, have dispersed. Why doesn't Felina call her to come home too. The hem of her faded gown sweeps the balcony dust. Her mother's rocking chair creaks. Afterwards she'll invite Raoul to join her for a cup of pungent, exotic Earl Grey tea. All dressed up with her blond hairdo and her jewels. Her clothes smell strongly and suffocatingly of lavender. And the puppies, all of a sudden, separate from each other on the bench. Dark, wet shapes. As if they have already accomplished their designs. They crawl to their wicker basket in the corridor. Above them, from the illustrated wallpaper, the birds look out. As if the starlings, in mid-flight, have frozen here.

Wave after wave the birds come to the cypress trees. Dafna gathers her dolls into her lifted skirt. She is twelve years old. Like me the first time in the courtyard. Standing in the grey, grimy, vaulted stone passage, with the sky above like a lake trapped between the walls. A very clear lake, pure and deep. By contrast the paving stones are old and worn. Sliding over them with a little shudder. A dull noise, an inner sound, erupts from them. Or maybe from the tunnels going down to the deep, greasy warehouses next to the wall. A revolting smell of urine and donkey droppings comes from them. Father's big warehouse is here, and inside it are mattresses and iron beds with their springs bouncing up and down, creaking in the hands of the porters. Old Samoori's donkey is here too, rubbing against the wall and pulling straw out of a torn mattress. Mute Sarah hits him encouragingly on the rump. Her awkward laughter stretches her wide mouth. Her sister Mary climbs the stairs holding a broom and a clattering tin pail in her hands. She emerges from the gloom of the tunnel into the light pouring with extravagant abundance from the lake of the sky. Her dress is wet, her legs are muscular and her feet are bare. She beats the donkey's back and her sister, the broom flies furiously. And then, to the sound of her shouts, Sarah and the donkey are sucked into the whirlpool of the houses. Its thin hairy legs gallop as if they are about to break. Mary grins. She sweeps the scattered straw into a heap, and stands flashing her eyes: The porters, where are the porters.

They're all grown up, with Morduch a boy among them. And so he is bare to the waist and in short pants. Climbing with acrobatic agility onto the piles of mattresses to straighten and steady them. His efficient, disciplined seriousness, without a word. And when he suddenly slides, lithe as an animal, down the side of the truck, his sparse, faded hair flutters in the wind. Give it to me, the Romanian porter jokes with Mary, taking her frizzy hair in his heavy hand. For your bald brother, for Morduch. He almost pulls her hair out. Slipping away from him, shouting and laughing, Mary escapes and he pursues her to the alcove in the passage wall. He hides her there with his body.

The smell of the big, hot, dusty stone. Her father puts his arm around her shoulders: Here you are, Felina. Big-bodied, the long elastic suspenders emphasize the sturdiness of his chest. His good nature, his friendliness. Chatting to the porters and calling them by affectionate nicknames. See here, Morduch my dear, just like I promised, a big, red watermelon. The knife passes from hand to hand and slices the fruit. The boy's eyes above the donkey's back, soft, melting. And as if he doesn't dare, his hand trembles, offering Felina the slice. Then he watches from the side, as she digs her white teeth carefully into the soft, juicy flesh. The knife is still in the hands of the laughing porters, they call to the Romanian: Have you finished. And kick the peels towards the donkey in the filthy passage.

His mother sits in the blue-painted doorway. A broad woman, wrapped up in summer too in warm, bright rags. The two pillars of her legs resting wide apart on a pair of stools. She doesn't move. Even when Mary drops down at her feet, covering her face shyly with the corner of her slipping robe, singing in a hoarse, tuneless voice: Who's that treading on my grave/Who's that disturbing my rest. The mother's face is quiet and untroubled as that of the ripe sunflowers swaying beyond the wooden picket fence in the evening breeze. It is I, your beloved/It is I treading on your grave, Mary goes on singing sadly. Her sister Sarah scratches the blue wall with her nails. She hurts herself and whimpers softly. No one takes any notice. Morduch ties the donkey's rope to the fence. He stands there for a moment, his back to Felina, without going inside. His balding head, his grey undershirt and the scarred, scratched skin of his arms. From behind the fence old Samoori curses: The donkey's hungry, Morduch. He shouts and still Morduch does not move, his back to her. And suddenly he's off. Running towards the vaulted passage, escaping into the gloom saturated with the smells of the marketplace: rotting vegetables and dust. His mother grumbles: Majnun – madman. But Mary hushes her. She raises her head and says to Felina: Go now. Your father must be worrying about you. And there's a strange coldness in her voice.

Three cups of tea on the low balcony table. A flowered china teapot, slender and elegant. In a little while Raoul will come. Mother cuts the cake. Lays the folded napkins beside it. Briskly her hands set the table. Her rings shine in the yellow light of the lamp. Its light splashing on the path seems to withdraw, gathering itself into its own borders. The rosebuds peep out of the darkness.

Where's Dafna. The car stops next to the broken fence and its lights go out. Raoul steps out, waves at the balcony. He came, Mother smiles triumphantly this time, too. She draws the tartan rug over her knees. Everthing is ready. Dafna shows the guest in and immediately retreats into the darkness of the house. His shadow dances for a moment on the wall. Then it climbs, brushing the table, to the empty chair.

A light goes on in the back room. It shows through the window on the side of the balcony wall. The evening breeze brings up a pleasant smell of flowers and wet grass from the garden. Mother asks about her business affairs. In spite of the divorce, she has placed all her property in Raoul's hands. In fact, he has been in charge of her affairs ever since her husband's death. The shop was sold, but most of the apartments are rented out for key money. And he tells her about the tenants. Old and immobile. The expenditure exceeds the income. Today, for example, he had hopes of making a certain profit. An elegant woman came to his office, a singer, she said. She wanted to put her apartment up for sale. To leave – to escape, you might say, her husband, herself. To emigrate to France. And she sat there for hours, crying, begging him to let her off from having to pay her part of the key money.

Cars nose into the alley. Momentarily, in a flash, illuminating the fence. Suddenly the lizard which had been nesting among its cracks, or another like it, appears on the balcony wall, behind Raoul's back. He does not notice it. His big, heavy hands lie on his parted knees. His square head thrusts forward slightly from the collar of his suit, as if he is trying to listen to the sounds of the night. The birds are already silent. And in the stillness the only sounds to be heard are his slightly grunting breaths, the murmur of distant traffic, the cup touching the saucer.

Scales. The notes of the recorder drip into the silence, delicate and tremulous. Gradually he relaxes in his chair. His tenseness evaporates slightly. His hands come together in his lap. Dafna's practising. She abandons the scales to attempt a short children's song. At the end she stumbles and climbs up again. And then in a burst of confident enthusiasm, as if something delightful and wonderful has been revealed to her. The same tune, over and

39

over again. Like a scratched, discordant record. He looks at Felina
expectantly, but she is silent. Her eyes are fixed on the scrap of
star-studded black sky between the buildings and the trees. From
the close, bird-laden branches of the cypresses a gentle twitter
rises, a murmur goes up.

'Yesterday Morduch came to see me in the office.'

Raoul's voice is unexpectedly loud. Intruding into the tremulous
notes of the recorder. Her mother's rocking chair lunges forward
and stops. Again the nape of his neck moves away from his collar.
In fact his entire back detaches itself from the back of the chair.
The legs of the chair creak beneath him. Thrusting forward like
a goring ox.

'I bought a few of his paintings a long time ago, to decorate the
office.'

A pause. Even Dafna stops. The silence solidifies. Her mother,
in particular, overdoes it. She turns her head away sharply from
Raoul. Stands up and clings to the railing with a desperate air. Her
thin, weak hand wrinkled as a chicken's leg, all knuckles and skin.

'Look, Raoul. You must know building workers,' she interrupts
him, speaking fast: 'We have to mend the fence.'

'Morduch wanted to see the paintings. He misses them, he
said. He just happened to be passing the building and the blind
was open.'

Opposite the balcony Persian lilac and pepper trees. Their
sharp, fresh smell borne on the evening breeze cooling her
burning face. Mother sails along the railing. Talking fast. Garrulous.
Trying to show Raoul, to prove to him: That low stone fence is
cracked. The whole building is dilapidated. A man is needed.
Energetic, enterprising. The neighbourhood is really excellent. A
quiet, pretty street. New buildings have been built further up the
road and the prices of apartments in the vicinity are soaring.
Nearby a historical site has been discovered, Jason's tomb. Once
there was a mosquito-ridden swamp there. They dug it up and
there it was. A beautiful tomb. They restored it and renovated it,
they even planted a park around it. And only this building. The
paint is peeling in the stairwell like leprosy. The old stones are
crumbling, and the winter and the damp have made things worse.

And maybe someone has damaged the fence, the workmen who mended the pavement. She doesn't know. One day the floor will give way under their feet too and collapse.

There's nothing for her to worry about. It's a fine, strong, stone building. If only it wasn't so cold and gloomy most of the day. Fact: none of the neighbours, the key-money tenants, want to sell. In spite of the neglected garden, the weeds, the dusty cypresses. He's already told her the same thing twenty times. And now he continues his story:

'I told Morduch that I like his paintings too. There's something simple and elemental about them. They remind me of Juan Miro.'

But since when has he taken any interest in painting. In art. This is something new. The stimulating smell of the pepper tree leaves revives her senses. When she was a child Mary used to pull off the narrow leaves and tell her fortune by them: Love, hate, jealousy, friendship ....

'Morduch wasn't pleased by the comparison. "You think I'm an imitator," he said.'

In the depths of the house the puppies growl. Huddled together and quarrelling over their places in the wicker basket. Filthy, woolly, what was the dream she dreamt. Dafna goes on trying to play the song.

'What did you say, Felina.'

'That you're right, Raoul. Morduch's an imitator.' Her sharp laughter is quarrelsome and provocative.

His face pales and recoils. His double chin quivers. With difficulty she swallows the provocative laughter. But why did he mention Morduch. Flattering her: he hung paintings in his office. Juan Miro. He should concentrate on his own affairs. The economic sphere: real estate. Apartments. For sale, for rent, and for key money. The fence. Workmen. I'll send them tomorrow. I'll speak to a contractor. Don't worry. You can rely on him. That's what her mother would say to her later in her room. He's always at your service when you need a man, pleasant, well-educated. Her skinny hand trembling on the tartan rug.

It's hot in Mother's bedroom. A stifling, sourish smell. Opposite the bed, on the little screen, a picture from the movie comes into her memory: he has succeeded in persuading the girl to go sailing with him. They set sail together, but not in the direction he promised. She insists that he take the boat back to the shore. Her beautiful face is arrogant and angry. What's the matter with her – she said before that she loved him. And now this adventure is not in the least to her liking. She might even hate him because of it. Her voice is sharp and supercilious. Felina's mother opens her mouth wide. Her lips are wet. Her bosom rises under the cover. The lovers' quarrel excites her.

I'll never be loved, said Raoul to Felina in the dark room. It astounded her. In the window she heard the wind sobbing in the trees. His sorrow contracted in his naked hairy shoulders. She felt tempted to respond to him. To embark with him on the little voyage.

Something shrill, stammering, bad, insinuates itself into Dafna's playing. She plays the wrong notes, stumbles, the recorder wails. The sounds are sharp and broken as the sounds made by a dumb throat. Dafna tries again, breathing wildly into the hoarse reed. Torturing it. To make there be a miracle, to make it produce a sound. Pulling the sounds to pieces like the dolls she shamelessly exhibited on the fence. To entertain the children in the street.

Felina shrinks in her chair. The soft warm cushion behind her back. Still there in the tree tops, in the dark, the birds lie in wait. Her legs are heavy. She is nailed to her place, stiff and cold. When will Raoul go, leave her alone. Her shoulders and her back bristle nervously. The pressure in her chest, like on long wakeful nights. Mother offers Raoul a cup of tea. Their voices recede and only the echo of the recorder pierces her ears.

The class finished earlier than expected. An opportunity to sit in the café for a while. From the corner of the street a man in a long, black cape loomed up in front of them. Morduch signalled Felina to keep calm: Don't be afaid. The man stretched out his hand, his long cape flared threateningly. Satan himself, Morduch chuckled softly. But to Felina it seemed that she had already seen him before, or someone like him, standing next to her sick father's bed. The waitress burst out angrily: Go away, madman.

But afterwards it was hard for Felina to concentrate on the students' conversation. He came here with us just because of you, one of the girls whispered to her. Who do you mean, Felina was alarmed. Morduch of course. And her friend added: He doesn't usually join the crowd.

His silence was oppressive. His forehead had grown high due to his chronic loss of hair. Suddenly she felt mesmerized. As if he had succeeded in transfixing her from his corner with his quiet, thoughtful look. He asked about Raoul. And his sisters, Mary and Sarah, how were they. He was surprised, did she really still remember them. Incredible. She tried to stop the commotion raging inside her, eroding the walls of her heart. An upheaval of emotion. She turned away from him to the group. Listening without hearing anything. Afterwards she would remember how his eyes had scrutinized her face. He did not join in the conversation, just sat and listened to them. And for some reason her own laughter then sounded crude and silly in her ears. At the café door she dared to offer him her hand in parting. Hating herself for her ingratiating smile, her patronizing behaviour: You don't say anything. You don't like us, do you. But his hand tightening round hers was narrow and blazing, like a white-hot bar of steel.

The living room is decorated with her large paintings. She looks at them as at alien objects. Their bold, pretentious colours give rise in her to revulsion and pain. Her faith in her own expressive powers suddenly seems childish and absurd. To draw in simple lines, like a beginner. Something modest. A view of a balcony. At first the delicate, shifting shades of the yellow, the blue and the radiant pink only at the edges.

Dafna has given up her attempts on the recorder. Now she is concerned only for the repose of the puppies. Standing with them in the corridor where she has been summoned by her grandmother to say goodbye to her father. 'Do you have to talk here too,' she asks. Raoul shrugs his shoulders. They part in silence and the frozen birds observe them from the wallpaper. Why don't they try to curb the child's caprices, it seems to her that Raoul is asking himself. And why does he keep on visiting them. What is it that draws him here. They were contagious as a disease.

Their impractical world, like the huge, eccentric blotches of colour staring at him from the paintings. Felina's hostess gown covers up her sick legs. Her mother strokes her old furniture affectionately with her emaciated hands. And the child, Dafna, is fonder of the animals than of her father.

The fence is visible from the entrance lobby. A ghostly blueish light streams onto it from the lamp. Her mother was exaggerating, it's only a little broken. It will survive. But it certainly looks very neglected. His hand strokes its rough chilliness. Catches on its bumps, its crumbling excrescences. On the balcony Dafna collects the tea things onto the tray. Felina's long silhouette still lingers at the railing. But she wanted him to go, she was waiting for him to go. And now she's watching him tensely, rooted to the spot. Next to the car, on the pavement, his long shadow hesitates too.

Dafna is demolishing the wall of empty clay pots. She carries them in her arms, pressed to her hips, along the garden path. Their empty bellies seem swollen. She tries to fill them up, with stones, with earth, with geranium plants.

Ever since morning this bustle in the garden. Around the fence and under the pepper tree and the Persian lilac, where the workmen have left their sacks and bundles. Suddenly you realize: this is not your corner. The sight of the familiar view which calmed you by the mere fact of its routine presence. Something foreign, or forgotten, has infiltrated it. Upsetting the balance, the hard-won harmony. The wish to embrace the blueness is rebuffed and dispelled. As if a flock of crows had landed here to peck at a desolate ruin. Fear flutters inside you. As if you were a branch of lilac broken by these workmen, its tender buds crushed. Especially disturbing is the youngest of them, the one with the peaked cap, its dirty-white emphasizing his swarthy skin. Under the shadow of the cap his look climbs to the balcony, clings to the hem of your gown.

For hours they sit in the sun. The hair of the older workman is covered with white dust. Between his parted legs lies the heavy stone and he chisels it with his thick short hammer. His ugly mouth gapes and grins spastically with the effort. Compared to him, the boy spends a lot of time resting. He sits in the shade of the trees, lights a cigarette, his cap slipping over his eyes, you can only guess what he's looking at.

At midday the boy comes up to her. He leans sideways against the front door and asks her in a velvety voice to make them coffee. Hobbling to the gas burner she tries her best to hide the weakness of her legs. He says to her: 'Raoul sent us.' And his accent is guttural and rolling. That was how they pronounced Raoul's name in the courtyard. Mocking him behind his back for his lordly attitude towards the porters. When he arrived in the country her father had put him in charge of the packing in his place. Felina remembers how he used to stand in the entrance to the warehouse supervising the porters for hours on end, as if drinking in their swift, strong movements.

'What's the noise?' her mother asks. In her room the shutters are still down. The sunlight, strewn with specks of grey dust, barely penetrates. 'Raoul sent the workmen.' Felina holds onto the doorpost. Her mother nods her head as if in confirmation: As usual, he keeps his promises. 'Come in, Felina. Why do you always wear that gown.'

In the room, the usual desolation of empty eau-de-Cologne bottles and crumpled papers. Piles of Hungarian newspapers and glass toys on the chest of drawers. Felina sits down underneath her portrait: a smiling little girl with fair braids, a hard hat and big butterfly bows. Mother sighs contentedly: Raoul didn't forget us. Every day I feel surer that he wants to come back. To you and to Dafna. Have you noticed how much prettier she's grown lately. So thin and ugly when she was born. And now she's shot up and filled out. Her bosom too. And her periods, earlier than usual. Only her arms and legs are too hairy. I wonder why. Suddenly she is silent. The old suspicion hovers in the air again. Like a light curtain billowing in the breeze, swollen out of proportion. And why did Raoul mention that painter yesterday. Did it upset you. Her mother speculates, confused.

Smells of cooking. Roast meat and fried potatoes. The table's dirty. The waitress comes and wipes it with an evil-smelling cloth. Let's leave, says Morduch. They stand in the street. The initiative for the meeting came from her. She had an idea, or perhaps she didn't. She was no longer sure. A deaf-mute couple were standing next to a nearby shop window. They spoke with movements of their hands and lips. Voicelessly. And another couple, not far off, she combing his hair affectionately with her fingers. Suddenly she turned around and without a word began to walk away from him. Glancing backwards, as if hoping that he would follow her. But he had already slipped into the entrance to one of the shops. Uncomplaining, she went on walking, alone. And in the bus queue a woman was talking about her gym teacher. Divorced twice, already a grandmother, she said, and soon to be married again. A real acrobat.

Hammering. The window full of white dust. 'Close it,' Felina scolds Dafna. 'The house will get dirty and Granny will be angry.' But the activities of the workmen fascinate Dafna. They fool around, splash each other with water from the hosepipe. Running feet on the path, wild laughter. The dogs bark madly on the bench. Dafna laughs and her laughter is as annoying as the mute Sarah's. The hollow plant pots in her arms. They'll fill up. Today. You'll see.

The silence of the house is broken. Throaty voices, jubilant shouts, and the creaking wheelbarrow trampling the path with its iron wheels. Piled with cement and heavy stones. In the warm air an unstable current makes itself felt, as if before the last spring rains. Big spring flies fly inside, their colour a brilliant green. Dafna's bare arms emerge from the dense foliage. Raking earth and cutting shoots. The puppies run behind her and shake the street with their barking. From time to time they disappear and appear again. 'Watch the dogs,' Felina calls to Dafna from the balcony. She doesn't know why. The wheelbarrow falls silent and the boy stops to look at Dafna and the running dogs. Then the wheels start turning again, but now their creaking seems more vehement.

The ferment in the mute girl's body. She would crawl into the cellar, between Morduch's paintings leaning against the blackening wall to dry. The colours, in a bright, astonishing mixture, illuminating the greyness of the courtyard stones. Ridges of paint jutting from the texture of the paintings. In the evening the boys would gather at his place. Crowding onto the bare mattress. The cigarettes smouldering in their hands and bodies. Their shadows on the high ceiling changing shape, expanding. Sarah was drawn to them. Her grunting laughter sounded like dried peas tumbling out of a torn sack. Morduch would stroke her head shorn because of the lice and speak to her in sign language.

Where's Dafna. A pungent, piercing smell of geranium leaves fills the balcony. It's already covered in mud. For a moment the flame of her red blouse flits through the white oleander bushes. The workman rolls the wheelbarrow down the path like an acrobat. His knit shirt is torn, it exposes the brown line of his waist. Why has he turned into the alley, why down the slope. There is another entrance to the building there, a back entrance. The workman disappears into it, hidden among the bushes. He'll throw his stones down there, dirty the garden, crush the flowers.

Her helplessness on the balcony. Her sick legs. They will do as they wish in the garden. Dirty and destroy. Raoul sent them without supervision. Busy as usual with his own affairs, more important in his eyes. He'll only come to visit them in the evening. To check up and see for himself: Yes, the fence is mended. But what is it that has been destroyed here nevertheless. Trying to compose herself she picks up a fallen geranium leaf, breathes in its smell. Is this what the adolescent Sarah's smell was like, or perhaps it was more bitter, like wild thyme, or wormwood. Felina breathes in deeply, trying to remember. When did she see Morduch's sisters last.

It was a short dry winter. Like crowds of white butterflies the almond blossom fluttered against the background of the blackened courtyard stones. On the white evenings flocks of starlings would fly down to them. Old Samoori would take two big saucepan lids and clash them like cymbals, to chase them away. And one day, at twilight, the Romanian climbed right to the top, breaking the slender almond branches with his crooked legs, and hitting the birds with his stick. Up they flew in great flocks. Like gathering clouds they surrounded the courtyard with anxious twittering. And down below Mary stood and laughed.

In the corners the fluff of the oleander seeds collected. The weightless almond blossoms drifted in the wind. Their sweet delicate scent faded. The end-of-season rains were short and angry. They poured down between the courtyard walls in a deluge. The water flowed and flooded the low tunnels. Felina trudged through the puddles in her high boots. She was already pregnant, her belly round and high. And Morduch came running towards her. He bumped into her and pretended not to see. A big sack in his hands to cover the donkey, to protect it from the cold. He embraced the long neck and shivering velvety ears. Slowly the animal collapsed in the stone arc. On lean bony knees. The sagging belly breathed heavily, the patient head drew itself in. The Romanian stood over it still, hitting it again and again with his stick to make it stand up. Stop it, Morduch burst out at him. Not taking any notice of Felina any more, the rain on his face like tears. What have you done to him. Mary squatted in the courtyard, her wet dress tucked between her knees, rinsing cold, dead fish in a basin. The mute sister twisted her face, not knowing whether to laugh or cry.

Dafna. Her heart is full of foreboding. The flapping crows set waves of shade in motion in the fading blue, blinding her eyes. Dafna's back has vanished long ago into the darkening bushes. The clusters of rose, geranium and oleander blooms have begun to lose their colours. Silence and darkness enfold the garden.

The hem of her gown trails in the mud and the clay pots get in her way. Full to the brim of dark loose earth. Hobbling along the railing Felina listens attentively to the rustling. Where's Dafna. Where have the workmen disappeared to. The creaking has stopped. The wheelbarrow is silent. Suddenly even the dogs are quiet. Following her with their tails drooping. The lump of fear chokes her throat. What are they plotting. They'll knock her down, they'll writhe between her legs, and no one will rush to her rescue. Mother's in her room and there's no light in her window. And perhaps her face like Father's has already turned to stone. She has been left alone. Even the birds have disappeared from sight. Darkness fills the balcony to overflowing. Snuffling and sniffing along the railing the dogs will not let her be. Watching her weakness, her collapse. What's happening. She'll call for help.

But her voice is dumb. Suddenly the breath of the night lies hot and blazing on her chest. Like Morduch's groping hand, like an incandescent iron bar.

She'll resist, come what may. The movement will startle them. And the crash. Dafna will hear it too and come back. One after the other the clay pots are sent flying. Smashing onto the garden path and even further, onto the mended fence. Her arms move freely and gaily. The oppression finds release at last. The whiteness of the new stone blackens with damp earth. The young plants are buried underneath it. But the sound of the breaking clay is dull and echoless. And the silence redoubles in the street.

Translated by Dalya Bilu

4

Twilight

by SHULAMITH HAREVEN

I

L AST NIGHT I spent a year in the city where I was born. I had
long known the password for getting there: Dante's line, 'I am
the way to the city of sorrow.' In a clear voice I said: '*Per me si va nella
città dolente*,' and time split open and I was there. In that one night's
year I met a man, married, became pregnant, and gave birth to a
murky child who grew fast, all without light.

The city of my birth was very dark, extinguished, because the
sun had left it and gone away a long, long time ago, and people in
the street walked swiftly through the gloom, warming hands and
lighting up faces with candles or matches. Here and there someone moved about with an oil lamp. The streets were wide, as I
remembered them, but many windows were boarded up, the
planks hammered in crosswise. Many other windows were
stuffed with rags and old newspapers against the cold. As there
was no light, not a single tree was left in the street, only black
fenced-in staves. Not one plant showed on windowsills.

I saw no one I recognized at first, yet everyone seemed very
familiar, smiling faintly. They never went so far as to break into
laughter. They already knew they would live without sun from
now on, forever more. There was an air of humility and resignation about them. They were as kind to each other as they could
be. Two acquaintances meeting in the street would warm one
another's hands with a shy smile.

They wore the clothes I remembered from childhood: you
could always tell a man's calling by his dress. Policemen wore a

policeman's uniform, of course; the judge went about as a judge, alighting from his carriage in wig and gown; the chimney sweep was always in his work clothes, and so was the coachman, and so was the Count. The children were dressed as children: sailor collars and lace, and the girls with knees frozen in dresses of stiff scalloped taffeta. Many wore school uniforms: dark blue or brown, high school badges embroidered on their caps. Everyone knew where he belonged.

In the city of my birth no one had died since the sun had gone beyond recall, and no one had had new garments made. Their uniformlike clothes were not quite tattered yet, not by any means; but they reminded one of the costumes of a theatre wardrobe worn over and over for many performances; somewhat graying at the seams, somewhat fraying at the sleeves, stale smells buried in each fold. And yet, such clean people. Clean as smoke.

I seemed to require no sleep or food in the city of my birth, but only speech. Now I have slept, I told myself, now I have eaten, and it would be as though I had slept and eaten and could go on. And on and on I went, through the dark streets, only some of which I remembered, and some of which were ruined and not repaired but closed.

One night I drove to the opera in a carriage. The horse defecated as it went, but the odour of the dung did not reach me. I realized all of a sudden that there were no smells in this city. The coachman wore an old battered top hat, and when I paid my fare he raised his top hat in greeting and cracked his whip in a special way, an expert crack in the air. He knew me for a visitor, but he did not know that I came from the land of the sun. Perhaps he did not know about the land of the sun at all, though it was so near, right beyond the wall, only a password between the twilight and it. Most people do not know.

At the opera I met the man I married that night, that year. They were singing Mozart on stage, and the audience was so pleased, so responsive, that at times it seemed audience and singers might be interchangeable. I myself, it seems, could have gone up there and joined the singer in 'Voi chè sapete'. There was a festive mood about it all, an air of goodwill, bravo, bravo, rows of women's hats bobbing joyously, how can one live without Mozart.

The man sitting by my side at the opera leaned over and said:

'We must leave in the intermission, quickly, because the opera will be surrounded by soldiers after the performance and this whole audience taken away to freight trains.'

I consented, though wondering how come all these people knew it and none escaped. In the intermission the man took my hand and we left quickly by a side door. Trucks full of bored soldiers were already posted in the square, the soldiers preparing to get off and surround the building. Their sergeants, papers in hand, were checking the order of deployment. A young soldier was whistling 'Voi chè sapete' and said to his fellow, 'How can one live without Mozart?'

In the dark light, the no-light, I asked the man holding my hand without my feeling its touch why people weren't escaping and he said:

'Why, this whole thing repeats itself each night.'

He drew over to a door, narrow as a servants' entrance, and through it to a slippery, winding staircase, mounting to a roof. The roof was amazing: we were standing at the altitude of an airplane's flight, perhaps twelve thousand feet, perhaps more, very high. Yet I could see every single detail in the opera square below.

The floodlights of the soldier's trucks came on suddenly, tearing the darkness, glaring and terrible, and with this evil light came the wails, the shouts, and the curses. Now everything happened very fast. The people in festive clothes piled up on the trucks, and there was no more telling them apart, batch after driven batch. Only the soldiers stood out clearly because they had light, then and now, and because they were shouting so.

'Operation Cauldron,' said the man by my side. 'Every night it repeats itself. Every night they are driven in trucks like that to the trains and do not return. In the evening they are back, going to the opera, and it all starts over again. The only difference is that the people are a little less alive each time. They fade, like pictures in an album. But the process is so slow it is barely noticeable.'

'And you – don't they take you in Operation Cauldron?' I asked.

'No,' he said, 'I'm already ...' he waved his hand and didn't explain. Then he added: 'You don't have to go either. Of course, if you want to ...'

The moment he said that, I was seized by a whirlwind. I wanted, wanted unto death to leap from this tall roof in the dark courtyard now filled with shouting soldiers, to go out to the opera square. Together with all the children. Together with all the neighbours, whom I suddenly recognized one by one: Mrs. Paula and Mr. Arkin and his wife, and Moshe of the haberdashery who used to give me pictures of angels and cherubs to stick in my copybooks, and Bolek the pharmacist's son. They were all being herded onto the trucks here before my eyes, fearful and apprehensive, the soldiers shouting over their heads. And I wished to leap and be with them. To be taken.

'I did not leap either,' said the man, very sad, as though confessing a sin. The whirlwind began to abate. I held on to the parapet and breathed hard. A fierce desire had come and gone and left me reeling.

One by one the trucks moved off with a terrible jarring noise. In the square lay a child's ballet slipper, a gilt-knobbed walking stick, and an ostrich feather that probably fell from the hat of a lady in the opera audience. Then they *are* somewhat diminished each night, I thought to myself, and my anxiety found no relief. The emptiness that remained in the square had drained my body to the core.

'Tomorrow it will all happen again,' said the man by my side. Grief was everywhere. It was all over.

'Could we get married?' I asked, like someone asking permission to take a vacant chair in a café, and he nodded and said: 'We could, yes.'

We did not know where we would live. That entire night we wandered through the streets, as there was no telling day from night except for a slight shade of difference in the depth of darkness; everything was shrouded in the same no-light of the extinguished city. That night we also crossed a park, which since the sun had gone had long ceased being a park; many marble statues were strewn over the ground now, statues of people, some of them smashed. One small statue was very like my grandfather's.

I wanted to take it away with me, but I had no place to put it. Once or twice I also saw a white marble statue of a horse, its haunch wrenched off and something like frozen blood on the marble. There had not been so many statues in my childhood days, not in the park or all over town. They had apparently turned the park into a dump, maybe for all the world. The presence of the kind people from the street was missing here, and we returned to the city that never slept, that always had men and women walking about, huddled against the cold – till we got to a smoky alehouse. A few people, their breath misty in the cold air, their spirits high, were crowded in the doorway but did not go in.

The man with me briefly considered entering the place, then as quickly dismissed the idea. There was a space behind the alehouse, a kind of small courtyard paved with concrete, and in it a tiny shed, which I took for an outhouse. He opened its door and we went in; but there was no end to the shed, and its far side had another door, behind which lay, suddenly, a vast deserted official residence. It had heavy, very rich furniture, a sideboard and carpets and enormous armchairs, and crystal chandeliers thick with dust and cobwebs. I had always known that this residence existed behind some wall or other, and that one day I would inherit it. Generations of my forefathers must have lived here, they and their wives, my grandmothers in their handsome bonnets. I went in, unamazed. The furniture was too large and unwieldy, and we decided we would use only one of the rooms, a plain and all but empty room with a kind of stove on the floor to be stoked with paper or wood. The man crouched and lit a fire, the heat of which I did not feel at all, and his shadow fell across me. I accepted. He blew on the fire a little, and when it was going somehow, he checked the window locks, then stood before me and said:

'The wedding took place this afternoon.'

I knew these words to be our wedding rites and I was very still, the way one is on solemn occasions. This will be my life from now on, I told myself, in a city without light. Maybe I will never leave this flat, that I will never enter its big rooms and stay only in this room, and perhaps one day the soldiers will come for me too, take me to the trucks, the trains, along with all of them, with all of them, with all of them. I shall say to all the children: Wait for me. I shall say: I am coming with you, of course I am coming with you.

All at once the room filled with people, women in shawls, neighbours. They came beaming, bearing gifts, cases, cartons. They all stood squeezed in the doorway, in the room, filling it, joyously offering their blessings in identical words: 'The wedding took place this afternoon,' they said and kissed me, 'the wedding took place this afternoon.' The room overflowed with people and with parcels. I opened one, and it held all the toys I had lost as a child. The neighbour who had brought them stood over me, smiling, angelic, and repeated excitedly, 'the wedding took place this afternoon'. She knew that her present was apt.

Afterwards the women neighbours left, their thin voices fluttery with a small, birdlike gladness, trailing down the staircase, and all the parcels remained: cases and cartons and beribboned boxes. I saw no need to shift them, though they hardly left us space to move about the room.

'This is where we shall live,' I told the man in the room with me, and he nodded his head in assent.

So a year went by. We lived like lizards, in crevices, among the empty cases in the the room. I do not remember anyone buying food, but every day I crossed the long corridor, past the large, imposing, unheated, and unlived-in rooms, to cook something in a kitchen that was like a large cave. Once we even went on an outing. Behind our apartment, not on the alehouse side but on the other, lay a desert stretching for many miles, and beyond the desert, in the distant haze, a range of mountain peaks, very far away. We stood at the edge of the house, a few dozen others with us, and looked at those faraway hills.

'Where is that?' I asked the people with us. They grinned good-naturedly and would not tell me, as though I should have known.

One of them said: 'Los Angeles,' but that was a joke.

I went in, back to our room, took off my shoes, my feet weary as after a long walk.

Now and then we would hear shouts from one of the nearby houses: the soldiers come for the kill. They never got to us. We would lie frozen, waiting for the night's Operation Cauldron to end, the leaden silence to return, the hollow grief.

Toward the end of the year I gave birth. The child tore away from me at one stroke; and I remembered dimly that once, long ago, in my other life, I had loved a man very much, and it was just this way I had felt when he tore away from my body: as though a part of me had suddenly been severed for all time. Then I wept many tears.

The child stood up and walked within a day or two. Next he began talking to me, demanding something in an incoherent speech I failed to understand; he grew angry, and I knew he would not stay with me long. One day he left and did not return. When the man came home he removed his coat wordlessly and we both knew: the child had run off to the opera square. And it had been impossible to prevent.

The days went by, day running into night without any real difference between them. Sometimes kindhearted neighbours called. Once one of them came with scraps of material, a dressmaker's leftovers; we spent a whole morning sewing children's frocks, except that at the end of the day we had to unravel them all.

One day I knew that time had come full circle: my year in the city without light was over and I was to go back. I said to the man with me:

'I'm going.'

He nodded. He did not offer to come with me. I would have to fall asleep in order to wake up in the other country anyway, and he could not accompany me into sleep. I think we never slept once in all that year, neither he nor I. Our eyelids were always open, day and night.

I lay down on my bed, which only now turned out to have wheels like a hospital bed, and the man I lived with set it going with one hard shove along the corridor, which turned into a steep incline, and the bed rolled into the kitchen. The kitchen, where all that year I had gone to cook, had changed: it had been set up as an operating room. I was not surprised. I lay there waiting, unafraid. All the instruments were apparently ready; only the big lamp above me was still unlit. A stern-faced surgeon in a green coat and cap bent over me, examined me at a glance, and said:

'Turn on the light.'

The big lamp blazed over my head, and I fell into a heavy sleep and woke up in my other house.

It was morning. A great sun shone straight into my eyes. Ailanthus branches gently swayed on the veranda, drawing curtains of light whisper-soft across my face. A strong smell of coffee hung in the air, but as yet I could not take deep breaths of it. My soul did not return to me at once.

Through the door came the murmurs of my husband's and children's voices, speaking softly so as not to wake me. I delighted in them but could not understand them from within yet, as though they were a translation that had not come off well. I lay still, waiting for my soul to flow full in me again, and I knew it was all over and completed: I would no more go back to the city of my birth, to the lightless city. Dante's verse dimmed, faded, returned to the pages of the book, a line like any other: its power exhausted. In a day or two I might even be able to read it without a pang. And sleep too, I told myself wonderingly, to be able really to sleep. My past was commuted. From now now on I would find nothing there but the stones of Jerusalem, and plants growing with mighty vigour, and a vast light.

I got up to make breakfast, my heart beating hard.

Translated by Miriam Arad

5

Nechama-Gittel

by HAYA ESTHER

PART ONE

EVEN MENACHEM-MENDEL had never seen what those walls, the single wire-netted window and the odd, watchful lizard saw of his wife, Nechama-Gittel, my aunt.

In the steamy room, silently observed by a small puddle of water on the floor, a curious crack in the wall and a black hair on the green expressionless water, a faint smell of chlorine. Far from clean. It was hard for my aunt Nechama-Gittel to be in a strange place.

Foreignness and displacement, feelings she feared above all, could overcome her suddenly – or not so suddenly – in any unfamiliar place. When that happened you did not need to try hard or to be particularly perceptive to observe how she struggled to lock herself away, enclose and protect herself. And all this with success, thank God.

Today, a Sunday after the new moon had been blessed at the close of Sabbath, Nechama-Gittel was with another aunt, Chava, at her home in an ageing quarter of town, named 'The Thread of Kindness', whose back leaned towards the quiet, modern streets nearby. Chava had that dreaded disease we shall not name; and Nechama-Gittel had come to help the sorry woman a little. That evening she would sleep at her home; and the day, the very hour, had now come to go to the ritual bath.

My aunt cared little for Scriptural injunctions, but believed profoundly in one teaching of the sages: 'The Torah says you shall be untouchably impure with menstruation for seven days, in order then to become as desirable to your husband as on your wedding day.' Which is why she went to the bath. She walked there, on a starry winter's evening, among gust-borne leaves, eddies of wind, and lost-looking puddles stripped of their usual midges. She decided she would walk there, to be purified by ritual immersion; walking with her consort of tears that attended her as weeping willows support those who pass by on trains. Sorrow, pain and their friends were still on the march. A single image came to mind. The evening before, at the close of the Sabbath, at the moment of blessing the waxing moon, she had been with those who followed Aaron-Moishe on his final journey. She had held grimly to the shoulders of Esther-Leah the tearful widow. She had glanced palely at the moon, torn by its veil of misty rain clouds. Had lowered her gaze to encounter the moon-lit faces of a crowd of men in round black hats; the congregation blessing the new moon.

Sounds mingled in the synagogue courtyard, which formed the continuation of Zelig Lieder Street: voices chanting 'Welcome unto thee!' to the moon of purity, and the soft, broken weeping of the dead man's wife. Almost taunting wafts of wine arose, not the ritual kind just used for marking the Sabbath's end and the week's return, but the rich aroma of a good vintage from the adjacent wine-press. But it was not this image that so frightened my aunt Nechama-Gittel.

There arose within her a half-remembered dream she had had at dawn; she whispered repeatedly, lips trembling, 'No dream lacks vain things.'

She did not want this image; tried to smash it to splinters, to turn its face to the wall, to plunge it into water, to tear it out of her. But it reassembled itself, floated. My aunt Nechama-Gittel mainly remembered the big toe of her mother, my grandmother. The toe had oozed blood whenever my grandmother Toiveh returned from the ritual bath.

Roughly every month the bath attendant trimmed the nail inexpertly with scissors she dug deep into the flesh. A sorry toe it was.

Nechama-Gittel discovered the mystery of the return from the bath when she was aged only ten.

She could recognise the signs: the first was that sad, oozing toe; and the second, unmistakably, was her mother's shining eyes, lit with a warmly watchful radiance, in which vast feelings swam caressingly, gazing timelessly on us all. A silence trembled mysteriously in the smoothness of her throat, a paler white than ever, etching the vault of her eyebrows with awesome delicacy.

The fog did not disperse. The weight in her legs became an ordinary ache that could be borne. When Nechama-Gittel rested her legs on a sofa she relieved the ache, suffused throughout the pudding-like mass of interlaced veins: the reward of five births, neither easy nor difficult.

The mist rose and reached for her heart, covering her face still clouded with fear and word-toubled thoughts.

From one corner she could hear an intense conversation, in another a heavy silence. Without wanting to join in, she tried to look at the other women's legs, as they leaned against the wall. Unsuccessfully. Her eye chased a lizard that stole in through the window.

Diminutively slender and serpentine it observed her blankly. It seemed to reach out a transparent tongue to entrap a minute mosquito, and mockingly danced about the strange strain on the wall before her. As Nechama-Gittel watched the lizard, she felt the shadow of a memory rising within her, lengthening and strengthening, blowing away some of the fog. It filled the picture-shaped window, the lizard's tail making time creep in reverse. A sharp pain ran through her and she stopped. Could that be a tear she was shedding? Tears are good for clearing fog. She saw herself with clarity; none other than herself, with Aaron-Moishe as a nine-year-old boy, one Sabbath eve like so many, in a window opening, trying to catch reflections in a window opposite, across the street. Playing guessing games, dividing passers-by into righteous or evil.

Yes, now the memory was sharp and bright.

How Aaron-Moishe one Sabbath eve had offered explanations

of the strange expression: 'Entering the ritual bath with vermin hand'.

She had not understood then, and still did not.

She had gazed at him then, and still gazed.

Remembering. The best part of Sabbath eve with Aaron-Moishe's grandmother, bringing her the stuffed fish, prepared in honour of the Sabbath. From the washing-line each Sabbath eve, hung lacy underpants, a black shawl and long black stockings. Remembering. The joy of fingers poked through the lace inside. Wrapping the head with the shawl. The gentle caress of long black stockings. Fixing shining eyes on the gaze of Aaron-Moishe's cat, Chedorlaomer.

The thread of time halted, gathering up Aunt Nechama-Gittel's solitary tear (tears are good for cleaning foggy soot); and she rose, turning away, sticking fragments together to make a whole. Clambering stubbornly from her grave.

She arrived, reached the black gate. She had to push the low gate and walk down the paved path flanked with bushes, to reach the door of frosted glass and its odour of mildew.

She halted.

She did not move on.

She could sense it coming, the fog of foreignness, there before her, spread beneath her feet. Rising and tepidly enwrapping her with its fingertips. One hand's fingers were damp with the cloudiness of cold mist. Its chill entered and fondled her breasts with a steely caress, wrinkling her nipples, penetrating to her heart and sinking there like a stone, bearing down on her belly from within her womb, pushing on her thigh and pressing again on the soles of her feet.

She knew him, this visitor, and waited for his other hand, the warm one. This hand was not bluish or grey, but the colour of orange smoke from a bonfire, of fantasy, of colourlessness. A wave of warmth rose to her mouth, flowing over her tongue and around the arch of her lips. It burst from her nostrils, and into circular floodlets spreading over her cheeks; into her eyes, darkening them; moulded to her brow from within; and bursting

61

suddenly from her vagina, lifting her soaring over the ground, leaving her suspended, detached – and came out of her sightless eyes. She blinked, tried to peer within herself, and there – alas for those fog-blinded eyes – she saw another Nechama-Gittel.

She raised smoke-wearied eye-sockets to the heavens, registering a patch of sky and a lonely star that blazed a path through the clouds, and found herself whispering mistily once again: 'No dream lacks vain things'. Somehow she pushed herself within, past the low gate, hovered over the paving to push the blank-eyed glass door, and found herself in the centre of the square waiting room.

PART TWO

Through the fog she thought she could see several women leaning against the wall. She dropped into a chair in the corner of the square room.

She shrank, repelled by the foreign smell.

The foreignness of women's sweat, a little diluted chlorine, a medley of undefined perfumes, and a repelling sourness of towels. Stuffy air; unaired clothes. She tried to unravel the skein of odours one by one. Maybe she could cling to a familiar one: the delicate, clean scent of fresh sheets and newly cooked noodles with cinnamon and a hint of pepper that rose when our grandmother Toiveh caressed our faces with her pure white hands, with their delicate joints and pale fingernails. (Such a scent would doubtless have helped her disperse the fog; but sadly it was not there.)

The bath attendant said 'Your turn, madam'. A bath attendant like any other, except that she dragged her weary feet.

My aunt went into an angled corner room with a yellow bath, at whose head were taps for eyes, that dripped lazily. This was inside.

Steamy room, silently observed by a small puddle of water, a curious crack in the wall, and a black hair on expressionless water.

She filled the bath, with the help of the alienating taps and undressed while, out of the swirling bathwater, peeped the twinkling eyes of Aaron-Moishe.

She removed her shoes, put aside her blouse, took off her black skirt and fine stockings, hung her belt on a hanger, and remembered his baths, in those days. The plaited sash belt and Sabbath eve eyes. He would raise his eyelids, give a penetrating glance, and tuck his fingers behind the silken sash. A look of farewell. Quickly removing all kinds of underwear she was naked, breasts heavy with the milk of her fifth child, weeping milky tears.

Standing.

Nakedness: white, peaceful, ripe, radiant, concentrated.

Her breasts wept with her, tears of dissension, tears for the day Aaron-Moishe married Esther-Leah.

A good marriage, a successful one, arranged propitiously by all those involved: matchmaker, worthy parents, and the Almighty maker of all matches.

Walls, wire-netted window, watchful lizard, crack in wall and puddle of water, all saw a painful nakedness – a nakedness that pricked the soles of one's feet with needles – with delicate, fragile toes slightly parted. It rose and enwrapped her legs with scalding, spiralling caresses, her legs those of a delicate girl. The rubbing of coarse soap, soft rounded belly; heartbeats pinching a ripe nipple. A living vision that penetrated and could be touched.

Yes. The fog dispersed for Nechama-Gittel my aunt, very slowly; and she wanted to sink into the bath that had filled with water. She entered and sank into that day of fathomless sorrow, Aaron-Moishe's wedding-day, when she took to her bed, sank into it and wished not to get up for days, weeks or months; floated or sank in a world of her own.

The wire-netted window was gradually steaming up. Nechama-Gittel carefully washed the tight curls that had not been shaved for several weeks now; a slightly boyish head. Lathered her fine, rounded shoulders. Rinsed, dried, checked herself. She was ready.

She opened the door a crack and called out: 'I would like to dip now.'

The short woman came from somewhere or other and looked in.

'There's a bell for you to ring,' she muttered, at once adding in a dry prickly voice: 'Wait your turn; I'll be back.'

Nechama-Gittel stood naked. But for the strangling pain in her throat she would have chatted to the lizard that twitched its tail like a snake near the strange slanting crack in the wall. Her eyes followed the lizard's blank gaze which she could see was fixed on the ceiling; and it was from there that the dream of Aaron-Moishe again descended on her, filling the room.

Before her stood Esther-Leah's husband, his face distorted by sorrow or laughter. His hands reach out and his eyes envelop her. He clasps her to his heart. He grasps her hand and hovers with her, turning round and round and round. He puts his head between her breasts, finally sinking onto her bed. The bed which belongs to Menachem-Mendel, her husband.

There is no Nechama-Gittel – just happiness. Happiness beyond the bounds of any one moment. Just eyes in which a face was inlaid: watchful, wide, grey, thoughtful eyes, with a heavenly softness, delineated with the brush of fine eyebrows.

One moment of unclothed nakedness was enough for Aaron-Moishe to vanish at the edge of the puddle, enough for the lizard to swallow the tiny spider that had meandered towards her, enough for Nechama-Gittel to close her eyes tight and seal her ears against the sound of the crack in the wall.

The bath attendant entered, short of stature, to turn her body gently round and check that not a black hair remained. Nechama-Gittel now went down slowly, step by step, into the water of the ritual bath. In the corner, Menachem-Mendel performed the dawn rite of hand-washing.

Semi-circles of water clasped her waist, as, with legs apart she sank into the water. She wants to remain there but cannot and she floats. She placed a towel over her head, crossed her arms before her and recited a blessing: 'Blessed art thou, O Lord, Our God, King of the Universe, who has hallowed us by thy commandments and commanded us to take the ritual bath.'

The blessing floated on the face of the water.

Then, like a flock of birds, the words took flight and scattered. The first three clung to the crack in the wall, striving to pass through it, shaking the stones, while the whole room quaked.

'... O Lord, our God ...', the anguished croaking burst outside, up and up, bearing steamy patches of ceiling.

'... who has sanctified us ...', adhered to her innermost heart.

'... with his commandments, and commanded us ...', clung to the lizard's tail.

'... the ritual bath', drowned despairingly in the puddle in the corner.

Again and again my aunt Nechama-Gittel immersed herself. She rose slowly; dripping, radiant, steaming. How beautiful she was! The bath attendant said 'Just like she should be', and disappeared. With wide, wonderful eyes she put on garment after garment, laced up the black shoes and tightened a black shawl that framed a pale face and fine trembling throat. Aaron-Moishe reached out again, his eyes met hers and gathered her soul towards him.

Thunder rolled out there in Jerusalem, the crack widened; she almost ran from the room.

The thunder moved stones, shaking them, making the lizard's tail tremble. It shifted the stone window frame.

My aunt ran, shutting the low black gate, stopping, looking back. No harm done. 'God be praised', not a stone had fallen.

Translated by Jeremy Schonfield

6

My Friend B's Feast

by YEHUDIT HENDEL

WHEN I CAME in I heard her saying from the room: And three kilos of onions, don't forget. She must have been afraid he hadn't heard. – Three kilos of onions, it's important, she repeated firmly. He was already in the corridor. – Don't worry, everything will be all right, he replied from the corridor.

Inside the room lay B, dying. Attached to tubes, all wounded, all bandaged on the veins and arteries of her arms and legs. In the flushed, immobile face, swollen with cortizone, only the glittering little eyes darted.

I hope he won't forget anything, she said.

He won't forget, I said.

You'll come.

Of course, I said.

Nira will cook the meal.

Naturally, I said.

I've given instructions about everything.

Naturally, I said.

When my brother Nahum's wife died, she made him swear not to get married after she was gone.

She made an effort to smile, but all you could see were her trembling, sensitive nostrils.

In my case Nira will cook the meal.

She made an effort to smile again.

She's a good cook.

I didn't know what to say. I felt her eyes fixed on my face, sharp and cold, like two steel nails.

Right after that I'll die, she said.

But B, I said.

The two steel nails turned red-hot.

Right after that I'll die. I'll hang on till Saturday.

Again she made an effort to smile.

I hope I'll hang on till Saturday.

Her eyes darted over me now, wild, as if she had four eyes.

I told him the exact menu. It has to be exact. It has to be just so.

I said of course it would be just so.

It has to be delicious.

I said of course it would be delicious.

I explained it to Alexander, she said, I explained that everything has to be just so.

He'll take care of it, I said.

Yes, I hope he'll take care of it. – All the time her eyes darted over me, wild. She said: The doctor's giving me two hours leave. I can leave the hospital for two hours. I'll hang on for two hours.

Of course, I said.

He'll give me an injection first. And he'll come with me, of course. I invited him and his wife, of course.

I didn't ask her who else she'd invited. She waited.

There'll be ten, she said. Actually, eleven. And there'll be one empty place. I like one empty place.

Again she waited.

And Nira will serve the meal, of course.

I didn't know what to say. I remembered how when I was a child my mother once told me about plants that bled a red juice when they were broken. She said: I explained to her exactly how to set the table.

Now too I didn't know what to say. She said: The injection will be enough for two hours. At four I have to be back here.

I told her that she would be back here on time.

Yes, I'll be back here on time, she said.

I didn't know what to say. There was silence.

And that's it, she said.

There was silence.

After that, that's it, she said.

There was silence.

You don't know what to say, she said. There was silence. It was evident that she felt confined inside her skin. She said: After that, that's it. And next week – she tried to move her head, which was heavy, and it was evident that she felt more and more confined inside her skin.

Everything will be settled quickly, she said.

I didn't ask what.

Her eyes darted over me again, rapacious, and I could feel the hot mud in her body.

Yes, everything will be settled quickly, she said and sank her head into the pillow as if there was an abyss of air there inside the pillow.

I looked at her swollen, exhausted face. Her chin was bandaged and I thought about the place where the animal's neck begins. I thought about the bones, the hair and the teeth. Her eyes ran over me so wild that for a moment I thought that she heard through her eyes. There was a pearl hanging on her chest. She said: I explained to her exactly how to lay the table. She breathed heavily. She said: You see, you turn into a watchdog.

Everything, like death itself, was clear and absolute. It was clear that she had taken care of everything, including what would happen afterwards. Unlike death it was clear that this too was planned. Suddenly I saw her strolling down the avenue with a white parasol. She said: I brought it from Japan but I look like a little Chinese woman. She had a sly laugh. She really did look like a little Chinese woman, strolling in the shade in the cypress avenue with a white parasol. I remembered the amusing stories of her travels, when she travelled round the world with Alexander, round the world more than once. It seemed to me that she was searching for a mirror, that she was avid to see her face in the mirror. Again I remembered, the story of the mandrake plant that screamed when it was uprooted, and how my mother told me that its root, when it was pulled up, was black. I looked at her wounded swollen veins and although she was all covered up I felt as if she saw through her whole body.

You can't get that thought out of your blood, she said.

She was very quiet now, as protected as possible inside the

pillow. She told me everything quietly, dryly. She told me how she intended to set the table, who would sit next to whom, and which table-napkins she had given instructions to take from the cupboard and where they were in the cupboard and under what. Which dinner service was to be used to serve the meal on and which to serve the coffee afterwards, what to make the compote from and in what bowl, and to take out the cutlery with the long white wooden handles and not to forget mustard seeds, it was very nice to put mustard seeds in a salad. Afterwards she explained what kind of soufflé she intended making, and the quantities of courgettes, garlic and onion, and that she had asked Alexander to make sesame sweets. He was a great expert at sesame sweets. He enjoyed making sesame sweets very much. There was nothing he liked better than making sesame sweets. The bandages on her arms were stained red and she looked as if she were simultaneously draining blood and words out of herself.

Enough, I said.

She didn't hear.

He's a great expert at sesame sweets.

Enough, I said.

She said: And I asked him to make sugar beet soup. Everybody likes beet soup. It's a pretty colour, beet soup.

She was speaking now neither quickly nor slowly. Her face was exhausted and only her eyes burned with the power of a force of hostile nature.

I asked if you liked sugar beet soup, she said.

A sudden cold blew from her, as if the fever had chilled her. She wiped her mouth with the tail-end of a bandage and sat up slightly. Again it seemed to me that she was searching for a mirror, that she was avid to see her face in the mirror.

I haven't got one on me, I said in alarm.

She asked what.

What? she said obstinately.

I said I liked sugar beet soup.

She looked at me and with one hand hit the iron bed, which made a sound like a musical stone. She was cruelly silent.

It's good, especially in summer, I said.

She was cruelly silent.

I'm talking nonsense, I said.

She went on being cruelly silent. – You thought I wanted a mirror, she said. No, I don't need a mirror.

She moved the infusion, holding her only luggage in her hand.

I'm glad you came to see me, she said. Yes, I'm certainly glad you came to see me. There was a kind of deep biological insult in her voice. She turned towards me, trying to smile.

Yes, it's good in summer, beet soup, she said. Again she tried to smile. Her voice choked and quivered and she swallowed her voice and looked at me quivering from the depths of the pillow.

I feel it approaching, she said.

I didn't know what to say.

It approaches in broad daylight, she said, it will come next week. She wept silently.

Not like a thief in the night, in broad daylight, she said.

I didn't know what to say. She wept silently. Her face was flooded, and it was hard to tell if it was set with tears or sweat. She looked so small now in the bed among the pillows, sunk into them as if in a narrow mountain pass, waving with the infusion in her hand, making an effort to open her arms and able to move only in one direction, like a bird capable of flying only in one direction. I thought: You can't get that thought out of your blood, that's what she said. I'm talking nonsense, that's what she said. The strong women, I thought, the strong women. My clever friend B, I thought. I didn't know what to say. I asked myself how many stones made a pile.

I definitely want it to be very festive, she said.

It was very festive. We arrived at one o'clock precisely. The other guests also arrived at one o'clock precisely. The table was punctiliously laid. I counted: there were eleven places. Everything was especially gay. The napkins were brightly coloured and flowered with little bouquets of little flowers clustered in tiny little goblets. At the door Nira received the guests. She was wearing a black dress with black lace, she had soft fair skin and the black lace emphasized her fair skin and the sympathetic melancholy of soft fair skin.

They'll be here soon, she said. Her face was tense and she made an effort to disguise the embarrassment in her voice. She said that there had been a problem finding something for B to wear and Alexander had driven to the hospital three times and three times she had sent him back to change the dress. One of the times she had asked for the gold sari-dress Alexander had brought her from India and then she had sent the gold sari-dress back. She said she had returned it because of the buttons which weren't properly sewn and they would open during the meal and instead of occupying herself with the guests she would be occupied with the buttons, and Alexander said: Thank God for small mercies, imagine her sitting there in the gold sari-dress, and it rustles too, Nira said, and they brought her the wide floral dress.

A faint blush appeared on her cheeks as she said this. – I hope she'll be pleased with what I sent, she said and added that it really was very difficult, because B, was very bloated. She spoke carefully, with the same sympathetic melancholy that added charm to her voice and she was incorrigibly sympathetic too when we heard the sound of the car approaching and when we heard it entering the yard and Alexander thundering: There, we made it, you see.

It must have seemed a little strange when we all formed up in a row. There was silence. She got out slowly and approached slowly. The doctor supported her on one side and Alexander on the other, and she walked silently down the long green garden path with her eyes making a big circle that instantly swallowed up all of us standing in a row. She smiled.

We're lucky it's a nice day, she said. She was wearing her jewellery and her eyes stood out in her face like big brightly coloured glass beads.

Wonderful, thundered Alexander, you see. There was a dead cigar butt in his mouth and his breathing was laid and excited. He was a big man with long legs and big steps and he always had magnificent wooden boxes full of big cigars.

I told you it would be a lovely day, he beamed.

She didn't look at him and only swallowed us all up as if we were some kind of shapeless stain. Then she took a small step forward. The she took another step forward.

Truly, what luck, a lovely day, she agreed.

You see, thundered Alexander.

She took another small step forward. Her head was heavy and she stepped carefully onto the lawn with one foot and then stepped carefully with the other foot as if there were shoe-mines on the lawn. Her bowed head betrayed the thin depleted hair and the ominous bald spots. She raised it, stretched, and hit her body with both hands. There was a metallic sound and I saw her standing in the gold sari-dress that Alexander had brought her from India with the power of a short queen who had lost her kingdom but not her authority. And she set off on her race, the sick old mare.

You mowed the lawn in my honour, she said.

In my childhood, in Nesher, I once saw a huge rock torn from the mountain. First it crumbled slowly, for days, maybe for a year, maybe for generations. When it fell it wasn't a rock any more. It only looked like one. In reality it was crumbs of soil.

But in my childhood in Nesher it hung huge in the air on the mountain and I thought that it was holding the mountain up. One day, at noon, in summer, when the sun on the mountain blazed and the rock was all gold like my friend B in the gold sari-dress she wasn't wearing, suddenly the rock tore. But in my childhood in Nesher it was still hanging there for years in the air holding up the mountain and at noon I would look for it on top of the mountain whirling and crumbling in the air all summer, and it seems to me the summer after that too. Afterwards came the winter and I asked myself how long it took for a mass of rock hanging on the mountain to fall off the mountain and I asked myself what material it was that held grain to grain and sometimes I remembered that when it fell I was afraid that the sun had fallen. Every day I looked at the quarry then.

The table, the table, said my friend B. This was after she had already crossed the lawn, still stepping on it with small careful steps, as if there were shoe-mines on the lawn. By then she had already extricated herself from the support of the doctor and the support of her husband, leaving the two embarrassed men behind her and us behind her as she proceeded alone along the narrow path, advancing with a tremendous effort forward into the house, her house. Her hands were limp, exposed and again she beat them like two wings against the two sides of her body as she approached the door and stood for a moment on the threshold and then entered with a sudden decision with a strong movement of a person setting out in stormy weather. It was hot. Her face was flushed. But it gave off a chill which was hard to bear.

Wonderful, she said.

She said this three times, in the same tone, but each time the temperature changed and the chill grew more unbearable, as if with each statement something was happening in her body. After that her eyes narrowed and she looked only at the table. Now she stood alone, apart from everyone else. She drew herself up a little, exhausted, and her eyes darted low, narrowed on the table. Everything was green. Everything was a lie. And she stood there, in the gold sari-dress apart from everyone else, and there was no way either good or bad. And only everthing was green everything was a lie. And apart from everyone else she began to walk towards the table as in ancient times those sentenced to die walked towards the hill.

Wait, raged Alexander.

Wonderful, she said.

She turned towards us, her confused audience.

Really, they've made it look wonderful, no? she said.

Her sick eaten body was already stretched as far as an eaten body could go and she stretched it further and further and further her eyes on every single one of us still standing there in that miserable row. And everything was green. Everything was a lie. And all that existed was only the chasm between one look and the next and one moment and the next and the passion and power which she now possessed.

She smiled.

She has a blue shadow under her eyes, and the smile took its time passing from one eye to the other.

Really, they've made it look wonderful, no? she said, drugged and poisoned, with the eyes of a she-wolf.

She knew the price of the performance.

Really, they've made it look wonderful, no?

She spoke slowly and it took time for her to get from word 'a' to word 'b', from place 'a' to place 'b', and the only thing she didn't have was time.

She knew that too.

The table really did look wonderful. It was covered with a red woven cloth with airy stripes woven into the cloth, so that the colour of the wood of the table showed through it. There were eleven places round the table, eleven little straw baskets for bread, and eleven slender-legged glasses with white garlands engraved around their rims, eleven tumblers of Hebron glass in purple, green and blue and a khaki colour for cold drinks. In the centre stood a huge glass jug with a silver handle and silver tongs and a heap of little square cubes of ice, and flat round slices of lemon floating in the water, and another eleven tumblers of low Hebron glass with a few low flowers stuck loosely in each of them to look like bunches of wild flowers dotted about, and then there was the dinner service, not the splendid one used for formal occasions, but the pseudo-simple, pseudo-crude one used by the family, a clay service in a clay colour with a narrow brown stripe encircling the plates like a slender ring, and of course there was the cutlery with the long white wood handles. The table was ready for the feast. On every clay plate stood a little clay plate and on it an artichoke, and scattered about the table stood saucers of a lemon and dill sauce for dipping. The wine bottles stood on a little table next to the main table, in front of the window, and there were plenty of salt-cellars, pepper pots and rolled-up napkins.

She was still standing at the door, flushed, examining the intricate colourful setting, which really was magnificent. Suddenly she took a small step forward, then she approached the table and stood there for a moment in agitation, and then she said that you didn't put red table-napkins on a red tablecloth and she had specifically asked for the antique-rose damask set. Alexander apologised and came back with the antique-rose damask set. She said: You put table-napkins in rings, don't you know that you put table-napkins in rings, what, didn't Nira remember? I specifically asked for it, she said. Alexander brought a pile of narrow wooden rings and inserted each napkin into a ring and she circled the table with little steps and examined the cards and the names on the plates. – It'll do, she said, and after that Alexander's voice rose thunderously and he called the guests in from the garden to the feast. B sat in her usual place, opposite the window. Opposite her sat Alexander, with his back to the window. Nira sat next to him as the guest of honour of the meal. They began with chilled wine. Alexander asked everyone what wine. There was Vermouth, a dry white wine and a rosé. B said: I want some too. Alexander fumed that it wasn't allowed. The doctor said nothing.

It's allowed, she insisted.

I knew it, he whispered angrily.

Full, she clamoured.

Her eyes were bulging and she tried to make her voice sound gay.

Full, full, she clamoured. She raised the glass carefully and set it down carefully.

In vain I try to remember what was said, I can't, but I remember exactly what we ate and even what every dish looked like, the colour, the quantities and the combinations, the gleam of the cutlery and the gleam of the glasses, and from which side they began serving in what order and what. There was nothing out of the way during the meal, everyone kept to the unwritten contract and nobody knew, or remembered or saw. B sat next to me, speaking now too neither quickly nor slowly, but laughing very slowly, with a kind of hidden violence, and it was clear that the same programme would go on running till the end of the meal and in this wretched lost battle all the data were positive, there was all the time in the world moving in endless directions. She let this be understood with every look, throwing out short, packed sentences, gulping water, jealously guarding the next wave of words. Her hands were wounded, and she made efforts to hide her wounded hands, trying to eat bunched up and move her fingers as little as possible. She tore off the artichoke leaves and dipped them in the lemon and dill sauce, and seated at the head of the table, at the most convenient vantage point, she didn't miss a move made by anyone. They said what a pleasant breeze. There really was a pleasant breeze. They said what a delicious sauce. The sauce really was delicious. After that they served the soup and she said to Alexander that she would dish up, and put the tureen next to her. To my surprise it wan't sugar beet soup. It was consommé. She smiled, inclining her head slightly in my direction, and it seemed to me that we both understood the code. The tremendous difficulty was the words. Today I'm not so sure about it any more, returning to the handsome dining room with the big wide windows, the bright locks of light and my friend B sitting there wearing her jewels and sweating under her jewels. She shifted them from place to place on her neck, and today when I read a little book about birds I remembered her, my friend B, sitting burning, with her shoulders slumped and her hands swollen, like a bird feeding on its own blood.

Consommé, excellent, she said.

She laughed.

There's nothing like hot soup on a hot day. She laughed again. – Alexander, the ladle, please. We'll begin at the end, Nira's first.

She said this slowly, quietly, and smiled a little smile, as if the fact that they had changed the soup made her feel especially gay. Then she sunk the ladle into the middle, making a little whirlpool in the centre, in the middle of the tureen, holding onto it hard, as if she were holding a heavy wooden stick in her hand. Her eyes bulged, glassy, two balls of celluloid, which did not move, fixed on the ladle, their gleam getting duller from minute to minute, and you could feel how from minute to minute, together with the cancer, the hatred of strangers bloomed her in body.

It's important to mix it well, to get the 'heart of the soup' into every plate, she said, and we'll begin at the end, Nira's first. She smiled a little smile again. Her forehead was bathed in sweat and she wiped her forehead.

Suddenly it's grown hotter, she said with the same little smile looking round the table from one to the next and suddenly she began to count aloud.

Don't worry, there'll be second helpings, she said and drew the tureen towards her, trying to increase the gaiety in her voice.

Over-enthusiam is weakness, writes Tolstoy in *War and Peace*, but my friend B, for all her cleverness, trapped in a narrow strip of life, for this one hour at noon, forgot, feeling, for this one hour at noon, her old power, trying, for this one hour at noon, to remove some misunderstanding as she ladled the consommé with her forehead bathed in sweat, and she wiped it away making the same movement over and over again but it kept on coming back. Her face was alternately red and white, and she dished the soup out slowly, plate after plate, stirring it with the ladle after every plate to make sure that everyone would get the 'heart of the soup', and everyone around the table held out his hand with the empty plate and then drew back his hand with the full plate and smiled and said: Thank you, you're wonderful, and she said: Marvellous, and everyone around the table knew that it was murder, the disease had murdered her body.

They ate and talked and ate and talked again. Someone said he had bought a movable air-conditioner and that a movable air-conditioner was a wonderful thing, and someone said that he hated movable things, he liked things fixed to the wall. After that they talked about how Haifa had become a dirty town. Someone remarked that it had never been clean and it had only had the reputation of being a clean town, and after that as usual they asked why we were still living in Hadar instead of moving up to the Carmel, there was nothing left in Hadar but for lawyers and prostitutes, and she said with a laugh that she knew Zvi would say that of the two he preferred the prostitutes, and she agreed with him, but at that moment precisely a wind sprang up and he asked something about the poplar.

It will have to be pulled up, said Alexander.

Someone asked why.

Alexander said that it would raise the house.

Someone asked how a poplar could raise a house.

Alexander explained that it had long roots and it could raise a house.

A house? the doctor asked.

Alexander explained that its roots were so long that they destroyed the foundations from inside the ground. The house remains whole but it has no foundations, it has nothing to stand on, it falls down whole, do you understand?

Strange, said the doctor.

Why? said B. She was apparently in pain. She smiled. – And it never stops shedding its leaves. It always seems that it's going to be left naked.

The doctor sipped his soup.

Yes, he said, growth.

B, turned towards him, leaned over to the middle of the table and took the salt-cellar.

It has to be strong, it acts as a wind-break, she said.

A wind-break? said the doctor.

She went on playing with the salt-cellar.

It has scars on its leaves. When the wind goes through it whistles.

It wasn't clear what the connection was, and she repeated: It has scars on its leaves. Haven't you noticed that it whistles? There was passion in her voice. She said: I'm very fond of the whistling.

You're tiring yourself for nothing, said Alexander.

She put the salt-cellar down immediately and pushed it to the centre of the table.

Yes, I'm tiring myself for nothing, she said, and she picked up the salt-cellar again and put it down again on the red tablecloth. Then she paused in order to gain control of her voice.

Her faced blazed.

The tamarisk tree has leaves with salt nodules.

Her face blazed even more.

Didn't you know that the tamarisk has leaves with salt nodules, didn't you know? It's doomed to die in the desert, she said. She asked if anyone had heard of the Dead Sea apple, the apple of Sodom. Haven't you heard of the apple of Sodom? The apple of Sodom, she repeated and Hell, haven't you heard of Hell? There are lots of synonyms for Hell, didn't you know? And the apple of Sodom, nobody's heard of it, nobody knows?

She laughed again. She had strong teeth when she laughed.

Once people believed that there was an animal that breathed for ever. Alexander, what's the name of the animal? They cut off its head, you know, and it goes on breathing after they've cut off its head.

We're in the middle of eating, Alexander thundered.

Oh, I forgot, we're in the middle of eating, I apologize.

Her face was full of blood. – I forgot, we're in the middle of eating, I certainly do apologize. She held onto her hands, which were trembling hard, as if an electric shock had passed through her body. – And a table like this too, with one's husband and one's best, one's dearest friends.

She looked around her, unable to control her hands. – Really, the best and dearest, I really do apologize.

You're going too far, Alexander thundered.

Yes, I'm going too far, I'm definitely going too far, she said. She said this now in a dry, matter-of-fact tone, and she still couldn't control her hands. – And the table-napkin, Alexander, you're dirtying the table-napkin, Alexander they're the old-rose damask table-napkins you know. It's my memory, you know, I've simply forgotten the animal's name.

Instead of eyes, under the forehead, her two celluloid balls bulged, blank, glassy, a foreign body in her face. Again she tried to make her voice sound gay.

You can serve the salads now, she announced, tugging at the wide flowery dress which revealed ravaged shoulders, all bones, the arms hanging from them as if they came from some other place. – I read this week, I don't remember where, that ever since 1945 the world has lost its stability.

Since '45? Alexander inquired.

Yes, since '45, she said.

Why since '45 precisely? asked Alexander.

She said: It's a fact that the world really has lost its stability. But nobody knows yet what the attributes of the new, unstable material are.

The two celluloid balls suddenly raced feverishly round.

And it can be anybody, she said. She spoke as if her voice had been wounded. – Materials engineering, it's a complicated business, she said.

Suddenly she raised her back, tilted her body backwards and

79

pressed hard against the back of the chair, raising her head too as she looked hopelessly in front of her for a moment, wringing her hands. – You can't live outside your home, that's what it is, I think that that's what it is, she said suddenly and straightened violently as if she wanted to increase the volume of air around her. She was breathing fast, and I thought that pain, like fire, reduplicated itself in the process of burning. She kept on wringing her hands. It's a cannibalistic thing, she once said to me. Living inside a sack, she once said to me. And all the time the leaves are rustling, she said.

She was still sitting erect like a dog.

The poplar has a concert voice, she said.

Around the table there was a sudden stir.

I've already said that I have great difficulty in remembering what was said during the meal, and yesterday I called someone to ask. She didn't remember either nor did her husband. They only remembered that nothing special happened until someone mentioned Beilinson Hospital, and B said: No, I'm not going to Beilinson. Alexander said that no one wanted her to go to Beilinson and she went on looking at her plate. Alexander said that she wouldn't even go into a street called Beilinson. Her face was full of blood now too. She bent over and began sipping the soup with small sips and said into the soup that nobody was going to call a street after her. Alexander shouted, but she didn't raise her face from the soup and said that that was what she wanted, not to have a street called after her. – You'll be able to walk freely in all the streets, she said. Alexander hastily removed the napkin from his knees. He stood up, but she went on eating her soup. – Like mountaineers, advancing by stages, she said into her soup. Then I didn't yet know the story and I only understood later that people, like history, repeat themselves. It was told me years later, on the telephone from Haifa to Tel Aviv. The lines were busy and I couldn't hear very clearly. The doctor joked that it wasn't so easy to get a street named after you. B didn't hear. She ordered the meat and salads to be brought but before that for Alexander to tell the story about the cobra. They all knew the story about the cobra but they all liked the story about the cobra too, and he lit a cigar, drew a breath and loudly and lustily recounted what he had already loudly and lustily recounted dozens of times before, how he had brought this cobra back with him from the UH Conference to the Tel Aviv zoo on the plane in a suitcase, and how over the ocean the cobra had escaped from the suitcase. It was night time. The passengers were sleeping. And when he opened the suitcase it was empty. And he drew a breath and went on telling how he had closed the suitcase, already knowing that the cobra was taking a walk over the ocean between the seats in the plane, and on all the seats people were sound asleep in the plane, and he drew a breath again and stretched his long strong legs, settling back in his chair, and she looked at him, her eyes concentrating more and more on one point of his face as she tapped her plate with the tip of her fork like background music accompanying his loud voice. You could see how her eyes grew smaller and smaller, narrowing on a smaller and smaller point of his face, moving along some strange, slanting, oblique line and after that this same oblique line moved around the table, passing glassily from plates to faces and faces to plates and together with it moved a faint little smile, but it was impossible to tell to which side.

You can serve the meat, she said.

The oblique line now moved onto Nira.

On the big wooden platter, she said and averted her face with the movement of a person crossing to the opposite pavement. – I hope the colour has been preserved, she said, cooking ruins the colours. She breathed hard. – Have you noticed, most vegetables go red when they're cooked, have you noticed? She breathed hard again. – The vegetable peel, it's all in the vegetable peel, she said, looking for words, but the words didn't meet, like objects that don't belong to each other. – You never know how materials will behave, she said. She laughed a little. – I like this dinner service, this clay one, she said.

Nira scattered the salads over the table (I've already said that there were mustard seeds). Then she served the soufflé and the quiche and a variety of baked goods, and added ice cubes to the beautiful jug for cold water. There was red cabbage cooked in wine, a dish of tiny onions in wine (a delicacy of which B was particularly fond), sweet and sour beetroot, and green beans with almonds. After that a magnificent platter arrived with a magnificent crown of rice decorated with mushrooms and almonds and raisins and thin slices of crystallized fruit. In the end came the meat, a huge joint lying on a thick board of pale wood and surrounded by pieces of chicken cooked in orange juice and wine. Alexander began to carve the meat and he asked us all what we wanted and B said that Alexander was a master meat-carver and all the time she followed his movements and looked at him. – The inner meat, the inner meat, please, she said and all the time she looked at him, and all of us knew that she was the one who took care of everything for him including the woman who would take her place, and she was the one who had brought her into the house, taught her the dishes he liked and how he liked his shirt-collars ironed. And she had learnt quickly. She had soft graceful steps and she passed round the table with the salad bowls and dished up with soft graceful steps, and after that she brought potatoes in aluminium foil with cream sauce and put them in the centre of the table and as she walked she bent over and the doctor asked if there was garlic in it. B said: Yes, there's garlic in it and so what if there's garlic in it? Today I'm eating garlic too today I'm omnipotent and she asked Nira to bring the peach-Melba and the apricot whip and the iced soufflé, and Nira went into the kitchen a few times with soft graceful steps and piled the peach-Melba and the iced lemon soufflé and the apricot whip in an exquisite black dish on the table and all the time B looked at the table and where she put everything down on the table and then someone suggested drinking a toast to her and everyone stood up and drank a toast to her and she stood up and drank it too. Her face was still flaming and you could feel the heat of her breath burning her.

We can begin the meat, she said.

She exhorted them not to forget the gravy and said that Alexander always forgot the gravy. Afterwards she said that the gravy was out of this world and suggested that after the meal we should all tell a story and Alexander would be first. He asked which one.

The one about the cobra.

There was silence.

The one about the cobra, everyone likes the story about the cobra, she said.

There was silence.

Why not? said the doctor.

She laughed a nervous laugh.

I forgot, you already told it, she said.

I can tell it twice, why not? thundered Alexander.

Of course, you can tell it twice, she said. Her voice sounded hoarse, like a sad croak, and she looked at him now, very concentrated, in the way a person might look at a point in a flashlight.

Never mind, she said.

The arteries in her neck suddenly filled with blood and she bent down and held the nape of her neck as if it were broken.

The meal, as usual, took longer than expected and I saw the doctor stealing a glance at his watch. She must have seen too, because she turned to me and raised her hand, making a sign with her hand. – No, the two hours aren't over yet, she said and went on staring distantly at her hand, as if it were the hand of some other body, and to this day her voice runs after me through the years: No, the two hours aren't over yet, and packed into this brief statement, like gunpowder, lay the entire foreseeable future. Her breathing was rapid, her eyelids pink, and she was already playing her role with only partial success, failing to fill in the gaps. After we finished eating she announced that for coffee and the sesame sweets we would move to the living room, and that Alexander had, indeed, made sesame sweets, he adored making sesame sweets. Here too everything was ready and waiting. There were eleven seats, a lot of little tables and a lot of bunches of flowers. The window was open, high, wide, and it was possible to see the sea from end to end, limitlessly. B sank into an armchair, slowly, laboriously, supporting one hand with the other. Then she relaxed her wrist, this too slowly and laboriously, as if it was the hardest thing in the world to relax her wrist. Suddenly she looked exhausted. Instead of the flush there were little brown spots on her face, like flakes of rust, and every time I remember that picture I think that there are machines that can withstand field conditions but not transport conditions. And moving into the living room, ah, no, with that my friend B could not cope, and how she got there making her head move and her hands move, advancing as if she were swimming by means of a strong backwards motion, and I said to myself something about the heavy soul in the light shell, I caught myself thinking: A deciduous tree, the poplar tree, I remembered the leaves with the salt nodules and how she said: The inner meat, the inner meat, please, and he said: But what do you want, and she said: My strength, I want my strength, and he said: What side should I begin on, and she said: The green-blue light the blue-green ray, the laser is a weapon that blinds, she said. Everyone remembers windows, doors, she said, everyone knows only a few details, the body is a particularly deep grave, she said brushing crumbs off the old-rose damask napkin, and I wish you all a pleasant day, she said, and to this day I cannot remember the second incident and only that a wind began to blow, the huge poplar trembled and a whistling sound came from the poplar and the table rose and the tablecloth rose the doors and the glasses and the chairs and the bottles and the antiques rose and my friend B remained sitting there next to an empty table in an empty room of a house being raised by a poplar tree.

Suddenly she said: Wait a minute, first Alexander has to bring the sesame. He hasn't brought the sesame yet. We forgot the sesame.

She laughed. As I said before, she had strong teeth when she laughed.

Everything's fading out like in the movies she said.

I didn't know what to answer and I smiled and she looked at me and to this day I can't forget the way she looked at me. Then she turned her head ninety degrees and looked at me again. Her face was strange now as if it was cut in half and like you sometimes see in the movies as if she had two faces one on the other and she no longer wanted to remove the second layer before the first. The faces were now facing me fully, two faces one on the other in two profiles with thick contours. It seemed to me that she was still trying to hide the fear but not the poisoned life, and that it was impossible to stand it for one more minute and I saw her suddenly bending the upper half of her body forward so hard that it seemed to me that the fear was cutting her in half like a butcher's knife. But she didn't say a word. One contour was distorted and underneath it a contour with strong teeth laughed. Again it seemed to me that it was impossible to stand it for one more minute but she stood it. We all sat and she stood. She even straightened up, stretched her neck and looked round for a minute at everyone sitting there with a soft look, a look like shot silk.

I'd like to hear a violin she said.

We can put on a record, said Alexander.

No, a live violin, she said.

There was silence. Her glance strayed round the seated square with a circular movement, one by one, with the face that recalled her face, its intelligence, and with the two contours that ran over it wildly with the tremendous desire to live. We were still sitting and she stood, looking at the tables and the cupboards and the antiques (I remembered how conscientiously she used to dust them) and all the fixed and the moving objects and the dozens of different signposts of time scattered here as if they were things forgotten somewhere by mistake.

Yes, a live violin, to see the fingers on the strings, she said.

Her look suddenly grew vague.

I'd like to hear a live violin, she repeated staring in front of her frozenly. Even her eyelids didn't move and it was clear that everything was behind her everything was over, existing in some distant time, old and buried, and only that tremendous desire to live was streaming through her arteries like a powerful shot of morphine.

She selected words as if they were precision instruments.

I stood up before the coffee because I wanted to say something.

Her face turned a silver shade.

My plan was –

Enough, roared Alexander.

She looked at him with a desperate squint, shifted from one

85

foot to the other and swaying slightly pressed both hands tightly to her body, as if she were wearing a strait-jacket.

My plan was –

I don't agree, roared Alexander.

She shifted from one foot to the other again, and the red blotches returned to her face and one eye suddenly grew black and swollen with a bruise under the eye. She looked as if she had been given a punch in the eye.

My plan was – she began again, but the words came out of her mouth strangely, as if they were going in the opposite direction, from the mouth to the heart, and had disintegrated on the way.

She began again: My plan was –

In the story, as in life itself, there's a moment when it seems unreal to die in the middle of summer, for ever. It's tremendously hard to bear the continuing dryness in the mouth, the burning in the feet, but it's unreal to think that suddenly thoughts stop and a human being turns into a corpse. But perhaps B was not concerned with all this. She was poisoned with morphine, her time was running out and she still wanted to say something. Again she shifted from one foot to the other, her one eye grew increasingly black increasingly swollen and her skin and her face were now completely opaque and their colour made you think of a material resembling coral.

She looked very exhausted but nobody dared stand up and the doctor didn't tell her to sit down either, and she stood there, with her one black eye, shifting from foot to foot, the other eye glittering big and open devouring the trees and the windows and the rays of light in the windows, unbelievably bright, transparent, endless, penetrating the surface of the skin without leaving a scar.

Nobody dared get up and the doctor didn't tell her to sit down either, and she went on standing and looking and seeing and looking, not moving, unblinking. It was hot. The poplar whistled. She made a strange movement with her head, the eye with the black bruise fixed on the poplar, the other eye in some other place low down on the trunk, as if she was trying to separate the shape from the background or the treetop from the ground. It seemed as if she was looking not at the objects but at the margins of the objects and everything looked really huge, really tiny, really split-second. Again she strayed over the faces of the seated people with staring eyes. Time passed. More time passed. And I saw her strolling to and fro along the long veranda opposite the poplar tree in the way you sometimes clearly see people you once knew in places where they have never been at all.

Have you ever looked at a plant after a chopper or a fire and what happens to the bitter hairy poisonous fruit? Have you ever looked at the hard round seed and what happens to the hard round seed? The fruit of the birch tree for example is ground up. Ground up it's used for rat poison or for spraying fish. Have you ever seen a bare tree blossoming? The tree shines, naked, pink, even the trunk is visible in the distance so pink and shining it is in its beautiful blossoming. Some people say it's the tree on which Judas was hanged after he betrayed Christ. Others say it was used to crucify Christ. Since no material is ever lost in the world perhaps a bit of it is still hanging on a tree somewhere and has become part of the naked trunk or the beautiful blossoming.

She turned to Alexander again, squinting desperately, and you could feel the wild cat bursting from her body.

My plan was –

Instead of contracting into a ball with pain, her body expanded and she opened her fingers, still able to fly, but they were heavy, swollen, made more of lead than blood, and she dropped them and remained standing for a long time without moving.

My plan was – for each and every one of the people sitting here – who are all very dear to me – she took a breath – to say one sentence to me – she took a breath – and also –

She took a breath.

My plan was – to tell each and every one of the people sitting here – who are all very dear to me – she took a breath – what role they played in my life – she took a breath – but it's impossible – it's impossible.

She took a breath.

It's impossible, I can't do it.

She took a breath.

In any case, I have to go, time's up, she said.

Her face was wet and she wiped it with her hand, like a little girl.

And in any case I'm burning, I'm on fire, she said and wiped her face with her hand, like a little girl.

When she was standing in the door she stopped suddenly, and turned round.

I'm sorry we didn't drink the coffee, she said, you'll have to drink it without me. Nira will serve the sesame and the cake.

In the middle, when she entered the living room, there was another incident that I forgot and skipped over. It was before she collapsed into the armchair. She asked Zvi to sing her a song. He asked what song.

Never mind, whatever you want, she said, and unable to keep standing she fell into the armchair. He knelt at her feet and began to sing:

> Seven mice and a mouse
> Are eight I suppose
> So I take my chapeau
> And I say goodnight.

She didn't move. Her hands trembled on her knees. They were cold and damp and stuck to her knees like clamps. She hummed:

> Seven mice and a mouse
> Are eight I suppose
> So I take my chapeau
> And I say goodnight
> I take my chapeau
> And off I go
> Where can you go so late at night
> All on your own.

A week later, on Saturday, we were there in the garden and there were a lot of other people there too who had come to condole with Alexander. He came up to us and stood with us for a moment next to the poplar tree.

I don't want you to hear it from strangers, he said, Nira's living here.

We didn't know what to say.

I thought you realized, he said. A strange smile crossed his face.
– That's why she had the feast.

We didn't know what to say. Zvi mumbled something. Then he said he would go and get us something to drink and I said: All right, I'll wait here, and I stood and looked at the beautiful garden and the beautiful woman moving round serving fruit and lemonade and iced coffee. Among the other antiques and jars and capitals there was a sarcophagus which I forgot to mention, made of wonderful white stone, standing open in the garden and my friend B would sometimes sit on its rim as if it were a bench. I couldn't resist the temptation and I sat down on it too as if it were a bench and looked at the beautiful woman moving round there in the garden and she suddenly looked at me like a small detail of no significance in the whole story, moving round the garden with little steps as if she had been moving round here all along. I've already said that she had a soft walk and a soft neck and I saw him standing in the kitchen passing his hand over her soft neck and I said to Zvi, let's go home. He said: Yes, let's go home. The poplar made a loud concert sound and on the bench sat my friend B. On the other side of the bench. Her black eye had disappeared and her eyes were china blue, a warm blue, sparkling on the rim of the sarcophagus, and inside it her head swayed like a giant marionette beating the stone of the sarcophagus. I was very tired. I said to Zvi, let's go home. He said: Yes, let's go home.

When we left he asked if I remembered what she had said. I asked what.

Translated by Dalya Bilu

7

Bridal Veil

by AMALIA KAHANA-CARMON

FATHER ACCOMPANIED her and sat with her on the Egged inter-city bus. Until the journey began. It was the bus before last. Because Father had taken her to the pictures. Now he was impatient. Irritable for some reason.

A group of UN soldiers were getting on the bus. One got on and Father said: 'Looks like Anthony Perkins, that one.' Another one got on. Looks even more like Anthony Perkins, reflected Shoshana but did not say.

For many hours she had waited for Father. An evening in another town. The park. Empty playground. Through branches and leaves, lights: dwelling-storeys. Residences, windows. Strangers' homes.

Since the early afternoon she had waited there. The gardeners were still having a rest in the shrubs' shade. Two long-haired vagabond tourists, one with hair like the sun in a poster, equal and matching tongues of flame in a blazing circle, with intense concentration measured and cut in two a single cigarette with a razor blade. Little boys and girls began arriving. Some of the little boys had their hair held one side by a hair-clip. Some of the girls had tiny toy handbags. Some little white woollies folded over the arm. Chilly in the evening in the mountain town.

Later on, deaf-mute children were brought to the park. With them two teachers. Or helpers. Very young, dressed like sluts.

The helpers went and sat on a bench. The mute children invaded the playground, swarming over every seat. Or, blank-eyed, violently spinning roundabouts, making swings and their sitters fly. The nice children scattered, scurried for mothers' or child-minders' laps. The mute children, like pirates, snatched at the vacated seats. Signalling to each other pleasure and delight; voicelessly, with gestures and grotesque faces only. Among them fully-grown girls riding the infants seats of the seesaws, on their faces the expression of mental retardation. One lanky boy, sombre, most obstinate, his shirt torn at the shoulder, kept on disturbing them. Trying to grab their rubber flipflops, rising and falling, while they draw back their feet and kick out at him lazily. Under his chin, in his stomach, his ribs, wherever the seesaw takes them. And whenever he, with his eyes shut, gapes in sound-less pain, one can see, his teeth are false.

The park emptied. Soon it will be completely dark. And now it is. The recorded voice of a woman trails past. Clear and vivid as though a singing siren were sitting on the bonnet of the passing car. Silence again. Then the trail of the familiar voice of an announcer, reading the evening news. From a first-storey balcony, across the trunks of the pine trees, once or twice, questions are asked aloud. Of members of a family, settling for the night. Then the vertical slats of the blinds were turned slightly, their backs inwards, their insides outwards, just enough to seal off.

Shoshana took out and started eating the food her mother had given her for the journey. Brown bread. A little smoked fish Lakerda. One or two apricots. A little halvah.

A man – an Ashkenazi, bald and pot-bellied in too-wide khaki shorts, once everyone sported clothes like that, with a shabby brief-case, like a middle-aged clerk – went in and out, in and out of the park. Earlier, when he had passed by her, she could still make out the grooved buckle, held in the last hole of his belt. Beads of sweat on his forehead and the front of his bald head. Also his eye, fixed on her sideways, like a rooster's. Fixed on her all the time. Later on, one could hardly make out the features of his haggard face. The darkness deepened more and more. Shoshana made up her mind and went to wait on the pavement, under the street lamp. She was worrying that Father might not find her, as he told her to wait in the park, in the playground, like all the children. And what if Father should come in through the other gate? What if he went away. But that's how it is. In another town. A strange town.

She stood on the street corner, peering furtively at the section of the main street, there beyond the alley. People were passing there. True, fewer people. But people were passing there. And cars. All along there had been some mistake, it was revealed to her now. She hadn't thought about it, but must have assumed that life outside came to an end when one went to bed, after supper. Except on special occasions. And here's something new, secret: there's the ordinary life of day. And there's the ordinary life of night. Life carries on at night. Differently though. At night everything is different. Houses, people, thoughts.

The bus lingered. Father started to grumble.

Since when do UN soldiers travel by bus, Shoshana reflected. Two were sitting in front. A third one stood over them, chatting.

Ice-blue eyes they had. And though they certainly had broad shoulders, something about them was as if narrow. And they were as though made of drier stuff. As though we, our end is to shrink, leaking a spreading puddle. And later on, when all but shrunk to thin skin, to get all wrinkled, to evaporate and be no more. But they, their end is to crumble, turn into dust, and be no more. And they were all similar, but each in his own way. Like guavas. They all taste good, but each tastes also slightly different, giving its own interpretation of the taste of the guava.

A man carrying a high cardboard box entered. On it, in big red scrawl, like a finger smear, it read: Parts – Incubators. He blocked the exit with it.

Again Shoshana was reminded of the story called 'Excerpt' in the 'Paths Reader Part Four'. A chick hatches out of its egg in the incubator. To whom will the chick turn its inborn human need for attachment. Will it turn to the electric incubator, it was written there, will it turn to the poulterer who breeds it in order to have it transferred to the electric poultry abattoir, to whom. The inborn human need, it was written. The human need of he who is not human.

From one of the seats could be heard the voice of a young man, of Oriental Sephardi stock, excited, even though whispering. 'Give it to me, let me be the secretary of the committee. No, not because you like me. Because I've got the hang of it. And you'll see if, within four years, I don't turn this place into a political springboard. First rate. If each one of them wouldn't need me, look for me, come to me for favours. Here's Ben-Dov. Who's Ben-Dov. Alright, he's head and shoulders above. Today. Fifteen, twenty years ago, what was he. A seaman. And today, you can see for yourself. And I, I'll get you the whole of the construction lot going. Think of it: power. True, true. But Anaby got demolished politically because he doesn't have the makings of a public figure. Just not a strong man. True, he was seen all over the place. Ran around. But he doesn't have the makings. It's a question of having an influence over people. You have to know how to get them going. How? Work at the source. Besides, you know that with me you'll get the works. Balance sheets, reports, deals, the lot.'

The bus lingered on. Father got up, parted abruptly, and left.

As soon as Father got off the bus, the UN soldier who had been standing up came over and sat down beside her. Perched on his seat, craning his neck forward, he picked up his chatting with his friends.

Freckled, young, good-looking. But the light went out and he stopped talking. Shoshana wondered about his sitting next to her. Moreover, she had noticed that before he sat down he had considered her, then the empty seat across the aisle, and making a quick decision chose to sit by her. And as soon as he sat down, it was as if a prize had fallen her way.

Even in the dark it was possible to see, his lips were finely drawn. The fleshy hand, grasping the rail of the seat before them, firm. And he's one of the boys. Very much one of the boys.

The bus started moving off. Outside, a tall woman passed, crossed its path walking very upright, and the driver cried out furiously: 'Great Garbo.' Shoshana peeped at the UN soldier, saw him smiling in surprise. Unaware, she too smiled inwardly. But now the strap of the flight bag – the blue El Al bag, with father's laundry, that Father had placed on the shelf above – slipped down, swung about and almost touched the beret of the soldier sitting in front of her. Meaning to put it back, Shoshana struggled to get up, tried to stand on the curve of the wheel at her feet. Trouble: the UN soldier was sitting on the edge of her skirt, Mother's wide skirt given for the trip. As the bus swerved to leave its bay by the platform side, Shoshana slipped, found herself in the dark waist up across a hard and alien knee.

'Sorry,' she cried out in Hebrew, reaching out with both hands, as if for a raft, to the rail of the seat in front, whilst the embarrassed UN soldier was saying in English: 'I'm sorry. I'm sorry. It's alright.'

Trying to stand up again, the UN soldier still sitting on the edge of her skirt, the bus swerving the other way, she flew to his knees once more. This time he hastened to help, to raise her like a package in order to put her back in her place. But with the bus jolting and straightening itself, he put his hand in the wrong place. 'Sorry,' he let go at once, alarmed. Straining to rise, Shoshana said: 'It's alright,' echoing his English, 'sorry.' And she tried a word from her school-days: 'Dress.' 'Dress? Oh, dress. I'm sorry,' his alarm increased and he rose. 'It's alright,' she mouthed in shame. The shadow of a smile was wiped off her face now. With it, her self-assurance.

Once, when Father still worked in Tiberias. A waitress, with a wink to her friend, volunteered to display her skills in making small talk. She announced, she'd ask a soldier if he was married. She couldn't find the word. Then she did: 'You, papa?' 'Perhaps I am and I don't know it,' the soldier laughed, very much taken by surprise. All the waitresses shrieked. What did he mean. Married or single. He invited the waitress to go out with him. 'Where to,' she asked. 'Dancing cheek-to-cheek,' translated Father, for all to hear the soldier's reply. What did the soldier mean. 'UN soldiers, they are like sailors of a ship,' Father had explained to her at the time. Father had a song in French, and once on a weekend, he translated it for us like this, with feeling: 'I see the harbour lights / Only they told me we were parting / The same old harbour lights / That once brought you to me / I watch the harbour lights /How could I help if tears were starting / Goodbye to tender nights / Beside the silvery sea.' And throatily: 'I long to hold you near / And kiss you just once more / But you are on that ship / And I am on the shore.' And again, as before: 'Now I know lonely nights / For all the while my heart is whispering / Some other harbour lights / Will steal your love from me.'

Along the nocturnal road were trees, nodding heads like

people. The light of the speeding bus falls on them, withdraws from them. And the vapour-veiled moon crescent is getting blurred. But why is her throat so dry – Shoshana gazed through the window for a long time.

Once, travelling home with Father's laundry, a nice young man, maybe a student at the Polytechnic, sat next to her reading a paperback. Entitled 'It Was Murder By Moonlight'. When it got dark, the young man put the book in his pocket and turned to touch her nape so artfully that until they reached the junction she couldn't make out whether he had, or she had imagined it. Then as now, at the first moment, the same panic. A blind panic. Like a wild animal's. Only this time there was no room for error. The UN soldier beside her is, he is, pressing his elbow on to her arm. This time she did not rise to leave her place and did not move to another seat. She sat on like a statue. Doing nothing. Gazing through the window.

Now, with his other hand he is seeking hers. And just as it's not for exercising their throat-muscles that people utter sounds. But for saying things with words, the things that matter. So it is here. He is seeking to say something, only in another way. What is he asking. Yes, I know. But it's clear what he is asking right now about it. And what does he expect from her. Hard to know, let alone when one is confused.

She stole a look at him. And learned that he was already sitting very close, much closer than she had realized. Deadpan faced, as though he had nothing to do with her. Passing his arm behind to surround her. UN soldiers in front of us, UN soldiers behind us. How does he have the nerve.

At the junction the lights came on. The UN soldier hurried, moved away abruptly.

Cheerful girl-soldiers boarded the bus. 'Smadar, Smadar,' they cried out to another who was still outside, buying something from a child-vendor. Good-looking, grownup, laughing. Here goes, reflected Shoshana, this will put an end to me. Besides, there's no escape: I know what he must think of me now – she didn't dare look his way. As he sat staring straight ahead, so did she. As he folds his arms, so she folds hers.

The girl-soldiers spread out boisterously over the vacant seats. The ticket inspector got on. And the UN soldier beside her smiled to himself, privately, tilting his chin a little, as a UN soldier seated distantly threw a side-comment in a loud voice, probably a joke. Shoshana took out the two tickets from the pocket of her plaid blouse. The return ticket and the late-night surcharge one, holding them both in her hand.

And she saw: the UN soldier who was sitting still grinned at her. As if asking permission. And before she could know what he wanted, he took her tickets from her hand. Holding them with his ticket, entirely together, he handed them to the inspector.

As ever and always she, the eldest daughter, has had to manage on her own – what is it that passed through her now, piercing through the bark, penetrating the sapwood, making it ooze. She felt herself shattered, knowing nothing.

Returning her tickets, he attempted to strike up a conversation with her:

'Israel?' he pointed at her.

Shoshana nodded.

He pointed at himself:

'Riff-raff.'

Where is Riffraffia, she tried to remember.

'Canada,' he smiled as if in confirmation, raising a shoulder to push his ticket into his pocket.

All she knew about Canada, she reflected, was what Father had once told them. A Canadian walked into the hotel kitchen. He sat down and said, to Father and the rest of the assistant-chefs, that where he came from, normally, they entertained in the parlour. But a specially welcome guest was always received in the kitchen. This was what the man had said, and dropped off. Totally drunk. Only later they found out he'd fallen asleep on the spice mill, which they had been looking for all that time.

The UN soldier pointed backwards with his thumb. To know whether she is a resident of the city they had left. Shoshana pointed ahead. The city they were heading for. He got it and laughed, as if by this she had proved herself sharp-witted. He pointed back again, shaking his other hand, as if enquiring.

Shoshana pointed at Father's bag. 'Papa,' she said. The UN soldier's face became respectful, and Shoshana felt pleased. Very.

Then she remembered. Tried her hand at making small talk: 'You. Papa?'

He didn't understand. But pointed at himself, and smiled: 'No papa. No mama. No brother. No sister. No wife. No children. Nobody,' he said. And he took off his beret. Put it on her bag. On her bag he put it. Now, with his red hair, he was better looking sevenfold. And as soon as the light went out he returned to her. Once the bus danced. And he, using the inside of his arm which was on her back, pressed it on her hard then, deliberately. As if to protect her, to spare her the bumps.

In the vicinity of the boundaries of the city, but a good way from the station yet, the road was blocked with buses and cars. 'A traffic jam?' people said, 'an accident?'

For a long time they waited there. More cars drove up, stopped. People began to get off the bus. Got tired and boarded it again. A man wearing the bus company hat appeared. A real veteran. There had been a road accident, he explained. They would have to proceed on foot. Passengers going further would be provided with transport. Saying this, he left. The driver translated it into English, and picking up his satchel indifferently, left too.

The UN soldier got Shoshana's bag down from the shelf, but people were shoving between them. Especially one woman, her fleshy bulks quivering, who kept on her conversation whilst alighting, as if incapable of stopping: 'Twenty years later I saw her, the one he left me for,' it was unbelievable that she was saying. 'Quite my look-alike. And he did the same thing to her too. The bastard, the worthless bastard,' she said. 'How do I know? He did it with me,' she spoke ordinarily. The ordinary life of night.

Almost the last one to get off, down there waiting for her was the UN soldier.

'Goodbye,' Shoshana was glad to have found the word. She took her bag from him, whilst here too was a novelty: the language not her own language in her mouth. A man-made contrived automaton. Look, as if at the press of a button it suddenly works, alive, performing: another secret new thing is revealed. Suddenly the world is full of questions and surprises. Meanwhile, she was overhearing a passing Israeli youth, who casting a glance at the UN soldier, was saying about him in Hebrew: 'A handsome corpse.' And it was as if it were her who had been paid a compliment.

The UN soldier did not go. He was standing, hands in the belt of his narrow trousers, and waiting. Shoshana pointed at his friends, the UN soldiers who were walking away, after they had set themselves apart and crossed to the other side of the road. He shook his head signalling no, and took her bag from her. Smiling and saying 'Little girl,' he pointed at his watch. Meaning, it's late and it won't do for little girls to be on their own.

They were the last ones there now. And as she turned to follow the crowd, which was making its way along the stalled vehicles, he stopped her. Catching her lightly by the edge of her sleeve. Tacitly, as if conspiring. And now that she had stopped with him, Shoshana felt that he had her consigned to his charge entirely. Under his patronage. Now she was his. All she had to do was to rely on him. For his part, his contribution or guarantees, were in evidence by the quality of the skin of his arms, for instance. Fine, sand coloured, strewn with freckles and as if brave, very appropriate. Or his watch, his square wrist-watch, this too was sort of appropriate, and by that an attested proof. Also his vest, like a white gym shirt, peeping out of his open collar. And so forth.

When there were no more passengers, the UN soldier pulled her to him, moved her to his other side, and led her with him down a path – many paths were here – leading toward the city. All went over there, whereas they go on a way that is theirs only. That too was right. She joined him unquestioningly.

From time to time he stopped her, hugged and fondled her. Once, kneading and kneading her, he said into her hair, slowly, so she would understand, 'You'll see. I'll be good,' and kissed her on her hair.

The words astounded her. Another secret new thing is revealed: this is what the grown-up girls are privileged to. Canadian girls. Blissful girls. Mysterious, haughty and deserving. Is it they who got them instructed, trained them. On evenings of paths through boughs in leaf, and lanterns hanging from branches amid twigs, foliage and tendrils. His chest in uniform, to which he held her when he spoke, belonged there too. His surprising chest, close, straight, all vacant and free; and how is this, a safe haven. But what had he said. As though she had been asked, in astonishment: 'All these years, and you didn't know? Did you really not know that there is, there is a Mediterranean Sea in the east as well?' Of course. A sea, and a beach. And why the scary relief. 'I didn't know,' I answer, and already am not sure: did or didn't I. But what did he say. Did he propose to her. A little girl. Does it mean he intends to wait until she grows up. To take her with him, in the fullness of time, to Riffraffia. Run along, days, run. The only thing unclear yet is how, without ever knowing me, he recognized immediately that I am Shoshana more than any Shoshana, and that is why I should be singled out.

In the floral skirt too large for her, made to fit her waist with a safety pin. In the plaid blouse too short for her, the sleeve not quite hiding the slipping bra strap. The same Shoshana. And another Shoshana. Mysterious, deserving. Beautiful girls, beautiful women, like beautiful fans. Always, whenever she perceives the beautiful, it's a pleasure. As if she partakes of their beauty, from a distance. And now, there she is, a proper partner herself, deserving. And at a threshold.

Like then, in the dream? I stand in a large public square. Daylight fades. A very beautiful African lady, an ambassador's wife, stands spellbound before one of the flower beds in the square. A corner of tall, giant funnel-like arum lilies. Gaudy. Striped, streaked and spotted, in supernatural hues. 'Harare-Horse,' she says in a low voice, 'Harare-Horse.' I too fall under the spell. 'Harare-Horse?' I ask. 'Harare-Horse: the piles of sweets in our marketplaces.' And someone comes to call her. To the airliner. To the night sky. Already studded with stars like jasmine flowers. Run along, days, run.

Holding her hand in his all the time, at the end of the path they came to a very tall wire-mesh fence. Looking new. They turned back. Over and over, at the end of every path, was the same fence.

Impossible to walk along it. Tall thorns, impassably tangled. No choice, the fence has to be climbed.

He threw her bundle over to the other side. Helped her climb the fence. Then joined her. He swung his legs over to the other side and jumped down. But she, she couldn't get down! Putting up his arms to catch her, she let herself go, fell into his arms.

Having received her, why didn't he allow her to go, steadily enfolding all of her, tightly against him. And why has he changed so. Why don't they keep on walking. And why is she suddenly again in the panic of a wild animal – she tried to free herself. But how very strong men are, it dawned on her. And he breathes as if he has a fit of shivers. Why did he abruptly fling her to the ground. And isn't it wrong to force down a person's head backward into the dust. Wriggling to set herself free, half of her trapped between his legs, and he keeps her legs clasped together, her top half locked in one of his arms, he only sprawled on her, hard, in his clothes and shoes, that's all, with his other hand, forcing her face towards his, seeking her mouth, as if looking for closeness and consent. Himself, giving, offering, donating his only pair of lips, the ones that matter to him, it must be, of lips that seem so well cared for. Yet, at the same time, he cruelly prevents her from freeing herself, as if forbidding her to make a move, what sort of a plan is all this, and he is sighing and is so worked-up. And suddenly he lets go. Everything isn't clear, isn't good. Haven't we been friends. And I, for his sake, I am no longer of Israel. I am of the UN.

Sitting beside her he asked, slowly, so she could make it out: 'How old are you?'

Shoshana showed with her fingers: thirteen.

He laughed. Buried his face in her shoulders.

'God,' he said, laughing, 'forgive me.' Now he tapped the top of his head, meaning: he had thought. To explain, he stuck out his fist three times, opening and closing it, and added fingers, meaning eighteen. He twisted his left hand, meaning: maybe. He stuck out his fist again and added with his right hand fingers, meaning: seventeen. Stuck out again and with one finger: sixteen. Thought it over, and only stuck out: fifteen. Shoshana was watching it all earnestly, patiently, trying to comprehend the sign language. But now he laughed, tapped her nose with his finger. Shoshana raised her head towards him, and he hugged her with one arm, drawing her to him. The private fair skin of his arms is nevertheless very appropriate. His chest in uniform, a safe haven.

'Mosquitoes,' he said. Of course, mosquitoes. He patted his back pocket, as if to check, brought out a crushed packet of foreign cigarettes. And matches, their heads a lighter colour than their bodies, attached in rows to a small book. He lit a cigarette. He pointed to the cigarette smoke and clarified: 'The mosquitoes,' making with his palm as if he is dispersing them. Smoke drives mosquitoes away, she learnt. He's a learned man.

He kept on smoking. Looking ahead. Turned and offered her the cigarette. Shoshana took the cigarette. He laughed and corrected her hold of the cigarette, encouraging her to smoke. But Shoshana gave him the cigarette back. And so, making a move to lean on her forearm, she gave out a small cry: she had laid the inside of her wrist on a piece of glass, and cut herself. She searched, picked up the piece of glass, clear glass of a bottle neck. He took it from her hand, hurled it away. 'Let me,' he asked to see the cut.

Shoshana hesitated. Put her hand behind her back, smiling at him shamefully. He resumed smoking, looking ahead. Shoshana brought out her hurt hand gingerly, sucked it covertly. He saw, laughed. Turning to her, he took the whole arm in his free hand. Could see nothing in the dark. Pressed her arm as if promising, and returned it to her. Having finished his cigarette, he stuck the butt in the ground. Rose up, almost without using his hands, she noticed. Went to fetch her bag, slinging it effortlessly over his shoulder.

He came over and pulled her up. 'Little girl,' he said tapping his watch smiling.

Shoshana rose up, yielding. He said something, speaking slowly, so she could make it out. And she couldn't. He repeated it, again and again, and she couldn't make it out. 'Never mind,' he laughed lightly.

Now houses could be picked out clearly. Everything seemingly colourless. And the street lamps' lights over there going out all by themselves. Is it so that in ordered way day after day the sky is rinsed white by the steadily increasing pure light, without hindrance, simply and in silence day slips out of night. A neat, uncomplicated solution. So very right. All the earth is full of heaven's glory. No need for witnesses. But the eyes see. Raising his hand, the UN soldier wiped off dust from each of her eyebrows with his thumb. In her heart it was as if he had sworn her in.

They were walking between the road and the line of trees along it. To the north-east, among the trees and across the flat roofs of the houses, she saw a reddening mark overlaying a suggestion of blue. And the clouds of reverence. The dwarfed cylinders of the solar tanks and their sloping panels, the ladders and spindly matchsticks of the television aerials, all blacker than black, against the background of incandescent sea, gradually igniting. It is of the revelations made visible, an inheritance in the possession of the sworn in, the initiated ones, to whom the mysteries of the world are everyday affairs.

Earlier, when they were looking for the way, they heard a gang of boys passing far away. Probably trainees at the vocational school. One was strumming the guitar, others singing indistinctly. She remembered that it had been the last day of school. The UN soldier even did a 'Bang-bang' in the direction of the sounds, as if holding a rifle in his hands. Now, in the light of daybreak, the boys were seen coming back. A reminiscence of colours: tight trousers, reminiscent of light blue; a belt, reminiscent of stripes of black and red; a shirt, reminiscent of yellow. Still singing, stopping to sniff each other's mouths, they were crossing the road, marching down towards the houses: the time is four o'clock in the morning, they'll wake up the whole street. 'I have no idea what I wrote in the exam. But what I wrote was the right thing.'

The UN soldier turned quickly, fixed her nimbly to one of the eucalyptus trees. Leaning against the tree with his arms held above her, he stood hiding her. She was astonished. By herself, it would never have occurred to her. She attempted to say something, but he put his hand promptly over her mouth, and she was breathing the fresh pungent tobacco smell on his fingers. Then he lowered his gaze to her, smiling amiably. UN-Soldier! – her heart clung to him. UN-Soldier! – thus she stood watching him all the time, her head tilted up to him her eyes staring wide-open at him, his hand on her mouth. Until, when the boys were not there anymore, and bending his knees, he held her by the shoulders, jokingly attached his cheek to hers. Remembering, he rubbed his hand against his cheek to show the reddish stubble which had started growing, grimaced to make her laugh, and released her. 'Little girl, good girl,' he said.

UN-Soldier! – Shoshana plucked up courage, put out her hands, took hold of his waist, did not wish to walk on. Then joined him, continuing to walk.

Free of any dependence known to me. Unknown dependences have lent here character and grit, without which you are not a person – he strides as though without moving his head. Regards everything before him as though all, and this means all, is equal and the same. And speech is not a must for him, with or without it will do. This, you can tell, is his natural state. There's a kind of admirable quality here, like a sort of luxury. Serenity arising from a reservoir of strength – Shoshana tried to match her footsteps to his. And all the while his face, arms, uniform – all of his familiar self, is both old and new in the new light.

A lorry, still nocturnal, its lights still on, passed them with a great clatter. Full of Arab labourers, stooping. On the other side of the road, the football pitch. The two goals, and the hard ground cleared of scrub, surrounded by a stand consisting of two rows of stadium benches, one above the other, like scaffolding. And a bus stop. The billboard. From here, whoever is not in the know couldn't have guessed that the dark rectangle on the billboard is the big illustrated poster of the Indian film. The girl has a red pea in her forehead, above her nose, and an amber necklace; the beads thick and squarish. While the man has an inclination towards a double chin.

The UN soldier scanned the highway looking lost, passing his palm over his ruddy neck. Inspecting her as if he's uncertain of her ability to lead the way. Perhaps he thought she kept looking at him all the time with great interest waiting for his resourceful-ness. But she keeps looking on at him as she walks only because she cannot take her eyes off him: I could not imagine him with a moustache, for instance, or with sideburns, or a beard. Now, that he is in need of a shave, I can. Or, here. Despite the peeling nose owing to this country's sun, here are the azure shards of ice-mountains. Shards from the faraway country where his home is, the keepsake imbedded in his face instead of eyes. His face, permanently wearing the sudden foreignness that a woman of ours has on her face, for a fleeting moment, when she first puts on her earrings. Like a foreign perfume. A foreignness that has a touch of class. Like fastidious sinisterness. Sinisterness that is the product of your own imagination, the product of your own effacement. Or his colours, for example. The colours of another earth, different – as far as the eye can see, other fields, different. With different electricity-pylons, vanishing into them. With different tractors and combine harvesters, looking minute when they pass through them. The men who drive them wear different overalls. Perhaps dungarees? Are their hats straw hats frayed at the edges? In the heat of the day in the field they all drink whisky out of jerrycans.

Shoshana stopped. To shake a bit of gravel out of her shoe. She tried to indicate that she was stopping.

He halted, smiled comprehension.

Shoshana resumed walking. The shards of faraway, they come complete with an arrangement of golden lashes. The colours, all the colours of a different, freckled earth, in the land across the ice-mountains: if you break with your axe a little ice in the valley, you'd be able to draw out with a hook a fish that is about man-size. And look lo and behold, they have arrived, fallen right here. Striding right here. With our very own football pitch behind us, and in front, our neighbourhood. All the birds in the boughs of the eucalyptus trees welcome the future sunrise in concert, but I know: it is also in our honour, also in our honour. Is there anyone like you in the world, that like you is just right.

And here's the neighbourhood.

A cat could be seen passing from a house roof to a shed roof. All the houses are deep in slumber. The end of the wooden cart is showing, laden high with watermelons. Of the first ones this season. But it seems, none of the Ezra brothers is asleep on the mattress over there. Even the hanging hurricane lamp is out of sight. In a slow death, devoid of any noble fortitude, the two abandoned houses crumble away. Cracks on the wall, the yards are thorn bushes. They say, among their foundations' low cement stilts there are snakes.

At the back fence of the house she stopped. Pointed at the house. But the UN soldier bent back his thumb and stuck it pointedly between his teeth, as he tilted his head backward, demonstrating to Shoshana, with eyes surveying around, that he wished to drink. She understood. Pointed at the tap beside the dustbin.

He rode the fence, then was over. The shoulder-line straight as a coat-hanger, the big shirt hanging down his back like a scarecrow's, he turned on the tap. Leaned forward above it, legs apart, and drank. A cat, probably lurking there the whole time, suddenly made up its mind, leapt out of the dustbin and fled to the neighbour's yard, hid behind the old icebox that lies there, its side on the ground. The UN soldier wiped his mouth with his wrist.

He came. Stood before her. Lifted the bag, hung it over her shoulder laughing, saying something in his language. Shoshana did not leave. He looked at her. Shoshana did not leave. With his finger he moved his beret from the back of his head too far forward. From his forehead too far back. As if mimicking someone, good-naturedly. Shoshana did not leave.

He started rummaging in his pockets. Took out the Egged bus ticket. Examined the Egged bus ticket. Folded it correctly, and folded it up again. Put the ticket in her palm and closed her fingers over it, grouping them together into a brown fist enclosing the ticket. 'Souvenir,' he smiled. Shoshana did not leave. He stroked her cheek lightly, and left.

When he could no longer be seen, Shoshana looked at the ticket. I don't know his name, it occurred to her now. He doesn't know mine, she looked at the ticket. Buried her face in the ticket. Then steadied the burden on her shoulder.

She entered home on tiptoe. Skirting the baby pram at the inside of the front door, she passed her sleeping brothers. Solemn, to the point of fear-inspiring, as if they are crucified. She changed in silence. And cautiously got into bed, together with her little sister, who was snuggled all curled up, and with her arms as if sheltering her head and face.

Her mother, her hair dishevelled, the eternal red dressing-gown is now thrown hastily over her nightgown, came in from the other room. Pushing aside the yellow striped curtain, she stood in the entrance: Shoshana looked her mother in the eye. Her mother looked Shoshana in the eye. Didn't say anything. Left. And Shoshana could hear how her mother was suppressing her sobs, over there, in her creaking bed in the other room. Then how the baby woke up. And fell asleep again.

She wiped her last dust-grain, or two, off her thin eyebrows, off the base of her neck. From behind her earlobe. Rosita is my name, I would have told him. A name to conjure with in the world. My birthright name, until it was changed into a Hebrew one by Hephtzibah's decree. Little-Girl my name will now stay. I've indeed shrunk to a small-finger size, yet have grown simultaneously by an arm's length: surrounded by the familiar, that at the same time is different. As with the girl Alice, in the show they sent us. For the adoption ceremony, when they adopted us on 'Love Thy Brother as Thyself Day'. And there were all those misfortunes. The loudspeakers went dead on us. Then the lorry broke down. And the guests fated to wait were irate: they were given tea, said thank you, but hardly touched it. Teacher Hephtzibah even organized us, the 'Clowns' choir, to start a sing-song, for them to join in. None of them did. Zvi performed for them his 'Dancing with The Lady Zvia' dance. In a lady's hat, a borrowed dress, a handbag and unshaven cheeks, he danced in ballroom style, embracing and stroking his imaginary partner. But some nervous ones whispered amongst themselves all the time: lorry – tow vehicle – a disgrace. Who's interested in these ones. Go on Mama, go on washing the laundry. Maybe in two weeks time, maybe in three: over there, where all of them are good-looking, all are kind-hearted, all loving, in their dashing greenish fatigues, in the barracks yard, in front of the grey pillared arches, taking pleasure and in no hurry, all of them will be watering with buckets, scrubbing or combing, each his own pet horse. One by one they'll stand still, their work at a halt. They'll be restored into motion again as I'll go on, passing along the fence, set on searching. 'Hail to my cousin / All ruddy and fair / Is he doing well / Our King David': the last in the row he'll be. Doing his work. Lovingly. Unaware. There I shall stand. Shall wait. Until he sees me. Recognizes me. He will put down his brush. Will come out to me. Bring me in. And everyone will laugh, but be glad, the Regiment's Sweetheart. In two weeks' time perhaps, perhaps in three, on an Egg'ed inter-city bus. With a blue El Al bag. To my destiny.

'But my name is Little-Girl / The Regiment's Sweetheart / And UN-Soldier is thine name / I see the harbour lights ...' And maybe, even in another twenty years. And even if I see those for whom they'd give me up. Those will be quite my look-alike. And they will be cheated on too. How will I know? for they will cheat on them with me! – She buried her face in the bus ticket. With a sinking heart. Sensing herself as one who is brought to court, and at the end the clerks had him a formidable paper to sign. And he signs. Among other things, also with a touch of satisfaction. A satisfaction which is not unlike a destruction wish, at once alluring and frightening. But the chick hatching out of its egg in the incubator, the one with problems, what about the chick – she was beginning to doze off. Prevented herself from falling asleep: as if without any restraints, how is it, suddenly a person is compelled to draw close. Extends attention, tokens of goodwill, of affection, pampers without reservations. Unafraid. Giving, getting exposed in front of a stranger. He ought to be fond of that stranger. Must be. Surely he needn't have anything to do with all this otherwise. Moreover, to do it willingly. Out of himself. He's fond, yes, fond. And sinking into sleep, like one striving laboriously, who towards the end of his journey is shedding any superfluous load, this is what she was left with: a person wants. Wants to receive, to give. A person extends, attention, care, is fond, makes one take part, as if they are not strangers. And then he leaves. Does not come back. She fell asleep.

She heard her mother getting up, passing into the kitchen. Mixing the feed for the chickens. In the heat that already filled the world, like laundry air, was all the humdrum of the drudgery of the newborn day. Born without a mask: no blessing, no chance, no reconciliation, no change, no novelty. No stir in the leaves of the creeper; this calabash-like, gourd-like plant, it decks out only the yards of the poor, as she had observed long ago. Twining over there, raising its yellow flowers, clinging to the posts of the pergola in the yard, its end can be seen from her corner in the bed. She heard her mother attaching the hose to the kitchen tap, to fill the two large galvanized laundry tubs and the pail for the baby nappies outside, under the kitchen window. The way she had told us once. Told us of a story that had taken place in their homeland. A story about a brother who strangled his adulterous sister and threw her body into a well. 'Blessed are the hands,' his mother had blessed him – she told us full of sacred awe.

But me, I am never more of this place. Ever more of the UN.

And the backlash swept her over. Like a forgotten melody. The burst of freshness of a power that draws one back, and anguish, akin to regrets, over that which is massacred here at your feet each time anew and gets trampled, you know not what it is. They recapture that which is extinct and by now is nothing but tenderness, all the tenderness. Yet in it are preserved all its lost flavour, fully retained, and its true colours – with a punch that is like a fist-blow to the jaw. In the great wide world only this time, only for me, only in my case – won't I, please – some day find you again.

Translated by Raya and Nimrod Jones

8

The Mystery of the Pigs' Heads

by ORLY CASTEL-BLOOM

'WHY NOW?' grumbled Yeheskel, stretching his limbs and letting go all of a sudden with a sigh, 'Just when I'm resting and relaxing?'

Moshe, a tall, moustached young man of his own age, dressed all in white, nevertheless threw the pile of cheques, the pocket calculator, the ballpoint pen and the scribbled papers one after the other onto the round table next to the armchair on which Yeheskel was dozing.

'In my exact estimation,' said Moshe with a nasty smile, 'you can afford to sacrifice a quarter of an hour of your life to examine these accounts. I made a miscalculation, and I've been racking my brains for half an hour already without finding the mistake.'

Yeheskel took the pile of cheques grudgingly and ruffled through them with a bored look on his face.

'How come,' he said as he did so, 'I always have to do things for you, and you, when I need you, always disappear and screw me?'

Moshe asked innocently when he had screwed Yeheskel.

Yeheskel quickly described two occasions, and thought of the third without saying anything. The first was when Yeheskel and Anat had just arrived in New York, two and a half months before and Yeheskel asked Moshe to lend him his van, because they had at least nine suitcases, and Moshe refused on the excuse that he needed the van to transport signs to some religious guy in Brooklyn exactly when Yeheskel needed it. The second was two weeks later. Yeheskel had asked Moshe to fix him up with a job in his workshop and Moshe had agreed to employ him (not before pulling a self-righteous face, in Yeheskel's opinion) at the starvation wage of six hundred dollars a month as a start. Yeheskel reminded him of this fact, and added that a number of weeks had passed since then, and Moshe had not only not given him a raise, but pretended to be dumb whenever Yeheskel brought up the subject with subtle or heavy hints. And now Moshe had the gall to come to him on his day of rest and ask him to check the accounts. Yeheskel announced that it was pure exploitation.

The third occasion, which was not mentioned, was five years previously. When Yeheskel had been about to confess his long-lasting love for Tzila, in a certain sooty boulevard in Tel Aviv, she had told him to his astonishment that she had already been in love with Moshe, his good friend, for four months, and that she was going to marry him, if only he asked her, and she didn't give a damn if he was only in it for the sake of her father's millions. Three months later Tzila and Moshe got married in an impressive and well-attended ceremony in a five-star hotel on the sea front, and Yeheskel was obliged to compromise on Anat, who had been waiting patiently for him for years.

Moshe listened to Yeheskel's complaints, which were made in a low voice, so that the others wouldn't hear, and said to himself that maybe Yeheskel could really do with a few hours sleep. He took the paperwork relating to May '87, and went back into his room to check it himself.

Yeheskel felt an uneasiness, which quickly turned to hunger, and he got up and went into the kitchen. Tzila skillfully prepared breakfast – eggs fried in sizzling butter, two for herself, two for Yeheskel, two for Moshe on a tray to his room, and two for Anat. The others had already eaten. Anat tasted one of the eggs and looked at Yeheskel. After all these years, she saw him casting a long, sad look of regret at Tzila, who responded with a smile, and Anat said that her two eggs were spoiled or something, in any case they had a disgusting aftertaste. Tzila looked at Anat, interpreted the gleam in her friend's eye as malice, said don't do me any favours, and threw Anat's two eggs into the garbage together with the plate that had cost two dollars.

Yeheskel asked Tzila in surprise:

'What have you done?'

Tzila said:

'I took Anat's two eggs and chucked them into the garbage. Have you gone blind?'

Yeheskel didn't answer, and looked questioning. Eviatar, who had been sitting to one side all the time jotting down notes like these, intervened and said to Tzila through the big doorway between the living room and the kitchen, that she had gone too far. Tzila shrugged her pretty shoulders. Anat, who was wearing a flowered skirt made in Hong Kong, stood up and went into the garden, where she met Yossi who was playing soccer with Tzila and Moshe's gifted child and concentrating on the game.

'Have you got a car here?' she asked Yossi. 'I want to leave. Everyone here's sick in the head. I knew I shouldn't have come to this idiotic weekend.'

Yossi said that he had sold his old heap a week before for a hundred dollars because he was stuck for food, and he asked her, after sniggering to himself, if she wanted to play a bit of football, and rolled the ball in her direction.

'Are you making fun of me?' asked Anat furiously, and she kicked the ball outside with all her strength. The ball hit the wind-shield of a parked car and landed in the street. Tzila and Moshe's child ran after it. A car stopped at the last minute with a screech. Anat turned pale.

'What have you done, you stupid fool?' said Yossi, flushing. 'You nearly killed the kid and you nearly busted my car window.' He gave her a light shove.

'I thought you sold it,' said Anat dryly.

'I sold it and I bought another one,' he said and kicked the post of an improvised goal. Tzila and Moshe's kid snatched up the ball and shouted hand ball, hand ball. He bounced it on the lawn as if it was a basketball and the ball bounced, because the lawn was hard and dry. The previous tenants before Tzila and Moshe played a lot of tennis on it and kept it in shape. In the end the kid lifted the ball to Yossi. Yossi headed it into the goal and shouted:

'Great! I was the forward and you were like the half-back. You made me a beautiful goal. You see? Now let's change positions.'

Anat got out of there and went back into the house.

Tzila was alone in the kitchen. She put the plates and other dishes into the dishwasher and cried. Anat saw her crying and said she was terribly sorry, she didn't know what was happening to her lately, life was hard and lousy, sometimes she really felt like committing hara-kiri. Tzila looked at her and smiled. Anat fastened her ponytail even tighter, and Tzila asked her why didn't she ever wear her hair loose. Anat giggled in embarrassment and said no no. They sat down in the kitchen and talked of this and that, and reminisced about the time when they were good friends, when they lived two hundred and fifty steps away from each other, and talked deep into the night about the third world war, atom bombs, ghosts and goblins and the signs of the zodiac.

A strong wind blew in through the open window of the living room and scattered Eviatar's papers. He stopped writing, collected them into a pile at the corner of the table, turned them upside down so nobody could peep, and put a heavy ashtray on top of them so they wouldn't fly away. He took a pack of cards and dealt three hands of poker. Moshe emerged from the study exhausted and unsatisfied, walked past Yeheskel who had gone back to sleep on the armchair, and switched on the stereo. The break-dance the kid had put on the turntable in the morning was still there, and the magnetic sounds filled the room. Eviatar pulled a face and said:

'Turn off that shit, Moshe. Put on something normal. Put on the Yellow.' He took a few coins out of his pocket and scattered them on the table. Moshe put on the Yellow and sat down, and so did Yeheskel.

They played until the record side was over – eight hands, and Moshe won them all. Eviatar said that he didn't feel so great and couldn't go on, and he went outside to let off steam by fooling around with the football and Yossi and Moshe and Tzila's kid. Moshe, who thought that his winning streak was due to the inspiration of the music, asked him to turn the record over on his way. Tzila and Anat came and sat down in the living room, at a little distance from the men, each of them with a cup of coffee, and Anat with a grilled cheese, as well, and they conducted a quiet conversation about expedient employment opportunities for Anat.

Tzila said that she had decided to send the kid to a regular American school, and Anat said that that was the only possible option. Moshe asked Tzila if she couldn't organize some coffee for them too, and Tzila didn't answer. He nodded his head in time to the music, made drumming noises with his mouth, and raked in more coins. Ilana came downstairs and everyone split their sides laughing. She had got mixed up and thought she was at home, and consequently she had come down in her night-gown and bumped into the wall, because in their place – so she explained later, holding her aching head and smiling – the wall was on the right and not on the left like here.

The poker game started up again, and Tzila asked Ilana if she wanted hard-boiled or soft-boiled eggs, because she was all out of butter for frying.

Ilana blinked and clicked her tongue, declining the offer, looked around and asked: 'Where's my husband?'

'He popped round to Monday-Basket to get a few things,' said Tzila. 'You've eaten me out of house and home,' she laughed and looked at her watch, still smiling. 'He should have been back by now.'

'Monday-Basket?' said Ilana quietly and glanced outside at Yossi and the kid, who had just shot a goal between Eviatar's parted legs.

'Do you shop a lot at Monday-Basket?' inquired Anat.

'Yes,' said Tzila. 'Especially on Mondays. You know, they give incredible discounts on Mondays. Sometimes fifty per cent.'

'Aha!' cried Ilana and the cry turned to a yawn, 'so that's why they're called Monday-Basket!'

'They had the right idea,' said Tzila and she got up to take her friends into the kitchen, after an impatient sign from Moshe. 'Everybody concentrates their shopping on the weekends, then Monday-Basket comes along and gives discounts on Mondays. Nice idea,' she pronounced. 'I think it's a nice marketing idea.'

'A very nice idea,' remarked Anat enviously, because she had always dreamed of specializing in marketing and advertising, but she couldn't get into the programme in Tel Aviv.

Tzila walked to the kitchen with Ilana behind her. Anat lingered in the living room for a moment to think about herself and hurried after them. Ilana sat down next to the table in the dining nook and asked Tzila to give her something to do, quickly, before she went mad. Tzila gave her a choice between two possibilities. She could clean the rice, or she could take the day before yesterday's bread and make breadcrumbs for schnitzels and hamburgers, because she hated fast food.

Ilana said, 'Bring me the bread. Ay!' she held her cheek, 'my tooth hurts. Have you got anything for toothache?' She turned to Tzila.

Tzila threw a fizzy dissolving aspirin into a quarter of a glass of water and gave it to Ilana. Ilana drank, but it didn't help her. The toothache got worse, and she asked for whiskey to numb it. After washing out her mouth in the whiskey and spitting it into the sink, she took another sip and swallowed it. She took another sip, from the bottle this time, and swallowed it. She left the bottle open and Tzila offhandedly brought her a clean glass. Ilana ignored both glasses and poured three big sips from the bottle down her throat and her eyes reddened. Eviatar scored a goal and the little five-year-old kid shouted And-the-ba-all's-in-si-ide, and he ran to the window to say that Yossi wanted them to put on a record by some David Broza. They put on the David Broza record and set up a speaker in the garden, and Tzila and Anat and Ilana hummed the words of the song: 'Who's looking down from above ...'

Mosquitoes and flies attracted by the heat bit them from time to time, but it didn't bug them one bit because they were happy. Ilana even stood up, crumbled the bread while swaying her body, and what a body she had, and cried: 'Oh, I never even noticed. My toothache's almost completely disappeared.'

Her husband came in holding a bag of groceries, and she stopped swaying and sat down.

'Ahipaz!' she cried, 'Where have you been and what have you been doing?!'

Ahipaz looked tense and exhausted and told them that he had had a flat tyre and a ballsup like they wouldn't believe. 'Where's Eviatar?' he asked.

'Outside,' said Ilana, and looked right into Ahipaz's black and sombre eyes, which stared back at her. 'You wanna go out and play a little football with him?'

'Okay, okay,' said Ahipaz quickly, 'I'll just grab a bite first. Tzila, for God's sake do me a favour and make me two fried eggs.'

Tzila lit the gas and Anat said: 'What is it with you people? All you want is two fried eggs, two fried eggs! Can't you eat something else for a change?'

'What for example?' asked Ilana.

'I don't know,' said Anat. 'Avocado maybe ... or almonds ...' she leaned against the back of the chair and closed her eyes.

Ahipaz ate the two eggs greedily and went outside.

In the living room Moshe and Yeheskel broke up the game to go outside and join the others in the garden.

There was a long silence among the women.

'Guess who I saw the night before last?' said Tzila suddenly.

'Who?' asked Anat curiously.

'Donald Sutherland,' said Tzila solemnly.

'What, in the street?' marvelled Anat.

'No no,' said Tzila. 'In a movie. I taped it for you.'

'You've got a movie with Donald Sutherland here and you keep quiet about it?' scolded Anat.

'Yes,' said Tzila and smiled. '"The Eye of the Needle".'

'"The Eye of the Needle"!' cried Anat enthusiastically. 'Oh, that's wonderful! That's great! Let's go to the living room,' she said and hurried into the living room.

Tzila wiped her hands on her apron, unnecessarily, and shortly afterwards, when she put the cassette into the video machine and pressed 'play' by mistake, a close-up of Sutherland at the end of the movie appeared on the screen. She looked at him from close up and cried in the direction of the kitchen:

'Ilana, Ilana! Come here! You have to see him. What an actor, what an actor!'

'I can't stand the guy,' said Ilana from her place at the table and pulled a disgusted face. 'I saw him in "Eagle has Landed" and "Don't Look Now" and I've seen this movie too and once was enough. Haven't you got a bit of grass for me?'

115

'No,' cried Tzila, 'I'm all out.' She looked at the numbers running quickly backwards.

Anat settled down in an armchair and absentmindedly ate the snacks left over from the night before.

'Maybe Ahipaz brought some?' cried Ilana.

'So ask him!' snapped Anat, who wanted the movie to begin already and for them all to shut up.

'Noooo,' murmured Ilana to herself and glanced outside at her husband who was arguing passionately with Eviatar and pushing him angrily while Moshe and Yeheskel intermittently joined in.

Two minutes passed.

'Ilana,' called Tzila from the living room, 'are you coming? I'm running the video. And this is the last time I'm calling you.'

'That Sutherland's just a sick creep,' pronounced Ilana to herself. 'You can see it in his eyes.'

'You're talking nonsense,' called Tzila, who overheard this remark. 'He's a good actor that's all.'

'A good actor, a good actor,' exclaimed Ilana angrily. She went on crumbling the bread and taking sips from the whiskey bottle. When Tzila and Moshe's kid shattered the kitchen window with a well-aimed kick, because nobody wanted to play with him any more, she looked indifferently at the hundreds of splinters of glass flying around. She was completely drunk. Tzila and Anat didn't hear the noise. They were watching their idol pushing the good guy, who was paralysed from the waist down, off the top of the cliff and sending his wheelchair flying down the steep slope straight into the sea, and Tzila said:

'Shew! How cruel that Donald is! You're right, Ilana, what a meanie! Ya-allah! Look how he pushed that poor cripple off the cliff straight into the sea just because he found out that Sutherland was a German spy!'

They went into the kitchen. Tzila stood in the middle of the room, very upset, and Anat leaned against the mezuza on the doorpost.

'Where do you get off?' cried Ilana. 'He simply fell in love with the cripple's wife and got rid of him out of jealousy.'

'What do you mean fell in love with his wife?' cried Tzila and began pacing up and down the kitchen, red and agitated, 'You didn't understand a thing. Altogether he fucked her once and goodbye, because she was fed up with her crippled husband, and that was only in a moment of weakness. I'm positive she regretted it later.'

'She didn't have time to regret it,' said Anat indifferently, to conceal how much she had been affected by the movie, 'because her husband was dead. That packs more punch than fucking Sutherland.'

'What are you ta-l-king about,' said Tzila and hit her temple with the palm of her hand, 'it's true that it packs more punch that her husband died, but now her whole life's ruined. From now on she'll have to live with the fact that half an hour before her husband was murdered she gave in to the temptation to go to bed with the murderer. You know how that feels?'

Tzila kept quiet and looked outside to see what everyone wanted to drink. The only ones there were Yossi and her son. They were both doing handstands and walking upside-down. Yossi hated the world and everybody in it. Sports helped to calm his nerves, which were in a bad state, which was why he was here now and not where he was supposed to be. He'd been thrown out on his arse, so he came to make trouble for Tzila. Tzila looked at the splinters of glass and bent down to sweep them up with a brush and a dust-pan. Anat watched her silently. There was a faint knock at the door. Nobody answered. The knock was repeated. Tzila asked angrily who's there. From behind the door a man's voice said confidently:

'It's Donald.'

An expression of amazement appeared on the faces of Tzila and Anat, while Ilana jumped up in alarm and cried:

'Oh my God, he heard what I said about him and he's come to kill me. Save me,' she begged.

'Pull yourself together, Ilana,' said Tzila, 'that doesn't make sense,' and she went curiously to open the door. On the threshold stood Donald, Tzila and Moshe Elias's black cleaning man, who Moshe calls Domingo, because he always came on Sundays. 'Here comes Domingo,' Moshe would say and clear off.

'Donald,' cried Tzila in surprise. 'But it's not Sunday today is it?' she turned to her friends, who shrugged their shoulders.

'I can't come tomorrow,' said Donald in embarrassment, 'so I come today.'

'Okay,' said Tzila in resignation, 'so let's clear the ground floor for him. Please,' she turned to address Donald, 'clean the kitchen good. Not like last time. I want it to shine like a diamond.' She stretched out her hand and showed him her ring, eight glittering little diamonds, and one big one in the middle. Donald nodded and looked at her. His eyes flashed, because he didn't have a servant's mentality.

Tzila hurried to join Anat and Ilana climbing slowly up the stairs. Ilana leaned on the banister so as not to fall, and Anat trailed behind her, in despair.

'Tzila,' said Ilana wearily, 'where's the embroidery you gave me yesterday? I told you I felt like embroidering a few cross-stitches.'

They moved away and disappeared into one of the rooms. Donald removed a scouring powder for cleaning and polishing sinks, a liquid for washing floors and a spray for shining windows, as well as a pail and rags from the cleaning-materials cupboard. He had already worked eight times for the Elias family and he knew exactly where everything was, because he put it there himself.

Upstairs the women got lucky and they found a matchbox full of dried marijuana flowers, apparently left over from Josephine and Richard's last visit, and Ilana shrieked with joy.

'Oh God, thank you,' she cried, 'this is fantastic! You want me to do it?' she turned to Anat who was sniffing the flowers. Anat didn't answer, and began rolling up the cigarette papers she took out of her pocket. Ilana began embroidering the piece of cloth with all kinds of gazelles and flowers drawn on it, which she was filling with cross-stitch instead of satin stitch. Tzila suddenly felt that she had to do something good, quickly, before she burst a string in her heart, and she asked Ilana if she had enough threads.

'Threads?!' cried Ilana magnanimously and pointed to the ex-cigar box, 'wait till I finish these.'

Anat lit the joint, took a drag and passed it to Ilana. Ilana took a drag and passed it to Tzila. Tzila passed the joint to her other hand, because she was left-handed, took a drag and passed it to Anat. Anat took a drag and asked if they shouldn't call the guys. Tzila glanced through the bedroom window and couldn't see anyone. In the whole big house there were only the three of them and Donald down below scrubbing and thinking sad thoughts in his mother tongue. Anat sneezed. Tzila said bless you. Drugs affected Anat badly and depressed her even more and she said:

'Say bless you to somebody else. Say bless you to your Yeheskel, Okay?'

'What's the matter with you, Anat?' asked Tzila. 'Are you freaking out again?' And she passed the joint to Ilana.

'Sorry, Tzila,' said Anat, 'don't take any notice of me,' and she withdrew into herself.

Ilana volunteered to go downstairs and bring them all a cold refreshing fruit juice drink. Donald looked at the sink and decided that it was clean. He filled the pail with water, squeezed in some greenish liquid for washing floors which also contained wax for polishing, and was about to pour it onto the marble floor which was full of the guests' footprints. His eyes encountered the bare feet of Ilana, who came into the kitchen with the fag-end of the joint stuck between her fingers, and he stopped himself.

'Hey, Domingo,' she said absent-mindedly, 'want some?' and she waved the remains of the joint at him.

'No, thank you,' said Donald.

'Why?' wondered Ilana, and she stepped between the pail and the floor rag to take the juice out of the fridge, and took a drag on the joint. 'You don't know what you're missing.'

Donald shrugged his shoulders and waited. Ilana bumped into the fridge door and juice from the bottle spilled on the floor.

'Oh,' she groaned, 'I feel so dizzy.'

She threw the butt of the joint into the clean sink. Donald pulled out the dry cloth sticking out of his trouser pocket and dusted the cookbook shelf.

Ilana poured the fruit juice into four glasses which she took out of the cupboard and went on standing there in confusion. She counted voicelessly and ticked off on her fingers: Me, Tzila, Anat, and stared at the four glasses in bemusement. She counted again, and again arrived at the number three. So why did she think she had to pour four glasses?

'Want some orange juice?' she turned round and said to Donald.

Donald shook his head without stopping his work.

'Why?' said Ilana and took a sip from her glass. 'It's hot today.'

'No, thank you,' said Donald politely.

'No, thank you,' repeated Ilana, mimicking his African accent, put the three glasses and the bottle on a tray and made for the door.

'You see,' said Donald. He stopped dusting, and Ilana stood still.

'I have to work. Work brings money. Everything that brings money is good. Next month I fly back to Ghana to get married. After, I come back to America with my wife. She will have to clean toilets too. But after, we go back to Ghana with ten thousand, even fifteen thousand dollars. We will be rich!'

'Get married!' cried Ilana. 'Nice! How is your wife?'

'She is black,' he said gloomily.

'Black, not black, what does it matter ...'

She lifted the heavy tray and the juice trembled in the glasses. She had just lost all interest in the conversation with the black man and she wanted to go back upstairs and give her friends the cold juice, roll another joint and smoke some more. When she entered the living room her eye was caught by a figure wearing black which crossed the window outside running from left to right. She approached the window, spilling juice as she did so, and looked outside curiously. A white man with long hair and a beard, about thirty-five years old, with a red ribbon tied round his head, aimed a pistol at her. He signalled to her with a quick, sharp jerk of the pistol to get back inside. She opened her mouth to shout for Donald, but the front door opened with a kick and the man stood in the middle of the living room and went on aiming his pistol at her, holding it with both hands. Ilana threw the tray with the glasses of juice and the bottle at him, hit his legs, and ran upstairs.

In the bedroom Anat and Tzila were sulking silently and waiting for her. Ilana managed to say: 'Anat! Tzila! There's a burglar in the house!' and Anat said indifferently: 'Ilana, is there anything else you know how to do besides crying wolf?'

The man came in, dragging one leg, and hit Anat hard in her surprised face. She fell back, unconscious. Tzila looked on aghast. Donald appeared, tied Anat with a rope to the foot of the bed and Tzila to her dressing-table chair, and gagged them with rags. The long-haired bearded man stopped Ilana's mouth with his hand and dragged her downstairs.

At the bottom of the stairs he let her go and pushed her, and she fell forward onto the carpet.

'This is not my house,' said the frightened Ilana. 'I don't know where they keep the money.'

The man sniggered and came close to her, raised her chin with his finger, and said in Hebrew:

'Don't pretend you don't remember me.'

'I've never seen you before in my life. What do you want of me?' she said.

Donald came downstairs and leaned against the front door, his hands behind his back, his eyes forward, like a sentry.

'Nineteen sixty-nine, Woodstock,' said the long-haired man and looked straight at her.

'Woodstock?' said Ilana in astonishment.

'Yes, Woodstock. You were there with a friend of yours, remember?'

'Me? Woodstock?' she frowned. 'I was never in Woodstock in my life!'

'Yes you were!' He threw his head back and laughed. Then he brought it back, looked serious, and said: 'Remember Jerry?'

'Jerry? Who's Jerry?'

'Jerry,' he said. 'You had a scene with him. You wanted to set up a stationery shop with him when it was all over.'

'Jerry ... stationery ...' muttered Ilana. 'I don't know anyone called Jerry.'

'Everybody knows someone called Jerry,' said the man angrily, 'which makes you a liar in any case. But why should I worry?'

He whipped the pistol out of his pocket. 'Anything you can't remember,' he said and closed one eye, took aim and fired one shot at the green wall on her right, 'I'll remind you of.' He looked with satisfaction at the little hole. 'Jerry had a wife. Her name was Caroline. A blonde with a ponytail. And she had a fever of forty degrees, and she was pregnant. In the third month. And you … and you …' He looked at her with hatred, 'hummed helpless helpless instead of helping her.'

'I'm very sorry to hear it,' said Ilana, 'but I've never been to Woodstock in my life, and I don't know any Caroline. Who are you? You've made a mistake.'

'What do I care what you think,' the man lost his temper again, 'the main thing is that I've got proof.' He clicked his fingers and Donald threw him a packet of snapshots held together with a rubber band. The man shuffled them as if they were cards, and held out one for her to look at. In the snapshot she saw her profile, a smile spread over her face, and she was sitting and singing. And all around her were hundreds of people, maybe thousands, maybe millions, also singing. Maybe I really was in Woodstock in sixty-nine, the thought crossed her mind, and she immediately shuddered.

'Listen here, you,' she said. 'I've never been to Woodstock in my life. I wasn't even in America when Woodstock happened. I was in Israel, a baby of twelve in primary school. I was planting carrots in the school garden with Noah, Yissaschar and all the kids. I don't know what you're talking about. This is … photo-montage,' she pointed to the snapshot. 'So will you please leave now?'

He fell on her and dragged her outside by her arm. Donald cut the phone cord with a penknife, smashed it against the wall, and ran outside after them. Behind a tree in the garden Ilana caught a glimpse of three figures and maybe a fourth sitting tied to each other, with one of them tied to the tree. The figures didn't move, and she couldn't see their faces, but by their clothes she recognized Moshe, Yeheskel and Ahipaz. She was shoved into a strange car, an old red model, and they raced off, Donald drove.

The man began drinking vodka from a bottle and offered the

bottle to Donald. Donald shook his head. Ilana tried to remember if and where from she knew the long-haired bearded man but her past offered her no clues.

'Where are we going?' she asked fearfully, but nobody answered.

'Where are you going?' she asked again.

'We're taking you to the Boss,' said Donald, and the long-haired man screamed at him 'Shut up,' and took a long drink and hiccuped loudly. Ilana turned her face to the scenery and sank into thought. After a while the man offered her the bottle and she declined with a shake of her head. He threatened her with his gun and she drank. After they had driven some way, she was already drinking of her own free will, and he smiled at her and exposed black teeth.

'That's the way I like you,' he said. 'Drinking from the same bottle as me and not being afraid of getting AIDS.'

Ilana moved the bottle away from her mouth.

'Have you got AIDS?' she said alertly.

'Maybe.' He snatched the bottle from her. The vodka splashed and wet her nightgown. 'But on the other hand,' he added, 'it may be just a virus. It may be nothing. I've just been feeling a little weakness and giddiness lately. So I thought maybe I've got AIDS. Because I'm a homosexual. You understand.'

'What do you want?' Ilana jumped. 'To infect me? To infect everybody? Is that what you want? To take everybody with you?' She lost control and tried to open the door of the big car. The long-haired man slapped her hard and she calmed down.

'I only said I might have AIDS, baby. Maybe. It's not definite.'

They gulped the distances. Roads, places and neighbourhoods where she had never been. The long-haired man no longer spoke to her and kept his eyes on the road. From time to time Donald peeked at her in the mirror.

In Tzila and Moshe's bedroom Anat opened her eyes and tried to get up. Tzila's eyes, which had been open all the time, looked at her anxiously. Anat tried to talk to her, but the gag tied around her mouth was too tight for anything except unintelligible groans to get out. She signalled to Tzila with her eyes to try to get closer to her, maybe together they would be able to free one of them to get help.

Tzila understood Anat's intention and tried to advance towards her by wriggling her bum, but she fell helplessly on her side and broke into throttled sobs. Anat made sounds at her through the gag and stamped her bound feet to encourage her to get up, but Tzila sat up and fell back onto her side with a loud thud. Anat looked outside through the window at the blue sky and wondered what had happened to the others. The thought occurred to her that they could die there from hunger and thirst if nobody turned up within the next few hours. From the house next door she heard the sound of Lionel Ritchie's latest hit and her brow darkened in rage.

The red car entered one of the slum districts. Ilana held the black velvet dress which the long-haired man had previously given her. His eyes were now scanning the shopfronts and looking for something. When they passed a café with the name 'Johnnie's Café' written on it he ordered Donald to stop. Ilana and the man went in, and Donald stayed in the car, wondering whether to run away. Nobody in the café took any notice of the young woman who came in swaying on her feet, wearing a nightgown, but when they saw that someone was pointing a pistol at her back they scattered quickly in all directions and the place emptied out.

In the women's toilets Ilana made haste to take off her nightgown and put on the black dress, which fitted her exactly. In the seconds which this took her the man tapped impatiently on the door with the barrel of his pistol. When they returned to the car the street was deserted. Her eyes were blindfolded with a black cloth, and she heard Donald whispering to her, 'Be good,' and the long-haired man screaming at him 'Shut up'. They went on driving and a few minutes later the car stopped again. An aggressive hand removed the blindfold from her eyes and she found herself standing opposite a big wooden door. On her left were three ruffians, one of them with an eye patch, who asked: 'Can we come in and fuck her too?'

124

It was a very old, run-down, single storied house. She climbed five steps, the man pressed the bell and there was a buzzing sound as the door opened. The room which greeted her eyes was big and very dimly lit. The heavy mustard coloured curtains were drawn, the furniture was old and some of it was broken and lopsided. In the middle of the room stood a black grand piano, more than half of whose surface was stripped and colourless. It was open and the keys were yellow. A jug with artificial flowers was standing on top of it on a little cloth. At the end of the room, on a chair standing slightly higher than the rest of the furniture, sat a figure with its back to the door and looked at the drawn curtain as if it wasn't drawn.

'We've brought her, Papa,' said the long-haired man gently, and he advanced and leaned his elbows on the piano.

It now transpired that the chair on which Papa was sitting was a swivel chair: an invisible push, perhaps with his foot, led to a creak of the hinges, and his body turned left one hundred and eighty degrees, until he was sitting facing Ilana at a distance of about ten metres, his hands on the arms of the chair.

An old man wearing a dark shabby suit looked at her.

'Bring her closer to me,' he said in a trembling voice, and held out both hands as if trying to get up, but then he gave up and let them fall onto his knees.

The long-haired man made a beckoning gesture with his hand. Donald hurried to bring her a chair and she advanced and sat down. The old man brought his face close to hers. His lips were trembling. His face and neck were so wrinkled and lined that his features were indistinguishable. His hands were covered with grey hand-knitted gloves, unravelling at the tips to expose pink fingers. Ilana looked him over and lowered her eyes. She had already experienced many trips in her life – but none like this.

'At last,' said the old man and nodded his head without stopping. 'I'm very glad to see you again, madam. My grandfather and your great-grandfather were very good friends. They met in Europe, when your father, who hadn't yet been born, wanted to set up a stationery store and make a decent living. Those were grand days, madam. You should know that.' He fell silent, making an effort to capture the dim memories, stopped nodding and looked at her. She looked exhausted, and the black dress added a melancholy note to her weariness. She looked like a Greek widow.

'You are very much like your father,' he went on slowly and quietly, 'and I'm proud to have found you alive and well, and now I can pay my great-grandfather back for looking after me and bringing me into the world. Relax,' he said gently after putting out his trembling hand to stroke her cheek, at which she recoiled slightly, 'you're among friends.'

'I don't like the look of you at all,' she said, 'please go away.'

'How could I bear your absence after seeing you, my dear? How could a miserable insignificant creature like me disturb the balance which the Great Power asked me to bring about? You've come to your rightful place. Very few people have succeeded in reaching such a unity of time and place. Columbus was one of them, but he didn't know it and he committed suicide.' He began nodding again and laughed a rusty laugh. 'And the great conquerors, Napoleon and Alexander of Macedon, tried all their lives to achieve unity of place, and they didn't take time into account, and they failed one after the other. There isn't one empire that didn't collapse at the end because of this mistake. Personally, I very much enjoyed witnessing the disintegration of the British Empire. That was a great experience.'

'What's going to happen?' asked Ilana and sighed.

'If I say revolution you'll laugh, Susan. And what will I get out of it apart from hearing your peals of laughter, tell me? First of all, understand that I'm your true father and these,' he pointed to Donald and the long-haired man, 'are your true brothers. When you were a little black baby you were snatched away from us by the Ku-Klux-Klan, who made you white. Your mother who was really black, sat not far from you at Woodstock, and watched you singing, and she told us what a beauty you'd grown up into. But what do the details matter? All that matters is that we've found you, and we love you very much. I love you.' He threw out both arms as if to embrace her and fell back exhausted, breathing heavily.

The long-haired man burst out laughing and ran out of the

room. Donald hurried after him, the old man looked after them sullenly.

'I'm not Susan,' said Ilana quietly.

'I know that the chances of your being Susan are one in thirty million,' said the old man. 'The years have simply wiped your real name from my memory.'

'Just a minute,' said Ilana angrily. 'Let's get a few things straight here. My name's Ilana, not Susan. I've never been to Woodstock in my life. When Woodstock was happening I was ten years old and I was planting radishes and carrots in the school garden with Noah, Yissaschar and all the kids. I won a prize for the best garden in all the primary schools in Haifa. I got a certificate of merit from the Education Department. They wrote about me in the school magazine, and when the teacher read out the bit about me, I hid under the table and the kids stared. It's a pity I haven't got the certificate here to show you, then maybe you'd believe me. Altogether I've only been in America for four and a half years, and now it's nineteen eighty-seven, right? Or maybe you're going to tell me I'm wrong. Maybe you think it's nineteen seventy.'

'I've been waiting for this moment seven and a half years,' smiled the old man, 'work it out for yourself.'

Ilana closed her eyes in despair.

'I feel ...' he said, 'I feel that it's April now, and I'm in love with Theresa,' he looked at her, 'your mother.'

He took a joint out of his pocket and began smoking it. Ilana looked at the walls. They were covered with pictures of deer, and completely yellow, with only the outlines of the deer in a reddish-brown colour. The smoke reached her nose, and she stretched out a long hand, because the smoke had a wonderful smell. He gave her the joint and she smoked it to the end.

'Enchanting,' he said excitedly as he followed her every movement, 'just like your mother at Woodstock. The same soft curls,' he touched her hair lightly. He took a harmonica and began happily playing a Russian tune from the old days. The long-haired bearded man came into the room and accompanied the old man on the piano, not all of whose keys responded to his touch. The music excited the old man even more, and he stood up and began to dance like a twenty year old, beckoning Ilana to join him. She didn't move and stared at him wide-eyed, her pupils getting bigger all the time.

'Tell me, did you fall from the moon?' she asked in astonishment.

'Yes,' he replied, 'but guess which moon. Oh,' he sighed, 'how I love you!' He began playing the harmonica again and the man accompanied him on the piano, in the wrong key. The sound of a woman groaning came from behind the walls, bringing the old man's playing to a sudden stop and making him lose his temper.

'Joshua!' cried the old man. 'Lower the volume immediately.'

'Joshua?' asked Ilana in surprise.

'My son,' said the old man, 'the seed of my loins. Your brother.'

'But I haven't got any brothers.'

'Nineteen forty-one. Bombay. Sailing on the Ganges. Your white hat. The uneducated one-eyed Indian who rowed the boat. Your yellow dress blowing in the breeze and exposing your slender legs. Your peals of laughter when we threw him into the river. My loud laughter when he tried to surface and we pushed him back in with your flowered parasol. His body floating on the Ganges. The way I fixed it with a small bribe to the local police. The great times we had there, the time of our lives. The act of love as a result of which your brother was born.'

'I don't know what you're talking about,' said Ilana.

'Oh Susan!' he cried and clapped his hands, 'you're trying to deny part of your past, but it won't be denied, it will float up to the surface, like the Indian ...'

He burst into loud laughter and pointed with his cane at the door from which the groans were coming.

'Go,' he said to her, 'go in there. Speak to your brother. After all, he was born only a week after you.'

Ilana stood up and advanced hesitantly toward the door. The long-haired man pushed her in and locked the door behind her. The room which greeted her eyes was small and dark and on the wall to her left a porn movie was being screened backwards. She searched for the spectator and discovered a man lying curled up on a mattress, his hair wild, and his terrified eyes staring at her as if he hadn't seen a human being for years.

'Don't tell me you're Susan', he said and his eyes flashed.

'I'm Susan,' said Ilana, 'don't tell me you're Joshua.'

'Joshua the wild man in person, but also Arthur, outstanding Marine, and also Joseph, double agent, and I've only just shaved off my moustache. But best of all I like being Simon, the crazy son hidden in the closet.'

'In other words,' sighed Ilana, 'you're schizophrenic.'

'Schizophrenic?' said the wild man in surprise. 'I'm schizophrenic? I've never looked at it like that.'

'Oh my God,' said Ilana weakly, 'so you're crazy too. There's no one to talk to.'

'Don't make the mistake of thinking I'm mad about this place,' he said and looked at the square of light left behind by the movie. 'Listen, that was a great movie. I've already seen it four hundred and fifty times and every time I see new things in it. I remember the first time I saw it, it was with the deer. Exactly where you're standing now, there was once a deer. What am I talking about a deer, the skeleton of a deer, with a bit of skin. She was with me here for five years until they took her away. Them,' he pointed painfully at the door. 'I don't know where they took her. Maybe to the zoo. They told me they let her free in the hills, but I don't believe them. I'll bet you whatever you like that they sold her to Richard the dead animal eater, and he ate her up. They'll do anything for money,' he said sadly. 'They took her away from me and they turned me into a deer-addict. I used to play catch with her. What am I talking about catch, from one end of the room to the other,' he illustrated the linear movement with his hands, 'games like that are never real. What do you think, if she'd wanted to she could have caught me easily. But she didn't want to. That was her greatness. She wanted me to feel good, she was real kind to me.'

He looked at Ilana's bare feet. She lowered her eyes and saw a little circle drawn on the floor with charcoal, and at a short distance from it another circle, and then another two circles, parallel to the first ones, all the same size.

'You want to hear something?' he asked and let out a long howl. 'You know what that is? I'm calling the wolves. When the deer was here I used to call the wolves, and I would sit and listen to them going berserk. I suppose you think I'm bullshitting you, wolves in the middle of New York, right? But no, I'm telling you: there are real wolves in New York,' he declared loudly, 'it's just that I don't know yet where they come from,' he said, angry at himself. 'We could hear them and she would shiver with fear. I called her Julie. I would go up and stroke her: calm down, calm down. In the morning she would fall asleep standing up in exactly the same place, until noon. Until one day I drew circles round her feet and ever since then – she never missed those circles once. And that's the answer to your question, what those circles are for.'

'I didn't ask that question,' said Ilana.

'Maybe you didn't ask, but you should have asked.' He fell silent. 'You know what,' he suddenly began rummaging in his pockets, 'I have to show you something.' He took out a ball of paper and threw it at her. She bent down and sat on the floor, undid the ball and flattened it out. There was a labyrinth drawn on it with arrows pointing in the direction of a door on which was written 'Out'. She looked at him in surprise. He opened his mouth to explain, but he didn't have the time. The door of the room opened wide and the paper flew away and disappeared behind a squashed cardboard box. Two steaming plates of soup were placed on the floor and the door slammed shut again. The wild man leaped on one of the plates and took it. When he passed her she noticed his features for the first time.

'Eat your soup, Susan, you must,' he said and ate his greedily. 'Afterwards you'll die of hunger, believe me, it's no joke.'

She picked up the spoon and drank more than half until she felt very weak, let her head fall back and closed her eyes.

'I feel so dazed,' she said with difficulty.

'Oh, that's nothing,' he said, 'they put something into the soup here. Something that neutralizes resistance. You have to get used to it. After a month or two it doesn't have any effect, but by then you don't try to escape anyway. You haven't got the will.'

'But it's so frightening,' said Ilana and curled up into a ball, 'I've never felt like this before. What kind of stuff is it?'

'I don't know, PR something. Dissolving tablets.'

'For God's sake, do me a favour,' she requested, 'tell them to fetch a doctor quickly to give me a sedative. It's too much for me. Tell them!'

'Relax, honey, it's all illusion. It's all in your head. Everything will pass. Just imagine,' he leaned over in her direction, 'I had to go through all this alone. Only me and the dark.' He kissed her hand, and held it gently.

'Oh Mama,' whispered Ilana. 'I can see terrible things. What is it?'

'It's all illusion, Susan. Relax. Joshua's here to take care of you.' Again he kissed her hand, and she pushed him away and stared into space.

'I see a desert. The Sahara desert. And they're going to shoot a camel.'

'Who?' he asked in surprise.

'The caravan. They're going to shoot a camel, what cruelty. Enough!' she cried.

'Shhh ...' he patted her back gently. 'It must be sick. They wouldn't kill it for nothing, they must be scared it'll infect the whole herd. Try to go somewhere else. Try to go to Spain. Try, I don't know, to change the camel into a bull.'

'What bull? All I see is caravans of lost camels that are going to be destroyed. It's awful.'

'Oof, why don't you see a bull?' he asked impatiently.

'Why a bull? Did you see a bull?'

'A whole bullfight. With a toreador and all the rest of it, applause and cries of Olé from the audience. I shouted Olé too, it was all so real and colourful.'

'So is something wrong with me?'

'I think so.'

'What do you suggest I do with all these camels?'

'If you know they're going to be destroyed, then destroy them in your imagination first, and I don't know, try to get to Spain. Over there I'll help you to escape.'

'I don't understand you.'

'I'll explain,' he whispered in her ear. 'Jump,' he kissed her forehead, 'over the Mediterranean,' he kissed her lips, 'and meet me in Spain,' he stroked her hair, 'not far from Gibraltar,' he stroked her thigh, 'I know a place there, a little abandoned motel whose owners are dying,' he loosened her clasped hands, 'for some couple to come to their special room. Outside the wind whistles, in the distance the sea storms,' he opened the zip of her dress down her back, 'the old people there tell,' he panted slightly, 'that anyone who goes into the special room doesn't come out the same.' He kissed her lips which responded to him. 'The name of the motel is "Mother's Legs", the name of the village is …'

The love-making began. During it the youth went on to tell her the funniest jokes she had ever heard. One joke, for example, was about this guy, who was very well established in life, a Western Jew with a car and a house and a family, who went to Lillienblum Street in Tel Aviv one day to buy black dollars. He went up to a certain Yemenite, and bought a bunch from him. And the Yemenite, after giving him his change, said to him: Guess what? And the buyer nearly wet himself, because he thought the Yemenite was going to tell him that the dollars were counterfeit and began to run, and it was a well known fact that you could never catch a running Yemenite. So the Western Jew asked the Yemenite in a panic: What? And that Yemenite said: Snot, and laughed fit to burst and told the Western Jew that he played this trick on everybody, especially on uptight German born like him. And another joke he told her, that made Ilana split her sides laughing, was about this woman who's on her way back from the Carmel market in Tel Aviv on Thursday with a basket full of tomatoes, oranges and tangerines and other fruit and vegetables, and she's walking down Rothschild Boulevard happy as a lark, as if she's just won a prize on a sweepstake, and right in front of her there's this other guy who's just come back from the market too, and he's eating one of the bananas he bought there because he can't wait till he gets home, and he throws the banana peel on the ground, and the woman doesn't see the peel and she comes a cropper with all her baskets and everything scatters in all directions, fruit and vegetables rolling all over the place, into the road as well, and a number five bus driving past squashed a tangerine and squirts the juice right into her face and eyes. Boy did Ilana laugh, laugh isn't the word, she nearly bust a gut, and the youth only smiled shyly, breathed heavily, zipped up his trousers and knocked on the door three times: twice and then once.

After that everything happened as quick as a flash. Ahipaz burst in, his black eyes glittering with jealousy, and slapped Ilana hard in the face. From the force of the blow she lost her balance, fell back and banged her head on the floor. Ahipaz let out three juicy curses one after the other and threw a blanket over her to cover her nakedness.

After him came Moshe and Yeheskel. Yeheskel looked at Ilana and smiled in embarrassment. Moshe turned to the actor, paid him a hundred dollars in one note and slapped him on the back. And when he tried to bargain for another fifty, Moshe pushed him roughly out of the room.

Before he went the young man turned to Ilana who was still lying on the floor and said: 'You're great. And if you ever want to see me again look for me in Albert Shushan's bar.' Donald came in and waited quietly to get what was coming to him. He pushed the money deep into his pocket and said to Ilana:

'Sorry, but I did it for the money.'

The old man came in, pulled off his mask, and Eviatar said:

'Sorry, Ilana, but don't be mad at Ahipaz.' He glanced at Ahipaz who was making an effort to control himself. 'It was all my idea. Ahi said it would never work out. I said to him: Give me a few hours and I'll bring you a one hundred per cent professional scenario. Don't forget you're dealing here with an artist of tomorrow. After that I said to the guys,' he indicated Moshe and Yeheskel, 'let's make a super eight movie, we'll act in it and film it with a hidden camera. But then Yeheskel said,' and Yeheskel nodded shyly, 'that from the philosophical point of view there was no need to film the movie. That we should do it for real, and I agreed. You understand, I'm going to change the concept of cinemas in the world. So I said to everyone, on condition that I'm the director. But actually, we did the whole thing for a joke. Are you trying to tell me that you never felt anything?'

'What difference does it make to you?' said Ilana with revulsion.

Ahipaz looked at Eviatar with hatred, and Eviatar smiled at him.

'Relax, Brother', he said, 'you got what you wanted. Ilana,' he turned to her, 'I think it was great. Your acting was out of this world. It's a real shame they threw you out of "Habima" theatre.'

'You're all sick. Really sick,' cried Ilana and got up and went into the next room. There she encountered Tzila and Anat. Tzila was sitting on the old man's chair, and Anat next to the piano.

'If I ever make a full-length movie,' Eviatar called after her, 'I'll take you as the star, I promise.'

'Tzila,' asked Ilana quietly, 'are you in on it too?'

Tzila didn't answer and hastily wiped away a tear.

'How could you have let them do it to me?'

'We didn't know,' said Anat in a hard voice. 'What do you think?'

'Honey, why don't you put something on? That blanket –' said Tzila.

'Yes, get dressed,' said Anat. 'Take it easy, but don't believe them when they tell you it was only a joke. It isn't true. I heard the whole story on the way here.'

'What's that?' said Ilana. 'What story?'

'Oh, Anat, why don't you shut up already,' said Tzila sulkily.

'Why should I shut up?' Anat flared up. 'If there's something I want to say, why shouldn't I say it? A person should know where he stands. Eviatar said that somebody saw you in a sex shop, in a porn movie, and Ahipaz wanted to pay you back in a porn movie with knobs on. They say that it was absolutely hard porno. If you ask me, I don't blame Ahipaz. If I took part in porn movies I'd understand Yeheskel if he did something like that to me. I just don't understand why I had to get a crack on the head and lie tied to the bed for an hour and a half until Moshe did us a big favour and let us go.'

'Is it true?' Tzila asked Ilana. 'Did you take part in porn movies?'

'Who cares if you did or you didn't,' said Anat without giving Ilana a chance to reply, 'in any case you have to know how to take it in the right proportion. And if people, never mind what they did or didn't do, aren't capable of understanding that they're in this world for two seconds flat and the act's over, then what are they worth as human beings? Tell me, Ilana, what are they worth?'

Her voice trembled with excitement. 'It's all part of this fucked-up life. So you can calm down and put it all behind you. And you've got two options in this life: either you can cry to the bitter end, or you can forget about the whole thing. Just forget it and...'

'Why don't you shut up already?' said Tzila sulkily.

'Who do you think you are anyway?' Anat continued passionately, staring at Ilana, 'We can all open wounds if we want to. You think I can't? I could tread hard on Ahipaz's own corns if I wanted to and tell everybody about how he seduced me,' she hit herself on the chest, 'on the Sea of Galilee in seventy-eight, and took me to the eucalyptus glade when you all went to swim in that lousy lake. But I don't do it, because in any case one day everything will come out and you have to carry on, until that day comes,' she concluded with a passionate cry to the room at large, and looked at the men who were listening to her speech from the next room, to see their reaction. Moshe clapped scornfully, Yeheskel looked at her without moving, and Eviatar was seen at the back of the room putting on his normal clothes. Ahipaz was nowhere to be seen.

'Ilana,' said Tzila, 'I just want to know. Did you take part or not in porn movies?'

'I won't tell you,' said Ilana. 'You'll die without knowing.' She went into the next room to take her dress, ignoring the long looks of Moshe and Yeheskel and the pale, gloomy Ahipaz, who was standing with his back to her and his hands hanging on the wall. She got dressed, turned to leave, bumped into Eviatar who was just standing there, and slapped him.

'I deserved that,' said Eviatar.

He crossed the room where Anat and Tzila were sitting, and left the house, unintentionally slamming the door.

Ilana returned to the big room, confused.

'I just want to know,' said Tzila, 'why you went to bed with that drip. He's disgusting.'

Ilana didn't answer and made for the door. She paused for a moment with her back to them and said:

'Ahipaz is a fool, and Eviatar is nothing but a psychiatric case who's got movies on the brain.'

She left.

Outside she fell straight into the arms of Yossi who was holding a bag full of warm cheeseburgers.

'Yossi,' she said. 'Are you in it too?'

'In what?' asked Yossi in surprise.

Ilana took off and ran down the road. Ahipaz came outside and ran after her, calling her name.

She turned round to look at him, dry-eyed.

'Ilana,' he said, 'I'm sorry. What should I do?'

'Mmmm ...' said Ilana reflectively.

In the distance Tzila and Moshe and Anat and Yeheskel came out and watched them, while Yossi begged them to tell him what was going on, why they weren't playing cards, why Ilana was angry, and what to do with the cheeseburgers, but nobody answered him.

'Come on,' said Moshe to Tzila, 'the kid's at the neighbour's.'

Yeheskel went to start his car and Anat got in. Tzila and Moshe's white Buick drove slowly past Ahipaz and Ilana who were exchanging broken words. Moshe drove and looked straight ahead, and Tzila waved goodbye with an anxious smile. Ilana looked at her, and Ahipaz nodded in her direction. Yeheskel and Anat's old car drove past them too, but neither of them looked at Ilana and Ahipaz. Yossi sat in the back seat, looked at Ilana for a moment, and sank into thought again. He had been the goalie in a grey football team in the national league in Israel which never won any titles and never managed to get into the premier league. Two months before he had hit a referee who had blown the whistle on him for a foul and wounded him, and he was suspended from the league for ever. The next day there was a caricature in the newspaper of Yossi standing in a goal full of footballs with his foot on the head of the referee who was lying bleeding on the ground. His arms were folded and he was looking at the audience with a proud expression on his face.

Four or five weeks later Ilana and Ahipaz were sitting in their house in Long Island, rolling joints of Columbian Gold marijuana, and talking quietly, and between one word of wisdom and the next, they wondered what they should have for lunch. Through the leaves of the tree in their garden sunbeams danced, and you wouldn't believe the stories they tell about the choreographer who asks the birds to fly from branch to branch. The birds flew from branch to branch, and all that's missing is for them to build their nest next to Ilana and Ahipaz's window sill. Because it's all very well, two birds fucking and one female bird laying eggs, and soft little baby birds hatching from the eggs, but why does it have to be next to my window? Aren't there any other window sills around? Let them go to Robert, let them go to Peter and Marianne, let them go to George and Cindy, or to that black couple at the end of the road. Let them go to hell.

Translated by Dalya Bilu

9

Male and Female

by SHULAMIT LAPID

AMNON DISAPPEARED without a trace in the middle of his wife's birthday party. Afterwards they all agreed that there had been no sign that something was about to happen. He was behaving quite normally, and he was surely a responsible person. It might have been understandable if some other member of the family had done it, but in Amnon it seemed incongruous. There wasn't even a motive in sight. He wasn't angry with anyone, hadn't quarrelled with anyone. He just went down to the street and got into his van, started driving and didn't come back.

It couldn't really be called much of a party. Rayah insisted that she didn't want any fuss. Fifty! What is there to celebrate? Eddie said, 'What's that supposed to mean? Having a mother like you, isn't that worth celebrating?' But Rayah planted herself in among the sofa cushions and covered her ears and cried, 'No! No! No!' until Eddie pulled her hands from her ears and yelled, 'Be careful, we might take you seriously after all and then what would you do?' Writhing under his big body and lashing out with her fists she cried, 'Get off me you crazy gorilla, I'm choking!' In the end she agreed to a modest party, but really modest, since she had no intention of announcing all over town that she had turned fifty. 'Even if you did announce it nobody would believe you,' said Eddie, and he began allocating tasks. Turning to his wife Milkah, he slapped her bottom and informed her that she was to prepare courgette quiche, lemon mousse and marble-cake, his brother Buki was told to fetch wine from Adler's, not just any old wine, but the very best – Yarden wine, and to Sharon, his sister-in-law, he assigned two or three salads. 'And what about me? What about me?' asked Rayah. 'You're going to sit there with a garland of flowers on your head and we'll throw you up into the air fifty-one times,' said Eddie. Amnon sat Galit on his knee and laid a big strong hand on Moran's head, and said to Milkah: 'I know you're all vegetarians but you can cook me a steak.' She smiled at him and said she was sure this wouldn't defile her kitchen.

Eddie suggested holding the party on the roof. The apartment was hot and stifling and on the roof there was a pleasant breeze, and besides that the little monsters would be free to run about instead of getting in the way and annoying everyone with their nonsense. Eddie always called his mother's and Amnon's children 'the little monsters'. He went up to inspect the roof and came down saying that it was covered with pigeon-droppings and if they'd had any sense they would have thought of scrubbing down the roof and anyway he didn't understand what the house-committee thought it was doing.

'Anyway, it would have been impossible to carry all the food and drink up to the roof,' said Milkah, trying to appease him.

'Impossible? Why impossible?' Eddie demanded angrily. There'll be one, two ... six adults here. Everyone could carry something. What's the problem?'

Milkah wondered whether to light the oven now or to wait until guests arrived. She didn't want to argue with him, knowing that once he got into 'that mood' there was no calming him down. After two years of marriage she recognized all the signs: the high voice, the pale brow, the blend of gaiety and anger.

He helped Milkah move the kitchen table and went to extend the dining table in the lounge. 'I should have bought the wine myself,' he shouted to her in the kitchen, 'I can't trust Buki with things like that. I bet he went to the Levinsky market to save a few shekels. Just like him to bring us some second-class wine.'

On the fridge door, Milkah posted a list of the dishes in the order in which they would be served, so she wouldn't forget anything. Once before, she forgot about a pie and remembered it only after everyone had left and she spotted it hiding behind a jar of pickles. She prepared the salad dressing and left the quiche on the marble counter to defrost. Eddie said that quiche tasted better when baked immediately before serving, but she was afraid something would go wrong, the oven, or the dough, and decided to prepare everything in advance. There was a clog in the sink and she poured boiling water into it and stood watching it bubbling on the little strainer over the drainage pipe.

Buki and Sharon were the first to arrive. They brought the pram and the shopping-trolley into the lounge and filled the fridge with the baby's bottles and bottles of white wine. Then Buki went down to fetch Sharon's famous salads from the car. Milkah apologized for the crush in the fridge and Sharon said, 'You should see our fridge!' She lifted Haran from the pram to give him a drink of water, but Eddie insisted 'Give him to me, give him to me,' and took Haran from her arms. He sat down on the sofa with an almost maternal air, concentrating all his attention on the swallowing and gurgling mouth and the eyes staring at him curiously. 'I forgot the glasses,' said Milkah, and ran to the kitchen. 'Bring the wine glasses,' Eddie said, whispering so as not to alarm the baby. Milkah took the wine glasses they had received as a wedding present from the top drawer of the wardrobe in the bedroom, and took them to the kitchen to peel off the labels and wipe them. She would have washed them, but now it was already late, the sink was causing problems and the guests had arrived. He could have mentioned it earlier, in the morning, or the day before, or week before, but not at the moment. How many times had she said to him, 'What about those wine glasses?' and he always said 'We'll get them down,' but he never did get them down, and now of all times he had to remember them when there was no time to wash them properly.

Mother and Amnon and Galit and Moran arrived just as Haran was beginning to reject the teat of the bottle with his little tongue. Eddie passed him to Buki for burping and went to open the door, and from the kitchen Milkah heard Eddie's whoops of joy and excitement at the sight of the new hairdo that his mother had treated herself to in honour of the new decade in her life. She had simply gone and got rid of her famous ponytail, all that long hair which had been gathered up and entwined on her nape since her secondary school-days, she had just gone to the hairdresser and had it all cut off and now she was standing in the doorway, blushing and excited as she took in the cries of surprise and approval and protest. Her beautiful hair was dyed blond. Cut in a straight line, it fell to just below her ears. Her forehead was covered by a wide fringe reaching to the begining of her nose, and her blue eyes peered out from under it with all the shyness of a teenager, and she pursed her lips and smiled at the uproar aroused by this silly gesture of hers.

'And what did Amnon say when you came home looking like this?' demanded Eddie. 'Amnon! What did you say when you suddenly saw her without her ponytail? She looks like Jane Fonda, doesn't she Milkah? I've always said that she looks like Jane Fonda. Can you see it now? Look! It's there – you can see it, can't you?' But no one said anything, simply because Eddie didn't let anyone else get a word in. He gathered up Rayah's hair on her nape and compared the new style to the old, and he made her turn round and round while he poured champagne for everyone. He had decided to buy champagne at the last moment in case Buki didn't bring the 'Yarden'. Now he poured it into the new glasses that Milkah brought in on the big tray, and proposed 'a toast to our new mother'. Amnon told Rayah she shouldn't drink too much, because sparkling wine gave her headaches, and she smiled at him and asked: 'Should we give Galit and Moran a tiny drop of champagne?'

'Is it French champagne?' asked Moran.

'Does he only drink French champagne?' Eddie cried. 'A fine upbringing you're giving your children!'

'Why not?' said Amnon to Rayah, but Eddie made a grab for the tray of glasses and said: 'Don't you try and take over here. I know what kind of host you are. Go be a miser in your own home, but not when I'm in charge. Come on kids!' and he filled all their glasses.

Milkah took the quiche out of the oven and Sharon cleared the first-course plates and the new glasses from the table and brought them to the kitchen. The children hadn't touched the champagne and Milkah drank what was left in their glasses, thinking it would be crazy to pour down the sink champagne that had cost forty shekels a bottle. Then she washed the glasses, quietly, so Eddie wouldn't hear, and laid them on the tea-towel. He didn't allow her to wash up between courses, but sometimes she got away with it.

The sink was almost half-full of water, and greasy gobbets rose from the drainage pipe and covered the surface of the water with black and yellow patches. If Eddie comes in now he'll realize I washed the glasses, she thought, and took out the rubber plunger from the cupboard under the sink and began pumping with it, up and down, up and down. The water frothed, and she didn't know if this was due to the plunger or because she'd succeeded in shifting the clog.

Amnon came into the kitchen and said 'Give it to me,' took the plunger from her hands, and pumped up and down, up and down, but the water in the sink remained at the same level as before.

'Come on! Come on!' Eddie burst into the kitchen, 'What are you doing? Milkah! Amnon! We're drinking a toast to Mum!'

Milkah and Amnon went into the lounge and they all raised glasses of 'Yarden' and congratulated Rayah. Then they gave her their presents one by one and kissed her.

'You're overdoing it,' said Rayah, wiping her eyes. 'I didn't want any fuss, didn't I say I didn't want any fuss? Don't you dare tell your friends that I'm fifty!' she warned Moran and Galit. 'They wouldn't believe it anyway,' said Eddie. 'Not now with that hairdo!'

Milkah returned to the kitchen. Amnon had removed the garbage bin from the cupboard under the sink and put an empty bucket in its place. The pipe was disconnected and water poured into the bucket, and streamed over the base of the cupboard covering the floor with sticky lumps and blobs of grease.

Milkah put the tray on the table, drank the children's wine, and ran to fetch the mop and rag from the balcony. In the kitchen the stench of rubbish and sewage blended with the sour scent of the wine and Milkah felt that she was liable to vomit at any moment. She was wondering whether to take the mousse from the fridge when Eddie came into the kitchen and asked: 'Where are your jeans, Milkah? The ones you bought in Medina Square?'

'In the bedroom closet, in the towel drawer. Why?'

Eddie's eyes were sparkling and there were red spots on his cheeks. Milkah wondered if he too had been drinking too much.

'No wonder I couldn't find them,' he grumbled and left the kitchen.

She began mopping up the water with the rag, but she couldn't reach the bucket, which was under the sink. She stood there helplessly holding the rag, dirty water dripping on the floor and the filth penetrating her skin.

'Squeeze that out in the bathroom,' said Amnon, and suddenly shouted 'Don't come in!' to Galit and Moran, who had appeared in the kitchen doorway. Water dripped on the floor in the kitchen, the hall and the bathroom. She squeezed out the rag into the toilet, then rinsed it in the bath and returned to the kitchen, mopping the floor again and again until it was finally clean and dry.

'Give me the female and the male,' said Amnon.

'What?' asked Milkah. Impatiently he grabbed the two sections of pipe himself, inserted the narrow section into the broad section and screwed it tight. Then he lifted the bucket, which was filled to the brim with muck, and carried it to the bathroom, leaving muddy footprints behind him.

Milkah bent down under the sink to clean the cupboard and put the garbage-bin back in its place. Then she stood up and saw that the sink was still full of filthy water.

'Look at her!' cried Eddie. 'Just look at her! Fifty? She looks thirty – forget forty!'

'Eddie, Eddie,' Rayah protested, 'you're nearly thirty yourself.'

Amnon came out of the bathroom holding the empty bucket and Milkah came in from the kitchen with the rag in her hand. They both gazed at the spectacle before them.

Rayah was standing in the middle of the room wearing Milkah's jeans. Her chin and mouth were wreathed with mischievous little smiles. She really did look young and beautiful in the jeans and with the new blond look, even younger than Milkah or Sharon. She raised her arms, twirled around, and peeped at Amnon like a bashful girl expecting expressions of affection from her first admirer.

'The clog is further along the pipe,' Amnon said to Milkah. 'I'm going down to the van to fetch a metal spring. Come on.'

Milkah washed her hands and arms, wiped them carefully and followed Amnon. He told her to stand in the yard, beside the drainage pipe, and tell him the moment she saw liquid flowing, while he went up to the roof and threaded the spring into the pipe. The scraping sound made by the metal spring set her teeth on edge and she rubbed her arms and looked up at Amnon. There was something reassuring in those strong arms moving up and down, up and down, thrusting the spring ever deeper into the pipe. She stood in the little parking space, between the water meters and the gas canisters, her mind a blank, her hands folded on her stomach, hoping that these plumbing operations would continue until the party was over and they had all gone home. Then she could clean the apartment, wash the dishes and sit down at her desk at last. Berman had hinted to her that if she carried on as she had started they would take her on as a partner when she had qualified. Berman-Schuster-Ishtar was one of the best firms in town, a firm in which any young lawyer would be happy to work.

The jeans Rayah was wearing now were the ones Milkah had bought for herself after the meeting with Berman. In the office she wore tailored suits and conservative dresses which wouldn't have embarrassed her grandmother, the kind of disguise that robs career women of age and sex, and suddenly she had felt an impulse to treat herself to something youthful, frivolous and unnecessary. Be a good girl – her mother used to tell her – eat all your food, do your homework, tidy your books, and afterwards you can go out and play. The jeans were her mother's promise, the reward for good behaviour.

The rasping sound emerging from within the pipe was replaced by a hoarse gurgling. Water began to gush, a thick and turbid liquid that had been suddenly released when the object blocking the pipe had been dislodged.

'Is it flowing?' Amnon shouted from his perch on the roof.

'Yes!' she replied.

At Milkah's feet lay a pigeon chick. Its open beak resembled little tongs made of yellow ivory, and black gunk stuck to the sparse plumage and wrinkled skin.

'I'm coming down!' Amnon shouted.

He closed the pipe carefully, screwing it tight with a big wrench, his movements strong and dexterous.

Then he saw that she was crying and noticed the chick. He embraced her suddenly, gathering her small body, all aquiver with weeping, to his broad chest. 'There, there,' he said, wiping her face with his dirty hands. Then he bent down and kissed her on the eyes, and held her firmly until her body relaxed.

'Go home', he said and strode towards the van. He tossed the spring and the wrench inside and shook the tool-box as if looking for something.

The sink in the kitchen was empty at last. She scrubbed it well and filled it with the plates and glasses that had been left on the marble counter and on the table, gulping the remainder of the wine from the glasses. 'After all no one's sick, thank God, and alcohol disinfects, doesn't it?' she muttered to herself as she went into the lounge with the mousse.

They had all left the dining table.

Sharon was standing there, pushing Haran's pram back and forth, shaking it firmly and energetically. Buki and Moran were arm-wrestling, pretending they were a fair match, and Eddie was sprawled on the armchair, bouncing Galit on his knee and telling everyone how he was going to knock a hole through the bedroom wall, join it to the balcony and build a storage room. He had all this equipment – mountaineering gear, diving gear, metal detectors, digging-tools, first aid – and he needed somewhere to store it all. He was always on the verge of starting or finishing some project or another, assuring anyone who would listen that next month, in two months at the most, he was going to write his 'magnum opus', a definitive study of fortifications in the middle Bronze Age.

'How do you put up with him?' Rayah chuckled, turning to Milkah who was standing at the table doling out mousse into the dishes. 'You're always tearing down something, Eddie. How can anyone live in a house that's in a permanent state of demolition?

You don't even finish anything. The wall in the bedroom is crooked. For a whole year you've had a crooked wall in the bedroom.'

'Milkah loves our crooked wall. Isn't that right Milkah, don't you love our crooked wall?' cried Eddie, throwing Galit in the air. He was tall and she almost touched the ceiling.

'Stop that!' said Moran.

'We've scared them, eh?' laughed Eddie, and tossed Galit in the air again, as she squealed and giggled.

It was then that they noticed that Amnon wasn't there. Perhaps because they all knew that Eddie wouldn't have dared to toss Galit around like that if Amnon had been in the room.

Rayah had given her sons what she called 'a liberal upbringing'. They were orphans and she decided not to force things on them and not to restrict them, because their early experiences had been unsettling enough. It was a fact that they grew up successful and handsome – none of her acquaintances had more loving and devoted sons – without needing her to dole out vitamins or say: do this, don't do that.

With Amnon it was a different story. He had ideas of his own about the upbringing of children. After the marriage he put a stop to Buki's and Eddie's habit of getting into their mother's bed on Saturday mornings, and after Moran was born he began restricting Rayah's contact with her sons.

'They're grown up now,' he said, 'and they have lives of their own. There's no reason why they should be getting under our feet.'

'It's just that they've got used to looking after me,' Rayah said.

'I am the one looking after you now.'

Buki accepted the new regime without argument, but with Eddie it was another story. Since his father was killed when he was ten years old, and his mother told him that from now on he would be her 'little Daddy', Eddie had become accustomed to looking after Rayah. Sometimes, when Amnon was out of town, Eddie would turn up just to see how she was, and they would indulge in their private nonsense as they had done before. He would open the closet in the bedroom and inspect her clothes, seeing what was new, what was missing, matching a necklace to a blouse, and belt to a skirt, prying among her handkerchiefs and boxes of earrings, sniffing bottles of perfume, making her wear something that he hadn't seen her wearing before. These meetings had the sweet taste of secrecy, something that was their own private reserve, and by unspoken agreement they were revealed to no one else.

Milkah explained about the clogged sink and how Amnon had gone up to the roof and removed the clog. For some reason she didn't mention the bird. 'In the middle of the party you send Amnon to fix your sink?' Eddie yelled.

'Why are you shouting at her?' said Buki, 'What do you expect her to do?'

Buki and Eddie debated the question of whether Milkah was entitled to ask for Amnon's help or not, as if she wasn't there in the room, or an inanimate object, or a deaf and dumb suspect accused of some heinous offence.

Milkah poured herself some of the 'Yarden' that was left in one of the bottles and looked at all the plates and crumpled napkins, the dirty glasses and the crumbs on the floor, and decided that today she would not wipe any of the dishes. She'd just leave everything to dry and in the evening, after the television news, she'd put it all away without bothering to wipe even a single fork. She felt her eyes closing and Sharon said, 'Come on, I'll help you clear the table,' but Eddie yelled at Sharon, 'You know I don't like that. Guests are guests. We don't help when we're visiting you and you shouldn't help when you're our guests. I want you to relax and enjoy yourselves. That's why we invited you.'

Then he went down to look for the van, but it wasn't in the parking-lot. Rayah phoned home but naturally there was no reply, and they decided to wait for the time being. Sharon took Haran out of his pram and began pacing around the room with him, rocking him and humming nervously. Buki said that Amnon had probably gone to buy cigarettes and Eddie told Milkah to tell them again exactly what she had been doing with Amnon while they had been sitting and enjoying their lunch. He interrupted her from time to time and his questions became increasingly unpleasant, and Galit suddenly began crying 'Daddy! Daddy!' and stopped only when Eddie gave her a ride on his back and leapt around the room with her.

'Put her down,' said Rayah. But Eddie went on cavorting about the room and shaking the little hump on his back, until Rayah stood up and asked Buki to drive her and the children home.

'Let me know what happens,' said Eddie. But his mother didn't answer. She was still wearing the jeans but her face was grim and taut and Milkah didn't dare ask her to take them off.

Milkah went to the kitchen to rinse the dishes and Eddie sat down beside the phone and called Rayah every quarter of an hour to ask if Amnon had turned up yet. After his fourth call she heard him slam the receiver down hard.

'The cheeky brat!' he said to Milkah from the kitchen door.

'What happened?'

'He told me to stop ringing. Said they'd let me know if Amnon comes back.'

'Moran?'

'Yes.'

Milkah finished washing the dishes and they filled the entire kitchen: the marble counter, the dining table, the oven cover. She decided to wipe them after all. When she'd finished putting the glasses in the cupboard she heard the chair creaking, and the sound of dialling, and Eddie announcing his intention of going round to Rayah's house. Then there was a tense silence and the receiver slammed down even more loudly than before. The silence in the room worried her.

'He hasn't come back?' she asked the shoulders and the back of the neck in the armchair. 'You can go round there if you like.'

'Thank you very much,' he muttered sarcastically. And then he turned and fixed on her a look in which hurt and bewilderment were combined. 'Mother's gone into the bedroom, she's lying on the bed, and she's told Moran to make sure no one disturbs her. "She told me" – Moran says – "That until Daddy comes home I'm going to be her little Daddy." And he thinks it's better I don't go round there now. They're tense enough as it is.'

Milkah looked at Eddie and didn't know what to say. She returned to the kitchen and went on arranging the dried utensils in the cupboards. Then she washed out the sink. The drainage pipe was working and the water flowed freely.

Translated by Philip Simpson

10

A Room on the Roof

by SAVYON LIEBRECHT

THAT SUMMER she sat on the patio under the rounded awning of the Italian swing, as the straw fringes interwined with the edges of the cloth dome rustled softly, sounding like forest noises, her eyes on the red glow flowing from the western horizon at sunset, her baby already standing on his own two, widespread legs, his fat fingers grasping the bars of the square playpen made of interlocked wooden bars. The rose-like hibiscus waved its circlet of toothed leaves bound in an envelope of buds, only their heads looking out of the long, laden calyxes, pouting like the lips of a coquettish girl, the abundant tranquillity all about deluding merely the part of her that was asleep in any case, not the part that was driven, tensed towards something beyond the apparent silence, knowing the restlessness of someone under eyes constantly prying but always unseen.

That early winter – the mud, the puddles of cement, and the rusty fragments of iron – already seemed distant and impossible, with the three Arab men giving off the stench of wood smoke and unwashed flesh. The men with their bad teeth and mouths, with high-heeled shoes that were once fashionable, now looking oversized, with the leather crushed under the heels.

In her dreams they still visited her sometimes, coming too close to her, which, perhaps, where they live too, could be interpreted as what they might have meant to hint, though perhaps it was done inadvertently. For a long time she wondered about it: did Ahmed draw close to her unheedingly, touching her legs with his rear as he dragged a sack of cement, with his back to her? And later, was it by chance that his elbow touched her breast when he passed by her, balancing the bag of lime on his shoulder, while she raised her arms to the lintel of the door to check the concrete rim as it dried? And did Hassan really believe that she would invite him inside the apartment, on that black night when he came back for his coat?

Sometimes she imagined that if she turned her head toward the corner, where she had placed the hexagonal fiberglass flower-pot in which she had planted an Indian alder, she would see Salah the way she'd caught him once when she'd climbed up to the roof unexpectedly: standing with his legs spread, urinating against the wall, holding his penis in his hand, looking down in concentration, aiming the foaming yellow stream at the line where the two walls met.

That summer, for a long time after they went off without ever reappearing, she avoided the roof when it was dark, fearing that they might pop up from behind the high potted plants. Sometimes, when she happened to wind up in the back corner, which was imprisoned within three walls and used, for the moment, as a storage area, and she saw the tools they left behind and never came back to collect, a chill would climb her back like a crawling creature with many legs, stirring a column of water in the depths of her belly like the pitching that afflicts you when you're seasick.

But there was no one to accuse. She had brought the thing down on her own head. And if her baby wasn't slaughtered, and her jewels weren't stolen, and nothing bad had happened to her – she should bless her good fortune and erase those two winter months from her memory as if they had never been.

Yoel, her husband, had been opposed to the idea from the moment she had brought it up, still just an idle word in her mouth and still lacking that fervour, that stubbornness, and that unyielding feeling of necessity which were later to possess her.

'A room on the roof?' He twisted his face and took off his glasses as he did when he was angry. 'Do you know how filthy construction is? Do you have any idea how many tons of soil and rocks will fall on your head when they break through the ceiling for the stairs? And I don't see why we need another room. There are already two unused rooms in the house. And if you want sunlight – you have half a dunam of private lawn.' Against her rebelliously pursed lips, which for a long time, until his patience first broke down, were to emit a defiant silence, he added: 'How is it you suddenly got the notion of building? What do you need that for, with a four-month-old baby?'

'So why did we bother running to the engineer and the municipality to get a building licence?' She countered his argument. 'And didn't we pay all the fees and the property improvement tax and all that?'

'So we'd have it in hand,' he replied, 'so that if we want to sell the house one day – it will be more valuable, with the licence already in hand.'

But the idea had already struck root, twisting up inside her with its own force, like an ovum which had embraced the sperm and was now germinating, and the foetus was already stretching the skin of the belly, and there was no way of putting that growth to sleep.

All that time she was wrapped up in her first-born son Udi, who summoned her from her dreams at night. She would come to him with her eyes almost closed, as though moon-struck, and her hands turned over the tiny baby clothes of their own volition. On her walks, pushing the baby carriage across broken paving stones, past piles of sand, she found herself lingering around houses under construction, raising her head to see the men walking with assurance on the rim of high walls, amazed, learning how storeys grow, windows square themselves in dark frames, shutters fan out panel by panel from the enormous yellow device looking like arm-bones with the flesh scraped off them.

From one of the yawning holes that would be a window, someone shouted at her with an oriental accent: 'You looking for someone to service you, lady?' She blushed as though doing something wrong and pushed her baby away in a panic. Near a building which she often passed, as he looked into the carriage, a contractor told her. 'Excuse me for saying this, but this is no place to wander around with a baby. Dirt and cinderblocks or pieces of iron sometimes fall around here, and it's very dangerous.'

After she started leaving Udi with a baby-sitter in the mornings, a woman who took a few infants in her home, she would go to those places in her old trousers, worn at the knees, climb up the diagonal concrete slabs, supporting herself on the rough rafters, grope in the darkness of stairwells still floored with sand. Here, she would later say to herself, she saw them face to face for the first time, in the chill damp peculiar to houses under construction. They came towards her from corners that stank of urine, all of them with the same face: dark, boiling eyes, sunken in caves of black shadows, hair cut in the old-fashioned way, shoes spotted with lime and cement, and dusty clothes. Here too their peculiar odour came to her nostrils: sweat mingled with cigarette smoke and soot. While she exchanged words with the Jewish foreman, the Arab workers would cast oblique glances at her; down on all fours laying floor tiles; panting as they transported sacks of cement or stacks of tiles; running to ease the effort; ripping out hunks of food with their teeth; half a loaf of bread in one hand, an unpeeled cucumber in the other.

Some foremen were irritable, refusing to answer her questions, dismissing her with a contemptuous gesture and continuing to give directions to their workers, ignoring her as she stood behind them, abashed, feeling how the Arabs were laughing at her inwardly, in collusion with their Jewish foreman, But sometimes the foreman would answer her willingly, watching as she took down what they had said in her notebook, like a diligent pupil. As she turned to leave they would say with amusement, 'So we have to watch out for you, huh, you're the competition!'

In her notebook the pages were already densely packed with details about reinforced concrete, the thickness of inner and outer walls, various gauges of iron rods, a sketch of the way the rods had to be fastened for casting concrete pillars, the ceiling, plaster, flooring, conduits for electricity and water, tar, addresses of building materials manufacturers. She hid her notebook from Yoel in a carton with her university notebooks. Once, when he said, 'What's going on? Avika said he twice saw you coming out of the building they're putting up on Herzl Street,' she looked straight at him and said in her usual tone of voice: 'Probably someone who looks like me,' and he responded: 'It's about time you changed your hairdo. Last week I saw someone from behind, and I was sure it was you. She even had the same walk and the same handbag.'

Afterwards, once she was ripe for it like a girl come of age, Yoel came back from work one day, and his eyes were troubled. He said, 'They want me to go to a training course in Texas for two months. We're getting a new computer. I said I couldn't leave you alone with the baby. Let them find someone else.' She answered firmly, alarmed at the swift feeling that leapt up in her like the shockwave of an explosion: 'I'll be quite all right – you should go.' And when the tempest had died down within her she thought: a sign had been sent from heaven.

The day after she saw him to his plane, David, the Jewish foreman came, accompanied by three Arab workers, members of the same family who looked amazingly alike. They all wore old woollen hats. They sat on the edges of the chairs, careful not to dirty the upholstery, with their eyes cast down most of the time. Only occasionally would they raise their eyelids and cast a quick glance at her and the apartment, squinting at the baby on her lap. David wrote down some kind of agreement on a piece of paper, explaining some sentences in Arabic, and they nodded their heads in consent. David copied their names from a form he'd brought with him and their identity numbers from the creased documents they took out of their pockets, a description of the dimensions of the room they were to build, detailing the thickness of the walls, and number of electric sockets and their place in the room, the break through the opening for the stairs, the type and colour of the plaster, and, beside these, the amounts to be paid as the work progressed. Before signing, she insisted that a final date be clearly written, obligating them to finish the work within two months, before Yoel's return.

Then the three of them stood up at the same time and headed for the door. There, on the threshold, after she thanked him for his good offices, David answered: 'Think nothing of it, dear lady. It's because I can see you're a fine girl, with a sporting character. Not many women would do something like this. So here's to you! And if you need something – ask for David in the Hershkovitz building any time. Good luck! They're good workers, up on scaffolds from the age of fifteen,' and, in her ear, softly, 'Better than ours, believe me.'

Sitting on the open roof that summer opposite the sky spread above her with rows of painted white clouds, hearing her baby babble, his voice rising and falling as he tried his vocal chords, she thought: how did things go so far that those men, whose gaze avoided her eyes, who shrank in her presence with shoulders bowed, as though narrowing their bodies, answering her questions with a soft voice, as though forever guilty; how did it happen that in November they sat on the edge of the chairs that first evening, and by December they were already marching through her house like lords, turning on Yoel's radio transmitter, opening the refrigerator to look for fresh vegetables, rummaging through the cabinet after fragrant shaving cream, and patting her baby on the head?

At first they still seemed to her like a single person, before she learned that Hassan had elongated eyes, whose bright colour was like the banks of wet sand at the water's edge. Ahmed had a broad nose, sitting in the middle of his flattened face between his narrow eyes and his lips thick like those of a negro. Salah's ears pricked up and his cheeks were sunken. Only the pimples on his face gave it some thickness, making it look like the thick skin of an orange.

On the first day, they arrived in an old pickup truck that had once been orange, but now on its dented face there were only islands of peeling paint, and its windows were missing. They got out and unloaded gray cinderblocks near the parking lot. Then the truck pulled away with a grinding noise, returning in a short while with a long wooden beam on top. After a short consultation among themselves, the truck was parked in the parking lot and the beam laid on an angle, the lower part leaning on the back of the truck and the top rising above the edge of the roof. Until the baby started crying inside the house, she stood at a little distance, her hands in the pockets of her slacks, and watched how one of them drew out a tangle of ropes with a saddle-shaped yoke at the end. He stood on the roof and harnessed himself with knots, looking like a coolie in a historical film. One of his mates loaded block after block in the basket on the rope, and the worker on the roof pulled them up along the flat beam, while the third worker, standing on the edge of the roof, leaned over and gathered the bricks one by one. Examining them from below, she saw how their faces grew sweaty with the effort, and their hands got dusty and were scratched by the rough blocks. By the time she had put the baby to bed and come out again, she saw they had unloaded the rest of the blocks on the lawn and disappeared with the truck, though she hadn't heard the sound of the motor. The next day, after turning the matter over during sleepless hours she decided she must demonstrate her authority over them, and she was ready and waiting for them in her window, cradling her baby in her rounded arms, anger breathing force into her movements. From the window she shouted at them as they approached: 'Why did you leave work in the middle of yesterday? And today ...' She looked at her watch with a clumsy movement, stretching her neck over the baby lying at her breast. 'Today you come at nine! You said you'd start working at six! This way you won't finish in ten months!'

'Lady,' said the one with the gilded eyes, insulted. 'Today was police roadblocked. Not possible we leave early before four morning lady.'

Something in her recoiled at the sight of the beaten dog's eyes he raised up towards her in her window, at his broken voice. But tensing her strength to suppress the tremor that awoke within her and threatened to soften her anger, she shouted: 'And yesterday what happened? Was also roadblocked?' Maliciously she imitated his grammatical error. 'You went away and left half the blocks down there on the grass.'

For the first time she saw the movement that was later to become routine: the jaws clamping down on each other as though chewing something very hard, digging a channel along the line of his teeth. Later she was to learn: that's how they suppress anger, hatred. They clench their teeth to overcome the wild rage that surges up, that only rarely breaks out and flashes in their pupils.

'Yesterday my friend Ahmed, he hurted his, the nail his finger.'

Behind him his companion raised a bandaged hand, and she looked out of her pretty window, framed with Catalan-style curtains, feeling how the three men in their tattered work clothes were defeating her, looking up at her from their places.

And two hours afterwards, she had fed and changed the baby and put him to sleep in his cot, her mind constantly on the uncomfortable feeling that had dwelt in her ever since her conversation with them, when she had spoken to them tyrannically. Now, knowing full well she was doing something she shouldn't, but still letting the spirit of the moment overcome the voice of reason, she went out of the front door carrying a large tray, with a china coffee pot decorated with rosebuds, surrounded by cups with matching saucers and spoons with an engraved pattern, and a plate of round honey cakes. She stood there holding the heavy tray, her head raised, debating whether to put the tray down on the marble landing of the stairs and climb up the wooden ladder that leaned against the building, reaching the edge of the roof, and to invite them down for coffee, or perhaps it would be better to call them from where she was. Constantly aware of her ridiculous position, she suddenly discovered she didn't remember any of their names. Then a head peeked over the edge of the roof, and she found herself calling to him quickly, before he disappeared: '*Allo, Allo,* I have some coffee for you.' Ashamed of the shout that had escaped her, she put down the tray and got away before one of them came down and brought her offering up to his companions.

That afternoon, placing her wide-awake baby in his cot, she put on old jeans and Yoel's army jacket and climbed up to the roof to see how they were getting along with the work. The tray with the rosebud pattern coffee pot and the pretty cups stood in a corner of the roof, cigarette butts crushed in the remainder of the murky liquid in the saucers. She stood and looked for a long while at the sight, which she would recall afterwards as a kind of symbol: the rich Rosenthal china from the fine collection her grandmother had brought from Germany heaped up carelessly, lying next to sacks of cement and heavy hammers.

'We finish the concrete rim,' said Hassan, who seemed to have taken upon himself the task of spokesman. 'Now we have to put water and it dry.'

'Is it twenty centimetre?' she spoke like them.

'It twenty to the metre,' he took a metal measuring tape out of his pocket.

'Is it two centimetres over the edge of the floor?'

It seemed to her they exchanged hurried glances, as if they had conspired together before she came, and she grew tense and suspicious.

'Did you bring it up two centimetres above the floor?' She repeated her question, her voice sharp and higher than at first.

'It twenty to the metre,' he told her again.

'But does it come out above the floor or not?'

'Level with the floor,' he spread out his hand to illustrate his words, with a satisfied expression, like a merchant praising his wares.

'That means it's no good,' she said.

'Why no good, lady?'

'Because the rain will leak in,' she said impatiently, her anger rising at the game he was playing with her while the concrete band was drying steadily. 'It has to be two centimetres higher. That's what David said to you, and that's what's written in the contract.'

'We say David twenty centimetre.'

'At least twenty centimetres,' she corrected him, her voice rising and turning to a shout. 'And of that, two centimetre above the floor.'

'There is twenty centimetre, lady,' he said again, his voice like a patient merchant standing up to a customer making a nuisance.

She pursed her lips as if to demonstrate that the conversation was useless. She threw her legs over the low wall around the roof and planted her feet on the rungs of the ladder.

'I'm going to get David,' she said to the three men standing and looking at her, anxious to see how things would turn out. 'If that's the way you're starting – then it's no good,' she added. She went down the ladder with a rush to show them the bellicose spirit that animated her steps, inwardly calculating how long it would take her to get to the building on Herzl Street and locate David, and whether it would be better to take Udi with her, or leave him in his cot and hope he was asleep. Planting her feet on the ground, she strode vigorously towards her car, determined to call David before the concrete band dried. Then she heard a thick voice calling to her from the roof: 'Lady, you don't need David. We add two centims.'

She turned her face upward, suppressing the feeling of relief and victory that surged up through her anger, seeing the three dark heads bunched together: 'Quickly then, before it dries,' she said in a loud, hard voice.

That evening, her sister Noa's voice came through from the public telephone in Jerusalem, mingled with those of other people: 'You made a mistake about the coffee. Let them make it themselves, and don't serve them anything any more. If they get into the house – you'll never get rid of them.'

'Don't worry. No one gets into my house without an invitation,' she shouted, over the strangers' voices.

But the next day Hassan, whose name she had learned, stood in the doorway. Smiling to her with his eyes as yellow as the winter sun, he said with gentle bashfulness in his voice: 'Yesterday the lady made coffee. Today I make coffee like in my house.' From a plastic bag he withdrew a container of coffee that gave off a fragrance like that in cramped spice shops where coffee grinders crush the dark beans into aromatic grains.

Taken aback by the friendly gesture, as though they hadn't sparred with each other the day before, as though she hadn't been racked all night long worrying about how she would mobilize the police and the courts if they tried again to violate the agreement they had signed, she took a step backward, and before she grasped what was happening, he slipped through the space between her body and the doorjamb, stepped over to the range, and put the plastic bag on the marble counter. With precise, expert movements he took out a long-handled blue coffee pot and a spoon, took a spoonful of coffee, added sugar that he poured out of another bag, and filled the pot with water. Then,

159

after fiddling lightly with the lighter and the knobs on the stove he lit and placed the coffee pot on the glowing ring. She observed his motions with astonishment, stunned at the liberty he took in her kitchen, her eyes drawn to his graceful, pleasing movements, knowing danger was latent in what was happening in front of her.

He stood on one foot, his other foot to the side, like a dancer at rest, peeking into the coffee pot now and then. A hissing rose from it, heralding the onset of boiling, and the spoon in his hand stirred without cease, with a fixed circular movement. He said: 'We put two more centimetre of cement from yesterday.' And she answered: 'Fine. I hope there won't be any more problems. David told me you were good workers – so do things right.'

Then she combed her hair and washed her face, and before she could change out of her soft mohair shirt, that had once been burned in the front by a cigarette, so she only wore it around the house, she found herself sitting at the table with his two fellow workers, for whom Hassan had opened the door with a hospitable gesture while she was spreading a cloth on the table in the breakfast nook.

'That's coffee like in our house,' he said, looking at her, the smile on his lips not reaching his eyes. She sipped the thick, bitter beverage, and smiled involuntarily: 'You mean the coffee I made yesterday wasn't good?'

'It was good,' he answered quickly, drawing the words out, alarmed at her insult. 'Thank you very much. But we like this way, strong coffee.' He clenched his fist and waved it to towards her with a vigorous motion, to emphasize his last word.

She heard Udi crying in the next room. This was when he usually had his first bottle of cereal. She excused herself and got up, feeling their eyes on her. She took Udi out of his cot, wrapped in a blanket decorated with ducklings, and carried him into the breakfast nook. The bottle of cereal she had stood on the windowsill having cooled, she placed it in his hands. Ahmed looked as though hypnotized at the sapphire ring Yoel's parents had given her for their engagement, and the others looked at the baby curled up at her breast in his bright blanket, drinking the cereal with his eyes shut. Hassan suddenly smiled and his eyes brightened. He enjoyed the sight of the tranquil baby, and he brought his face close to him and said fondly, 'You eat everything – you be strong like Hassan.'

Months afterwards she would remember that morning with dismay, when she had sat with them for the first time, as though they were at home there, drinking from cups like welcome guests, eating off the violet lace table cloth her mother-in-law had brought from Spain, looking at her baby over their cups. She sipped the bitter liquid and only part of her, the part that didn't laugh with them, thought: could these hands, serving coffee, be the ones that planted the booby-trapped doll at the gate of the religious school at the end of the street? Her heart, which had been on guard all the time, began to foresee something, but it still didn't know: this was just the beginning, appearing like a figure leaping out of the fog. From now on everything would grow clear and roll down like boulders falling into an abyss. The future would clearly be a fall – and no one could stop it.

In the afternoon, as she gathered the toys Udi had scattered on the carpet, there was a knock on the door. Hassan appeared with a sooty aluminium pot in one hand and a plastic bag imprinted with the name of the supermarket on the main steet in the other, a friendly smile of familiarity on his lips, and he said: 'Excuse. Can put soup on fire, lady?'

She tarried in the opening, defending her boundary with a hand extended to the doorframe, as though she wanted to stop them from coming in. But the look on his face and the way he had asked the question didn't leave room for refusal. The blocking arm slipped down, and, with cordial hospitality, as though to mask her hesitation, she moved her hand in an arc and said, 'Please, please.' Anger at herself welled up inside her for treating him, despite herself, as a welcome guest.

She went back to gathering up the toys, stealing a look at the way he put the pot under the tap with steady movements, like an expert, boiling water in the blue coffee pot that he pulled out of the bag, finding the barrel-shaped salt cellar in the right-hand drawer, knowingly manipulating the knobs of the range. While she arranged the toys in Udi's room, as he slept between the duckling blanket and the Winnie the Pooh sheet – still faint, still resembling discomfort – there stole into her a fear born of having people trespass, pushing her boundary back and pretending they were unaware.

When she returned, the other two were already with him in the kitchen. One was cutting vegetables into her new china bowl. The other was standing at the open refrigerator, his hand in the lower vegetable drawer. By the look on his face she could tell he'd been caught in the act. His hand, rummaging among the vegetables, stopped where it was.

'Need cucumber, lady,' he said, stepping back.

She went to the refrigerator, slammed the drawer home and took a cucumber out of a sealed bag in the rear of the upper shelf.

'Take it,' she said.

'Thank you very much, lady.' He took the cucumber from her hand.

'Lady drink coffee?' asked Hassan from the stove, stirring his coffee pot and smiling at her from the side.

Confused, fighting to control the muscles of her face, she said, 'No thanks.'

'Is good coffee,' Salah, who spoke only seldom, tried to persuade her.

'Thanks, I don't drink coffee at midday.' He wouldn't let up. She, already feeling the teeth of the trap closing on her, said, almost shouting: 'No!' She saw Hassan open the china cabinet and take out three plates.

A moment before abandoning her house and baby – fleeing to the bedroom, locking the door and breaking out in silent, suppressed, helpless weeping, into which dread was already creeping – she told Hassan in a soft, commanding voice: 'I'll thank you not to make any noise – my baby is asleep.' A few minutes afterwards, when she left her room, her eyes already dry and her voice tranquil, though her heart pounded within her, she said: 'Maybe you could cook your soup up there. I'll give you a small camping stove. It's inconvenient for me here.' Salah threw a malevolent glance at her over his steaming bowl of soup. And

Hassan said politely, 'If you please, lady, thank you very much.'

For five days she heard them arriving, but by the time she had fed Udi and put him to sleep in his cot, her workers were no longer on the roof. Angrily she calculated that in the past two days they hadn't raised more than a single row of blocks above the stone rim on top of the window. Suspicion stole into her heart that they had taken on another job and to make sure it wouldn't slip through their fingers before they finished the work in her house, they had taken it and bound themselves to another boss. That was the way they did things, as the bank teller who knew about her project had taken the trouble to warn her. But at mid-day shaken at hearing the familiar noise of the pickup truck and composing a few harsh sentences to reproach them with, she saw the truck was laden with iron rods, thin and thick. The three of them got out of the cab and set about unloading the truck and passing the iron rods from hand to hand up to the roof. Calm now, from her window, she watched them at their work. She decided to rest until Udi awoke from his afternoon nap.

For a while she heard them walking around the roof, dragging loads, their voices reaching her through the closed blinds of her room. Later, there was a lot of stubborn knocking which she first took to be part of a dream, and then she heard them at the door. When she opened it the three of them were standing close to each other. With Hassan half a footstep in front. He said, 'Hello, lady, how are you?'

Inwardly bridling at the familiarity he permitted himself in asking that polite question for the first time, and keeping her face frozen, she ignored his question and asked: 'Yes?' guessing they would ask permission to heat up their meal.

'Lady, we need money.'

Her sister had warned her about that in their last conversation: You mustn't pay them before they've done the work as agreed. She tensed. Her voice rasped more than she intended: 'Did you finish putting the iron in place for pouring the concrete?'

'We put band around roof.'

'You did the band, but I'm asking about the iron. Did you get the iron ready for pouring the concrete?'

'That's tomorrow, lady.'

'You'll get your money tomorrow.'

'We need some. Maybe you'll give us lady ...'

'Tomorrow,' she said firmly. 'Anyway I don't have so much now. I have to go to the bank.'

'Really, lady,' Hassan said, looking straight in her eyes and pounding his chest with his fist. 'Lady believe. We coming tomorrow money or no money.'

'No money,' she said, knowing how Yoel would smile when she told him about this occasion. Hassan turned to his friends, and they put their heads together and whispered. From where she was she saw the back of his neck, his dusty hair, looking grey under the woollen hat with the tattered edges, frayed yarn twisting down. His mates' brows darkened. They put their heads close to each other, taking counsel. One of them pulled a creased wallet from his pocket and seemed to be counting the banknotes in it. He had a worried expression. Within her she was already prepared to withdraw from her position and say: 'Look, if it's something pressing, I'm prepared to give you what I have in my purse now ...' He suddenly turned to her and asked, 'Can wash hands in water?' He surprised her so much with the question that, like the morning when he had stood before her with a cooking pot in his hands, she said: 'Certainly, certainly,' pushing the door open wide, while her only wish was to slam the door in their faces.

They entered hesitantly. Now she saw that Salah was holding a large army knapsack, the kind that Yoel used to extricate from the storeroom when his unit was called for manoeuvres. Hassan led the way to the bathroom, looking at her as though asking permission, and the three men made their way in and locked the door: for a long while she heard the sound of running water and the men's boisterous voices. Walking to and fro in the living room, looking out at the large garden, across from which no other house was visible she was gripped by sudden fear, thinking of what might be in the big knapsack. Perhaps they were assembling weapons there, spreading the steel parts out on the carpet, as Yoel had done once, kneeling on the floor and joining the shining parts one to another. Maybe they would come out in a little while with their weapons drawn and threaten her and her son? Perhaps they would take them as hostages in their covered pickup truck? And what about Udi? She had already run out of his special flour, and she wouldn't be able to feed him when they kept them there in their broken-down shacks in Gaza, among the muddy paths. They had shown those shacks on an American television documentary. Maybe, the thought flashed through her like lightning, she should snatch Udi out of his cot and flee with him, lay him in the back of her car and drive immediately to the police station in the main street.

Hassan came out first, and she was startled at his appearance. For a second she imagined a stranger had come out. For the first time she saw him without the woollen cap pulled down over his forehead. His hair, surprisingly light, freshly combed and damp, was brushed to the side, well-combed, and pulled back over his temples. He wore a dark, well-pressed jacket over a white shirt and tie. His black dress shoes were highly polished.

He told her: 'My friends come out minute, lady.'

'Aren't you going home?'

'Have wedding from our aunt in Tulkarem. We today in Tulkarem.'

At that moment the baby let out a screech more piercing than any she'd heard since the morning he had burst out of her in the maternity ward: high and prolonged, followed by a sudden silence. She herself let out a scream and rushed to the room, pushing his rolling highchair out of the way as she ran. Udi was prostrate on the floor, lying on his stomach, his face on the carpet spread at the foot of his crib, with a toy between his fingers. She bent down and picked him up, carrying him in her arms, and he looked at her with cloudy eyes. She hugged him close to her body and started murmuring things without knowing what she was saying, her heart pounding wildly, making her fingers tremble. After a long while he burst out crying, resting his head on her shoulder in sobs.

'Is okay, lady,' Hassan said from the doorway, and she looked around in panic, not realizing he had followed her.

'What?' she asked fearfully.

'Is okay he like so, lady,' he traced his fiinger along his cheek and made a crying expression. 'Is nothing. He good that way.'

'What's good?' she asked as the baby trembled in her arms.

Hassan approached her and gently lifted Udi from her arms. 'Lady get water,' he said softly. 'He need drink.'

In the kitchen, her hands still trembling, she stood still for a long time, trying to remember where the sugar bowl was. She heard Hassan talking softly to the baby in Arabic, like a man who loves to talk to his child, in a caressing voice, the words running together in a pleasant flow, containing a high beauty, like the words of a poem in an ancient language which you don't understand but which well up inside you, Udi, lying tranquilly on his chest, reached out towards Hassan's dark face, and Hassan put his head down towards the little fingers and kissed them. She, stunned by the sight, stood where she was and looked at them, as the tremor inspired by fear gradually died down, and another, new kind of trembling, arose within her, seeing something which, even as it happens, you already long for from a distance, knowing that when it passes, nothing like it will happen again, and, as though dividing themselves, her thoughts turned to Yoel, whose eyes examined his son from a certain distance. He was careful not to wrinkle his clothes or have them smell of wet nappies.

Hassan looked up at her and said, 'Hassan have like this at home in Gaza.'

'You have a baby?' She was astonished. 'You're married?'

'Also like this. Four years,' he said proudly, placing his hand parallel to the floor to measure the height of his son.

'You okay,' Hassan said in his soft voice, turning his face to the baby. 'You big – you doctor like daddy, yes?'

With the bottle of tea in her hand, she was shaken as though by a distant alarm. Troubled by the suspicion that he knew more than he should, she said, 'You can read Hebrew?' and he laughed. 'I read one word, another word. I see Doctor on door in English.'

'You can read English?' There was some mockery in her voice, like an adult talking to a child about grown-up things.

'I can,' he answered in English, smiling, for the first time, with another hidden smile, without the forced humility she was familiar with.

'Where from,' she asked, also in English.

'From the university.'

'Which one?'

'The American University of Beirut.' She recognized his good accent from having heard it on television when Arabic-speaking intellectuals were interviewed. She hadn't been able to shake off her Israeli accent in the two years she had lived in Texas, while Yoel finished his degree.

'Really?' she returned to Hebrew.

'Really, lady. I in Beirut two years. Maybe I be doctor that way, of babies.'

'Why didn't you complete your studies?'

'Hard. Can't talk.' He looked down at his hands, whose nails were free of lime. 'Life like that.'

Shortly after he left, joining his comrades who were waiting for him and watching him from the door, also scrubbed. She thought: they were nameless and ageless for me, in their faded black sweaters and their dirty elbows and stocking caps. They had a single face and uncouth words came from their mouths. Suddenly they became different: in white collars and jackets, their cheeks shaven, with a wife and baby and a child of four at home.

Even before she heard the bell ring she knew he had returned.

'My jacket, lady,' he said and went to take his jacket, folded carefully on the back of the chair. And, at the door, with his back to her, he turned around with a carefully planned motion that made itself out to be spontaneous: 'If lady want I stay now.'

'Where?' she asked in astonishment.

'With lady,' he answered seriously. 'Mister of lady no here. Maybe need something ...' And she, stunned at the very words, frightened that he knew of her husband's absence, wondered if he meant what she thought she had heard. She said, 'But you're going to a wedding, aren't you?'

'Going to wedding. But if lady want – I can be here ...'

After she had locked the door, still staggering at his suggestion, she suddenly noticed: Yoel's smell drifted from them, the odour of the delicate fragrance on the shelf of the right-hand cabinet next to the mirror. They had used her husband's toiletries, dried themselves on her towels. She carefully put Udi down in the cot and hurried to the bathroom.

With convulsive movements, like a madwoman, she gathered up the towels and threw them all, averting her head with a bilious feeling, into the washing machine, throwing the new soap into the garbage pail. She began polishing the taps and sink and scouring with disinfectant the floor which their feet had trod on.

But towards evening a tense quiet descended on her, something new. At night, before falling asleep, she remembered how Hassan had held Udi close to his chest and spoken to him in Arabic that sounded like a song; his long fingers, clean for the first time of spots of paint; the English he had spoken, sounding like human language for the first time instead of the broken phrases he knew in Hebrew. Yet his offer to stay with her she preferred to set aside and disregard. She thought back over things, seeing that she had been hard on them. They had gone to a wedding in Tulkarem. Maybe they had asked for money to buy a present for the newly-weds, and she had behaved unfeelingly towards them. The unease that gripped her was assuaged when she promised herself that early the next morning she would take Udi in his carriage and go out to the main street and, in the elegant store that had recently opened, she would buy clothes for his two children. Then she thought: it would not be right to offer him a gift, as a declaration of a special relationship, and not to honour his cousins. Generously she decided she would buy something for them as well. Maybe cologne like the kind Yoel kept on his shelf. If the weather was stormy, she'd take the car. An hour later, she suddenly interrupted herself as she read: if it rained hard, she'd leave Udi at the baby-sitter's.

She waited for them until noon, their gifts in pretty wrapping paper tied with curling ribbon, lying on the cabinet next to the front door, and the white envelope with their money next to the packages. At noon she began to worry: maybe they had drunk too much and had an accident. What if the police came? She panicked. Maybe it wasn't legal for her to employ them. If they were badly injured and couldn't continue the job, the construction would be delayed and maybe not completed by the time Yoel returned. In the afternoon, tired and angry at her helplessness and concern about the future, she decided to go to the building where David was working. Maybe some members of the same family were working for him, and they too had been invited to the wedding in Tulkarem, and she could find something out from them. For a long time she waited for David, pushing the carriage back and forth on the battered pavement in front of the building site. When he came, he told her that the wedding hadn't been in Tulkarem at all, but in a village near the Lebanese border. They would be coming as usual the next day, he reassured her, seeing her worried face. Afterwards he scratched the nape of his neck and asked: 'So it's okay, the job they're doing?'

'I hope so,' she said.

'What are they doing now?'

'They're setting up the iron rods to pour the concrete.'

'Are they doing it right?'

'I don't know. I trust them.'

The next day, anger making her fingertips tremble, so troubled her breathing was affected, she waited for them on the roof in the morning after leaving Udi with the baby-sitter and arranging to do so again during the coming days. By the time the sound of the approaching pickup truck reached her, her nerves were already in an uproar. Hassan got out of the cab and smiled brightly at her. With his filthy woollen cap and his shoes down at the heel he was once again what he had been.

'Something happen, lady?' His voice betrayed his surprise at finding her on the roof at that early hour.

'A great deal has happened,' she shouted to him, leaning over the wall at the edge of the roof.

'What's the matter, lady?' he asked, climbing the ladder on his way up to her.

'First of all, you lied to me.'

'Lied?' The shadow of his smile was erased.

'The wedding was in Tulkarem?' She flung out the words, her

hands on her hips, like a mother arguing with a child caught out in a lie.

'No, lady. Wedding not in Tulkarem.'

'That's what you told me.'

I said. My aunt from Tulkarem, The wedding there in village near Kibuss.'

He turned to face his comrades, as though asking, and Ahmed said. 'Kibuss Ga'aton.'

'Ga'aton,' Hassan repeated the name of the kibbutz, looking at her again.

'But you didn't say you wouldn't come to work yesterday.'

'We think sleep in Tulkarem and come work yesterday. No possible.'

'That's one thing,' she ignored the explanation. 'Another thing, David was here yesterday and he said you didn't do anything well. You didn't raise the concrete band two centimetres the way we said. And you put in number eight iron rods instead of number twelve, and you made one wall with fifteen centimetre blocks instead of twenty centimetres ...'

'That wall has window, lady. Must to be little.'

'You need a number three block near the sliding window,' she exploded at his effort to fool her. 'But the wall is an outer wall. You were supposed to use twenty centimetre blocks ... ' She added, scolding him, watching the colour ebb from his face, and how his comrades froze behind his back.

'We do everything good. Lady want – David come here. We talk.'

'I don't want you to talk!' she screamed. 'I want you to work. You've been working for a month. What you've done could have been done in a week. You just drink coffee, slip away, and work somewhere else.'

'Somewhere else?' he asked in amazement.

'On Monday. Where were you?'

He wrinkled his forehead in thought. 'Monday we bring iron.'

'Fine,' she said, raising her chin and walking forward with vigour and sitting on the edge of the wall. 'I want to see how much you get done today.'

170

For seven hours she sat on the wall, without moving, not going down to turn off the water heater she had lit in the morning suppressing the hunger that awoke within her, the need for a cup of coffee at the hour when her body was used to one, and, in the afternoon, fighting the pain in her back, which cried out for something to lean on, watching as they worked angrily, talking little, boiling water in an empty can on the camping stove she'd lent them, sitting down to eat with their legs crossed, close to each other, whispering to each other. All those hours she watched them as though riveted to the spot, only occasionally looking away from them, allowing her eyes to wander to the tops of the cypress trees and the purple mountains in the distance, the view of which, some other day, at a peaceful hour, she would enjoy. Later, when she recalled that morning, she would tremble as though the event were not irrevocably in the past: how had the courage to treat them that way been born within her? They could easily have come and pushed her, and she would have fallen and broken her neck. By the time anyone found her among the iron rods in the back yard, she would no longer be alive.

Occasionally Ahmed cast a glance at her, like a fearful child checking to see whether the ghost he had seen was still hovering in the area. But Hassan didn't look at her once. Seeing him, his clamped lips, and the line drawn behind his jaw, above his clenched teeth, she knew she had deeply wounded him, but she felt no remorse for doing so. Only the sweet consolation of someone who deals justly with himself, a feeling that rose and fell within her great anger.

They raised the iron rods over the edge of the masonry walls and laid them crisscross at regular intervals, tying them with thin wire. Afterwards they crowded steel struts into the room to support the wooden forms under the network. When they finished, they consulted among themselves for a moment and headed for the ladder, parting from her with a slight nod.

'Wait,' she called to them. 'You've earned your money.' She followed them down the ladder and went into the house. When she came out she put the envelope in Hassan's hand. Only after they had left without a word did she remember she hadn't asked them to sign a receipt for the money or given them the wrapped parcels from the cupboard.

The next day, after leaving Udi with the baby-sitter despite a reddish rash on his skin showing he hadn't been changed in time, she was already waiting for them on the roof as though spoiling for a fight. Today, she thought, stunned at the idea, they'll pour the concrete for the roof. The network of iron rods was prepared and the steel struts were in place. The wooden forms were raised, the buckets of gravel and sand were covered under plastic sheets, and the sacks of cement were arranged next to them. Today they would pour the roof, and the weather was fine. The transparent clouds didn't herald rain.

When she heard the sound of the pickup truck she leaped to the edge of roof, and even before she actually saw them she noticed his absence. Three men sat in the cab, and he wasn't one of them. Salah and Ahmed got out of the left cab, wearing gray woollen hats. Then a man with a shaven head got out of the truck, looking like a fugitive she had seen in an Italian movie, who had made his way to a widow's home in a village and laid siege to it. In one look she took in his black eyes, like the maw of a coal mine. His eyebrows meeting over the bridge of his nose. A strange feeling overcame her, like when all her girlfriends had been asked to dance, and she was left alone sitting by the wall, looking at the legs moving in the dark.

'Where's Hassan?' she asked Ahmed.

'Hassan no come. This one come, Muhammed.'

Observing from the corner on the wall, trying to repress the desolate feeling that grew stronger within her, she watched them put on rubber boots and mix the concrete with shovels, adding sand and gravel and pouring water, stirring it to produce a thick grey mixture in the square they had enclosed with wooden beams. Then Muhammed climbed up to the edge of the roof. Ahmed handed him bucket after bucket, brimming with the grey concrete and he swung and emptied them in big arcs over the network of iron rods, while Salah quickly filled in the space between the two wooden planks below, to stop the concrete from dribbling out.

Sitting majestically erect on the edge of the roof, her knee swinging, her arms crossed, she felt her anger give way to disappointment at Hassan's absence. Suddenly it became clear to her that he had come between her and them, serving as a kind of protective barrier from them. Here she stood exposed to the three of them: Salah stole furtive glances at her, as though already hatching a foul plot in his mind; Ahmed smiled right at her, baring his yellow teeth like the fangs of a beast; and the new worker, standing high on the upper concrete band, his body tense, his hands on his hips, stared at her openly. From where she sat his figure looked mighty, and his shaven head resembled a crooked egg against the background of the sky above him.

She sat where she was for hours – no longer emboldened with the anger that had gripped her the previous morning, making her decide to sit and see with her own eyes how well they would work under supervision – but now out of fear to get up and raise her legs over the edge of the roof in front of them. They worked without stopping, diligently, bringing up the contents of the big pool of concrete and spreading it on the network of rods. From time to time they would consult each other, exchange shouts in Arabic, sing a line or two, laughing out loud into their hands. And she, sensing they were laughing at her, was angry, insulted, and fearful. She watched them cook their meal, kneeling next to each other on the torn mat, tearing with their teeth at loaves of bread they held in their hands.

'What now?' she turned to Ahmed, keeping her voice steady.

'Now must dry.'

'If it rains?'

'Now two hours – good. Not two hours – no good.'

'The roof is twenty centimetres?'

'Yes, yes,' he said, and she thought: since that morning she hadn't heard them say 'lady'. She turned, pointed at the floor they had left spotted with cement. 'Wash that down before it dries,' she ordered, pretending she still had strength.

'No dry. We put water.'

She stepped to the edge of the protruding ladder and grasped

173

the wooden rung, and, as though incidentally, turned to them. 'What's the matter with Hassan?'

'Hassan no come.'

'I see that.'

'This one Muhammed come.'

'Will Hassan come tomorrow?'

'Tomorrow, tomorrow, tomorrow – Hassan no come.'

'Did something happen to him?'

'He not here.'

She carefully raised her legs, and when she had descended, even before her feet touched the ground, she heard their deep, guttural laugh, and she blushed. That's how men laugh at women when they speak ill of them.

The next day, waiting at the window, she knew why her legs had taken her there, why she had arisen early to prepare the kitchen, why she had checked how much coffee was left in the bag he had brought with him from home.

Salah and Ahmed came alone. She, knowing in her heart she wouldn't see Hassan again, was glad that the shaven-headed Muhammed wasn't with them. Swallowing her pride she went out and stood before them.

'Is Hassan sick?' she asked.

'No sick.'

'He won't come to work?'

'He work someone.'

'Why isn't he working here? Three will finish faster.'

Salah, perhaps seeing through her deceptive sentences, smiled somewhere in the depths of his eyes, the mockery of someone careful not to be tripped up.

'He no want come to lady.'

'He doesn't want to get his money?'

'No want,' said Salah, and she imagined she heard an echo of triumph in his voice.

'He doesn't want to get his money?'

'No want money, no want lady,' he said. She no longer had anything to say after that sentence, but she spoke in her normal voice: 'Very well, then finish by yourselves. You can make coffee in the kitchen if you want. There's still some of the coffee you brought.'

Salah and Ahmed kept coming for a few more days after the concrete on the roof had dried, removing the steel struts that held up the forms. They put on the door and bars over the window and broke through from the upper room into the break-fast nook. She didn't ask about Hassan again, but they sometimes volunteered that they had met him. She, stirred by the sound of his name, gave in and made the final payment before they finished the work. Perhaps they would run into Hassan and tell him of her generosity. But they never came back. They left the walls unplastered and forgot their tools behind the wall. Shaken with fury, again pushing her baby carriage, she roamed among the construction sites and hired workers to finish the plastering; they tarred the roof, and installed the electric wiring.

By the time Yoel returned she had a new hairstyle. They stood on the stairs leading to the bright, pleasant room on the roof, with three barrels in the corners from which palm trees sent up sharp bayonets all about, their fronds growing like a conjuring trick. He stood in amazement before the new structure then burst out laughing. 'Well, I'll be ... You leave a woman for two months, come back – and the world's changed!' On the roof, his arm around her shoulder in a gesture of appreciation he wandered from one corner of the roof to another, inspecting the landscape, and sliding his hand along the walls: 'I didn't want to do it, I admit, but it's really nice. Was it very dirty?'

'Not so terrible.'

'You found good workers?'

Stroking the rough wall unawares she said, 'They were relatively decent, workers from the territories.' 'What, Arabs?' he asked, looked at her reproachfully, getting serious.

'Arabs. You can't find anyone else. But every day a Jewish foreman came to keep an eye on them, the one working in the building at Herzl Street.'

'They behaved all right? They didn't make trouble?'

She took a quick, deep breath, with a whistling sound, and –

restraining the whirlpool of emotions stirring within her, looking away, clearly seeing Muhammed standing on the edge of the upper roof, staring at her with hatred, and the flash in their eyes when she got up and stood in this very place and accused them – seeing Hassan's fists clench and the crease along the line of his jaw when he clasped his teeth shut, hearing the rumble of the men's laughter when she raised her legs to climb down the ladder – she said, 'They were fairly decent. Once Udi fell down and I was really alarmed. One of them picked him up so gently and calmed him down, you wouldn't believe it. He spoke to him softly and kissed his fingers. Then it turned out he had studied medicine for two years. He wanted to be a pediatrician but for some reason he didn't finish his degree. He has a baby Udi's age and another boy of four ...' Suddenly she noticed the softness flowing into her voice, betraying herself to herself, and she added loudly, more stridently than she intended: 'But once they made some trouble about the money and tried to trick me by putting in iron rods that were too thin. Arabs, you know ...'

Translated by Jeffrey M. Green

11

'Will Somebody Please Shut the Gate'

by MIRA MAGEN

A FEW MONTHS before Mother's madness was officially announced, there were hints that something out of the ordinary was happening, and our daily routine suffered small blows, but life went on and the days were all pretty well alike.

She spread slices of pickled cucumber on the windowsill and said that once the sun dried them out pure cucumber would be left, that there was enough water in the tap anyway and it was just inflating the cucumber, but the sun shrivelled them into transparent greenish rags spotted with dried seeds which she ate and ate and her mouth reeked of rotten bay leaves and neglected teeth. Then there was the business about the windows, that we mustn't close because there wasn't enough air for five pairs of nostrils and if everyone exhaled their carbon dioxide into the closed apartment the air would be poisoned. But when the strong autumn winds blew through the rooms and the windows swung wildly on their hinges, banging the frames and rattling the panes, it was clear that something new was happening.

Father oiled the wood of the windowsill because the vinegar from the pickles had erased the paint and eaten away the glaze. He didn't tell mother to stop it, just as he didn't tell her that the cold coming in through the open windows gave us goose flesh. Just as he didn't tell her that there was nothing wrong with her stomach, but the more she folded her hands over her stomach and said how she was wasting away, the more reason he found to look after his Subaru. He tightened bolts, stretched belts, wiped

177

the panes with damp cloths until they shone like mirrors and you could see the neighbours' houses reflected in them. He shook out the rubber mats and spread them on the asphalt driveway and he scrubbed the headlights with the green washing-up soap, and only when the darkness thickened so that he couldn't tell the pliers from the screwdriver did he close his toolbox, gather up the rags and go upstairs.

There were no signs that Mother was wasting away. After all, when someone is wasting away they get smaller and smaller, but not one centimetre of Mother's metre sixty-two was missing, her ring stayed attached to her finger like a thin gold canal between two banks of thick flesh, her belt was buckled as always on the third hole and as always, when she leaned against the doorjamb the top of her head reached the bottom nail of the *mezuzah*. I believed that she was wasting away from the inside, that her instestines were growing shorter, her blood drying up, her heart shrinking and only her outer skin remained blown up and covered the general withering away taking place inside her.

So many things changed all at once that from fear I began to count the things that were still the same and did not panic because of sudden tears or shrieks that turned into laughter. One of those things was Talia's morning. She would stand in front of the mirror combing her hair to her heart's content, the black plastic comb shifting and rearranging the varying shades of brown and gold and the steady rhythm of Talia's hand remained constant despite Mother's screaming enough with that mirror. The shouts grew louder, rattling the mirror, but Talia would slowly and painstakingly continue to arrange each strand of hair. When it became unbearable Father would try to imprison the noises and violated the latest decree by closing the kitchen window but the insulation was less than perfect and the neighbours heard. The Baumans' curtains moved and half of Mrs Bauman's face filled the slit between them, then the opening narrowed to the width of her ear and she had to decide whether to devote it to her eye or her ear.

I didn't understand how Talia was able to wrap herself in a kind of membrane and detach herself from the screaming and how day by day she perfected this membraning ability of hers. I thought that if I tried hard enough I could be as good at it as she was. When I wrapped my sandwich in waxed paper Mother screamed that I was getting on her nerves with that noisy paper and enough and get on with it, I couldn't go on like Talia and I didn't finish folding the paper over the sandwich and the mayonnaise dripped on my fingers and then she screamed you think I didn't see you wiping your hands on your dress, and I didn't answer. The truth is that I didn't wipe them on my dress, and when I bit my nails in the first lesson the nail slivers I swallowed had enough mayonnaise on them to last me the whole lesson.

With Talia and me Mother's nerves were like a lizard's severed tail. Only Uli didn't irritate her, and when she ran her fingers through his soft hair they stayed straight and didn't curl on his forehead and didn't feel his hot scalp and all the fears accumulated inside his little skull. He sat on the living-room floor for hours lining up a long row of red Lego pieces, attaching one to the other, making sure that their sides fitted together without a crack. When there were no red pieces left he pulled out his shoelaces and tried to thread them through again, pushing the hard plastic tip of the lace into the holes until the plastic began to split and spread from so much pushing and wouldn't go through and Uli tried again and again and the tips of the laces broke altogether, and finally he went to kindergarten with his shoes untied and the teacher glued the split plastic, re-threaded the laces and tied two bows.

Those shoes of Uli's had a function, those two little brown things were part of the arrangements I made to maintain order amid all the changes taking place in the house. Every evening after he fell asleep I pressed them together between the legs of his bed and every once in a while I checked to see that the angle hadn't changed, that the soles touched each other neatly with the little hollow in the middle. Those shoes that had taken the shape of Uli's feet were a kind of good-luck charm protecting me from the chameleons of that house.

More than once I woke up in the middle of the night and heard the bats that had deviated from their usual route and were flying through the yard upside down like a plane that had been hit, crashing into the window, their black bellies gleaming in the dark, and the moths began hovering backwards, their antennae gone. I threw off my blanket and ran to Uli's bed to check if the shoes were obeying the order I had imposed on them, to be sure beyond the shadow of a doubt that they were still in the same position, the heels a centimetre from the edge of the floor tile, and then I went into the kitchen to see if the tap was still dripping at the same obedient rate, Talia said that the tap got on her nerves and when on earth were they going to fix it, but I hoped they wouldn't fix it so that I would still be able to hear an old familiar sound amidst all the new sounds that cropped up every day in that house.

Official confirmation of madness arrived on the Sick Fund's white stationery, with the words Mental Health Clinic printed in blue on either side of the red emblem. Father ran around with it to the National Insurance Institute and the municipality to arrange for allowances and discounts, and from being opened and refolded by a lot of clerks it became smudged at the edges with brown finger-prints until the letter looked like paper which had been left to spin in the washing-machine and came out wrinkled like an old cotton handkerchief.

You could say that that paper reorganized our lives and the days took on a new routine. Even Uli knew that Mother was in a special hospital and that if the Baumans or other neighbours asked any questions we were to say that she had stomach problems. Father stopped taking care of our Subaru, and the back window was once again covered with dust – children printed the word slob and all kinds of other remarks in the dust and during the damp nights water dripped onto the windshield from the roof leaving muddy brown circles.

We only visited Mother once, and in honour of the occasion I picked an anemone from the flower bed at school. Talia wore a tight-fitting denim skirt and a black blouse, her brown and gold hair combed back and resting on the back of her neck like a honey-coloured scarf, she rattled the house keys and hurried me with come on already so we can catch the three-o'clock bus. I put the anemone in a glass jar that had once held olives grown in a kibbutz, and we left. The bouncing of the bus shook the water in the jar and a woman said little girl what's that, you shouldn't take water on a bus, and when we got off a little water spilled onto my shoe and my sock got wet but the anemone stayed fresh and its leaves stood up so straight in the sun that you could see the thin veins that criss-crossed them.

Mother, wearing her green track suit, was eating chicken and rice, and some rice had fallen onto the suit and some was hanging from both sides of her mouth, she didn't say hello to us or sit down or anything. The man sitting next to her had the same exact food on his tray, and he was chewing on a chicken bone and Mother smiled at him and put the remains of her rice onto his plate saying take it, eat and she arranged his plate separating the rice from the gnawed bones and he scraped the rice from Mother's mouth with a long yellow nicotine-stained finger. Talia twisted the strap of her handbag tightly around her thumb, her nail was turning blue, but Talia didn't stop and she stood there as taut as an ironed sheet and when Mother said again eat, eat, she shouted hello Mother in a voice I had never heard before, three patients stopped eating and stared at her with empty eyes and rice fell from their spoons suspended in the air on the way from their plates to their mouths. But Mother didn't hear and kept on with her eat, eat and her thigh inside the green track suit brushed against his blue trousers. Then he pushed his plate to the middle of the table, and when he took Mother's hand and placed it on his knee and began to move it ever so slowly up over his thigh to the unmentionable place on his trousers, Talia pulled me out of there and water spilled out of my jar onto the bathrobe of one of the patients. Talia was silent all the way home and didn't wipe the tears that fell onto her cheeks, once the wind blew one of her tears onto my chin and I didn't wipe it off either, there was practically no water left in the jar so nobody scolded me on the bus but two women stared at us and whispered to each other, I don't know if it was because of how beautiful Talia was or because she was crying. Talia remained silent and I noticed that the black eye of the anemone was watching the leaves the whole time but it couldn't prevent the widest one from starting to wither.

During that time there was no one around to demand explanations when I was late from school. And that's why I could take all the time I wanted between one step and the next on my way home. I stood for hours under the almond tree watching the wind blowing the flowers about, thousands of pieces of white blossoms floating down to the pavement and I gathered them up into the empty bag that had held my sandwich and when I opened it at home, the delicate scent of almonds drifted out, overcoming the smell of mayonnaise, and I crushed the petals and spread the damp essence on my forehead and throat. There was a kind of relief about this blossoming of the almond tree, it was so completely certain that every year in January the branches would be covered with that white plumage which would then change to green, always always in the same order and at the same time. An almond tree is not one of those things you can surprise – what does it care if the wind bangs the windows that cannot be closed for fear of carbon dioxide, it doesn't count the loaves of bread growing more numerous every day because there is no hot food. I was so jealous of the patience of trees and the exact order in which things happened to them, I walked around outside for hours in order to gather up more proof of this. After the almond trees of January, anemones bloomed in the flower beds at school and then tulip bulbs thickened under their winding green leaves and during Passover vacation the school yard was all yellow with mustard plants and chrysanthemums. Under my bed, fig leaves piled up and yellowed still hanging by their stems, Talia said that I should throw out all that junk but I knew that when the windows started banging and the noise hurt my ears all I had to do was look at those leaves and I would calm down.

One evening Father came home from work, stuck his head in the kitchen sink and turned on the tap full-force and the water from his tangled hair dripped down onto the floor and the counter and he wiped himself with a used kitchen towel and said children Mother's coming back tomorrow. His face was red from being wiped and his hair stood on end like a porcupine's and once again I could hear that noise that made my ears hurt because the kitchen window was banging like crazy. Uli stopped chewing his bread and ran to his Lego and Talia wrapped herself in her membrane detached from Father's words, her face closed up tight, her eyes staring at a colour photo of a model in a magazine. I tried to learn from her whether this was good or bad news but I didn't succeed I only saw how her jaw protruded, and I knew that she was clenching her teeth very hard. During the long silence it seemed to me that the walls were breathing, small squeaks could be heard, cracking noises, I was sure they were groaning under some terrible burden and I couldn't stand it anymore, so I said too bad that she's coming back, my hand moved of its own accord to defend my cheek against the expected slap, but Father didn't slap me, he stood as unmoving as a troll doll, a large drop of water glistening on his earlobe like an earring.

Why now I thought, maybe we can stop her, maybe somebody can run over there and close the heavy gates. Why right now when I have almost completely managed to quiet the commotion in my head and I already have a few ways of calming myself down, and I have even got used to the glittering eyeballs of the neighbours peering out at us from the peepholes in their doors, they haven't bought the story about stomach problems for a long time now. I wanted the days to continue as they were and there really was a kind of uniformity to them, and all of a sudden, she's coming back.

When we heard the doors of the Subaru slam shut we stood in the hallway like an honour guard, Talia first, me after her, and Uli after me, standing very close to one another, because I was in the middle I could feel the heat coming from both of them and also the trembling. I had some chinaberries in my pockets for security and I kept stroking them until they were warm and damp, they helped me to overcome the terrible ringing that sent sparks flying up into my brain and stopped up my ears.

I didn't give Mother my hand when she came in because it was in my pocket clutching those berries, and when she bent over Uli I saw that she had become thin, her bones were sticking out under her purple blouse, Father led her into the living room as if she were a stem of glass, his large hand encircling her white elbow, she let him lead her to the biggest and fanciest of the three

183

armchairs we had. She sat down very slowly without moving her head as if its position on her neck were permanent, she only bent her body into a sitting position and said, I'm terribly thirsty, those pills dry me out altogether. Taila rushed to the kitchen to make lemonade, Uli sat on the floor near the TV and played with his Lego and I stood still with the chinaberries in my hand and no idea what to do. Father helped her unbuckle her shoes, red marks showed on her white feet where the straps had been and I decided that the best thing to do was to concentrate on this leg thing and not think about anything else.

Why are you afraid of me, she asked and all the windows banged at once, don't be afraid, I take medicine and I'm fine I just need to get stronger, and I saw that her ring had slipped down to her knuckle and she was twisting it around and around on her finger. Get a hold of yourself, I told myself, think about all the patience of the old fig tree and go to your room and touch the leaves, but the space under my bed had been emptied and cleaned, Talia had thrown out everything.

They didn't suspect anything at the grocery when I took five jars of pickled cucumbers and said that Father would pay later. The jars were much heavier than I had expected and my right shoulder hurt. Everyone was still sitting in the living room when I spilled the contents onto the windowsill in the kitchen, five rows, ten pickled cucumbers in each row placed very close together, dark green, shining in the sun, the strong wind blowing outside ruffled the Baumans' curtains, now and then enlarging the opening between them. I had been careful to open all the windows earlier even the very small one we never opened in the bathroom, I had opened all the cabinets and all the drawers, everything was open in order to expand the space and lessen the danger of carbon dioxide, now that everything was open and air flowed freely through the house I could allow myself to stand quietly in the kitchen and look at what was happening outside. The Baumans' curtains fluttered like a giant butterfly, thin fringes of pink gauze flew about in the wind like Talia's hair, I think Mrs Bauman's eye was blue or maybe it just seemed that way because of the sky that was reflected in her glasses.

Wind blew through the space between our building and theirs, the last thin rays of light played on the walls, I waited for darkness when the flight of the bats begins, they take off all at once from the south side of the building and the moon lights up their heavy stomachs. Strange creatures, thick membranes connect their digits and they fly through the yard in total blindness, and maybe this whole thing about flying is not as complicated as I thought, and I took the chinaberries out of my pockets to get rid of excess weight and they bounced against all the neighbours' windows below us until they finally landed on the ground. I rolled up my sleeves to expose my elbows and started to move them up and down in a uniform, controlled motion and I felt that if I could only get a little better at it my flight would be as transparent and gentle as a dragonfly, and Mrs Bauman's shouts, help! the girl is jumping, didn't divert me and the motion of my elbows became smoother and more delicate and more exact, almost perfect.

Translated by Sondra Silverston

12

A Hat of Glass

by NAVA SEMEL

THIS IS NOT the whole truth. Just bits and pieces of it sloughed off over the passing years. As I gather them up, they seem at times like crumbs from bread that's turned mouldy. Whenever I've tried to see the whole of it with my own eyes, it's been like walking backwards. I take care not to bump into the wall behind me. It's an ache I've known before.

'Clarissa,' I called after her in the street.

I think about her sometimes. Never actually forget her.

I started running after her, but stopped. She'd become no more than a speck of grey that kept getting smaller and smaller. Something turned inside me, then turned again and again, until it reached all the way back to the way things were at the beginning.

It was three months before the end of the war, but we didn't know it yet. I had no recollection of my face; hardly remembered my age either. I had no way of knowing that the man I'd married three years earlier and had lived with in Western Hungary had been consumed in a cloud of smoke.

Nor could I conjure up the dead foetus I'd been carrying inside me for two whole months – the soundless, motionless load that left no trace save a hidden line curving its way across my stomach. The body was one I hadn't seen in all those years since the war began. Even the menstrual blood, dependable as the seasons, the blood that might have assured me that at a time like this the sun was still revolving on its axis and that the universe was following its usual course; it too was taken away from me.

Janine, the French girl, said they were adding some sort of potion to the watered down liquid they used to shove at us announcing: 'Soup.' Except that for me, to know that the bleeding had stopped was undeniable proof that time had frozen, and that something was guarding the straits, lest even the slightest rush of hot dust push its way through and dissipate the heavy slumber. Those who had been consumed through the chimneys were the only ones to rise away, to beg for mercy.

In the long line that shuffled through each morning, only one thought kept flickering in my mind. I longed to spot those bombers in the sky zeroing in on the cursed spot and wiping it away, like someone who wipes a spot of blood after being struck across the mouth, then wipes it away again, until the only traces are the small drops on her hand, not a sign of it remaining on the mouth. But the wound kept oozing, and there was nobody to rise up and put a curse on the place; to make certain that nothing ever grew there again.

When my son went to see it, only one generation later, he returned heavy-hearted and told me: 'Mother, the ground is covered over with grass.'

I asked myself, what kind of a short memory the Creator must have, to be so good to that soil and not to have damned it. Planting a seed in it, no less, never felling its grass. He may go so far as to add some flowers just to please it. He did not even bide His time until those of us who curse it would no longer be here to watch.

It was my last *Selektion*. Who knows, perhaps the face unwittingly etched on me by my father and mother was what had kept me alive. Even now, when I study the rounded lines that frame my children's faces, I wonder whether that was what made me seem healthy enough, still fit.

Five hundred of us were chosen and taken to the sealed railway car. The doors were bolted and just beyond them we could hear the horror-stricken voices of those not chosen.

'Don't go near the door,' the Kapo said. 'They're finishing off the ones left behind.'

Then they hitched the sealed car to the back of the train. For four days we travelled, us chosen girls, our bodies deep in excrement and degradation. The stench was polluting the planet like the detritus of giants, bound to fall like ripe fruit and be utterly shattered. A few loaves of bread tossed inside just a moment before the train pulled away represented the innermost wish of someone hoping to buy us a little more time. Between the slats in the sides you could catch a glimpse of the earth moving. Were we going around in circles, only to wind up back where we'd started? The passing of time was marked by the jerking of our bodies packed together like worms, coupled with the relentless churning of the wheels as they thrust us forward along the overworked tracks.

Many hours later the train stopped. Its doors opened suddenly, but instead of daylight we saw the dusk of evening. A rush of cool November air clashed with the stench. That was when it hit me full force, as palpably as when a cripple fingers his deformity, only to be overcome by excruciating shame. We stood there in the big station, and the darkness cringed before the blade of light along the tracks. Trembling we stood, exhausted from the trip, our rags clinging to our bodies, enveloped in stench. I had no idea what phantom world they'd brought us to and where they'd be hustling us to next. The end was near, but we didn't know it. A man stepped out of the darkness and started in our direction. He was tall and his white locks glistened as they fell neatly over his forehead and temples. He was wearing a Wehrmacht uniform without the SS skull and crossbones. Five hundred pairs of eyes looked at him in mute terror. I heard a sigh, but it may have been a delusion. His face was clearly visible in the light of the emerging moon. Incredulous at first, he soon turned his head away in disgust. Later I saw the sorrow too; he could not wipe it away.

'Women,' he muttered and his face cut through our tightness. 'You've arrived at a labour camp. You are in Germany and this is Zittau.'

There was a wrenching moan of anguish. He came a step closer and the front row of women moved back, pushing the ones behind. He held out his arm.

'You women have nothing to be afraid of. Nobody is going to harm you here. This is a labour camp.'

We'd heard about those by now. We'd already been in another camp. I couldn't believe it. The old man in his elegant uniform did not conceal the surge of compassion that swept him at the sight of the tortured creatures before him. He took another step and touched one of the women standing near him, then fingered the frayed edge of her dress.

'It's a disgrace,' he said. 'It's a disgrace to look this way. *Das ist eine grosse Schande.*' He brought his palms together. 'Women,' he said again, 'I was an officer in the First World War. You were brought into the Reich in order to work in the factories here.' With a flourish, he motioned towards the large barracks whose silhouettes stood out against the darkness.

'So long as I am here and you apply yourselves to your work, nobody will harm you. I give you my word – the word of an officer who fought in the First World War.'

Then he turned on his heel and hurried off, disappearing in the darkness.

'It's a disgrace,' he had said.

We're nothing more than a criss-crossing shadow, a huddle of humanity with a flimsy breath of life still flickering inside us. The old officer was not with us long. Some SS women assigned to guard us let it be known that he was too soft, and that the surge of pity had been his downfall.

I don't know what they did with him. A solitary ray of light had touched the darkness, only to be extinguished. The selfsame darkness was free to reassert its haughty sway over a locked planet. We are still no more than prey, I told myself, still not members of the human race.

At four-thirty, with the morning still reluctant to unfold, we would rise. Treading gingerly, we made our way to the washroom at the end of the corridor. Shaven scalps bent over the basins. Every time I brought water to my mouth, it worked its way into the spaces where I once had the shiny, white teeth of a young girl. When they took me from my home, the Nazi struck me, and during those first few hours, fragments of teeth kept rolling about inside my mouth. I could neither spit them out nor swallow. All I drank was my blood, and its taste was peculiar.

At five, the kitchen workers would haul in a large pot, holding it by both handles and dragging it along the floor. One at a time, we filled our dishes and sipped the murky liquid in short gulps. It had neither smell nor taste, and only the heat of it reached our bodies. We'd stand there, in rows of five, in the doorway, pressed up against each other, huddling tightly to keep warm. The prisoners' uniforms hung loosely on our bodies, and the stripes outlined our emaciated forms. Over our shrivelled breasts, there was a grey stripe with our badge, the yellow Star of David, on it, and a number. Even in the darkness it lost none of its shine. Two, nine, six, three, four.

'Who are you? Who are you? I don't know. I don't remember.'

I would recite my number over and over again, like a dybbuk slipping out of its bottle, then back in again.

We would stand there tensely, side by side, in frozen anticipation. At a quarter to six we heard the sound of footsteps – master of the woman. What an icy expression God has given him. Never a twitch. Nothing ever fluttered, or glinted. He would flash a look in our direction as though seeing the scum of the earth. Marching behind him was his bevy of women officers, his chorus, in their spotless uniforms and shining boots, taking count. Day after day, the same count. Next, one of them would tour the rooms, inspect the pallets and depart. Then he would move on. Sometimes he would crack his whip; he'd never use his open palm. The very touch might be infectious. The overseer's entourage included one golden-haired officer, Brünnhilde of the Black Forest. Utterly untarnished, without so much as a furrow near her eyes or cheeks. Only the slightest rosiness, as if to say – how healthy I am, Oh noble beauty.

The rows extended as far as the eye could see in either direction and the only sound was that of plodding footsteps. The women's arms drooped like two extra stripes, like flaccid worms.

In the large workshops, along the workbenches, were the airplane parts for us to polish with whetstones and wheels and assorted implements whose exact nature baffled me. Nor did I know just how to fit them together. And in my dreams I found myself holding a shiny metallic object and struggling to fit it back where it belonged, but it resisted. I tried to force it but it refused.

Until suddenly it dissolved and the molten steel slithered across my fingers and up my stripes, reaching the back of my neck, where it settled, trying to strangle me.

She hardly said anything. Only the bare essentials. Mingling among us and watching. A broad-framed woman, she wore a prisoner's uniform like the rest of us but she was different. Imprisonment hadn't clung to her.

Janine the Frenchwoman, whose pallet was next to mine, said: 'This Clarissa was a "Fronthüre".'

I tell my children that she was a whore sent to the front more than three years earlier as a diversion for the soldiers. Several others like her had already thrown themselves against the fence to sever the frenzied memories. Others had turned into wild dogs, directing their humiliation and disgrace at women as yet unafflicted.

But not Clarissa. The way I remember it, the torment never took hold of her.

Day followed day in confusion. There was no keeping track. One morning I awoke on my pallet, but it felt like smouldering stones. There I was in a vast desert, the furnace overhead sapping whatever precious fluids still flowed inside me. I implored it to take even more.

Janine dragged me off the cot. 'Get up,' she said, almost shouting. I didn't budge. The goodness of the desert was what I wanted. She prodded me, but I couldn't move my legs. They were drowning in the desert sands and I didn't have the will. Janine beat me with her fists.

'On your feet,' she said, 'or you'll be missed in the roll-call. You mustn't be sick!' she shouted. 'Mon Dieu, you just can't take that kind of risk.'

'Leave me alone,' I begged of her. Janine persisted and forced my feet towards her, tying my shoes on.

And above, out of the fiery skies, came a different voice. 'Leave her alone!' Janine pounced on her.

'Monster,' she yelled. 'She'll die if she doesn't get up!'

The vast desert drifted away. I opened my eyes, which felt like tiny flames. Like one from days gone by, Clarissa's voice lacked the parched sound that comes from unremitting hunger and a wilting mind.

'You fool,' she said to Janine. 'You know I wouldn't let her die. Just leave her here.' Bowing to Clarissa's authority, Janine loosened her stubborn grip.

'Now leave,' she ordered.

Clarissa knelt and took off my shoes. She lifted my spindly legs back onto the cot.

'I'll be back soon,' she whispered.

I didn't know where she went but she did come back and in the hollow of her palm were some tablets, gleaming. A kind I had never seen here. Perhaps she's out to poison me, to embed her evil in me, to scar me with her shame I thought. But I kept still. Like an obedient child, I opened my mouth and swallowed. Into another desert I sunk. There was the hint of a breeze brushing its precious sands, stirring up pillars of dust.

For three days she kept coming, putting the medication in my mouth and disappearing. On the fourth day, as Janine told me, Clarissa stood during the first roll-call at the end of the corridor and waited. Then, when the golden-haired officer arrived, Clarissa stopped her and whispered something in her ear. The officer approached her master and he took the roll-call, but not a single woman was missing.

I was not the only one that Clarissa took charge of at the moment of collapse. There were others like me. She brought medicine to the ailing, and solace to the dying. Wetting their foreheads with soothing compresses until the end.

For Sara Mendelssohn who came down with the sailors' disease, scurvy, she brought fruits and vegetables.

The only islands of potatoes we ever saw floating in the lake of soup appeared on those rare days when the factory owners came to see the prisoners. That was how we found out about the orders to give us more and better food to make us more productive. But the SS men would fish any morsels of vegetable and shreds of meat out of the soup leaving us nothing but the greasy water, without a trace of the nourishment it once contained.

When I tried to thank her, haltingly, she brushed me aside with a flick of her hand, and turned away, as though it was more than she could bear.

Late one night, the door came open quietly. Clarissa got up and walked towards it, treading very carefully, as though on sizzling embers. She made her way to the pale slit of light, and as the door opened wider, I could make out the shadow of the golden-haired officer. She was standing there blocking the light. As soon as Clarissa crossed the threshold, the officer turned on her heel, and Clarissa followed. The door closed silently, as though it had never moved. I fastened my head to the hardness of the pallet, and as I turned back, I found Janine's eyes, like a cat's slicing through me in the darkness. I turned away. The silence hung so heavy that I could almost hear the Frenchwoman's eyelids batting, and the sound of my own breathing rumbled in my ears.

Other times she would be gone all night. We knew well enough where she slept those nights. Nestling in the embrace of the woman officer, her gateway to the world. Sometimes, she would be allowed to hear a Chopin polonaise or a Wagner symphony, resting her back against crisp sheets. And the Brünnhilde would offer her soft clothes, wash her body in a tub, shampoo her hair. Clarissa would lie there with her legs curled up, and her mind closed within itself. At the morning parade, a telltale nerve would twitch in the officer's cheek as she passed by Clarissa.

Clarissa never said much during working hours. Only once, she started singing in a deep, low voice, like a husky gurgle. She fought back the strange sound but it kept pouring out of her, unchecked, spilling on to our workbenches.

Unable to continue joining the airplane parts with that terrible sound, we stopped. It was like a mute straining to use his voice, the tremor of his vocal cords causing his listeners to shudder.

One night I awoke and found that Clarissa had returned to her cot from the hidden room. But instead of stretching out, she was sitting there like a statue in whom life had frozen, staring out into the darkness.

I could not stop myself from going over to her.

'Clarissa.' I spoke softly, 'What does she do to you?' Suddenly her face contorted with a pain so intense that I recoiled. She turned her head slowly, as though a key had been inserted in her back and said dryly:

'She doesn't do me any harm.' Then she touched my head. 'You're young,' she said.

'Why, I almost had a child, and my youth is gone.'

'You'll have other children.' She touched my forehead. 'I never will.'

Once a fate is sealed, wherever the body goes, that fate precedes it. People shy away as they would from someone with a dreaded disease, but the body has its own truth to tell. It follows its course, spinning and stumbling, without distinguishing. Once she was branded, the stigma could never be wiped away. Clearly, she would never be disengaged. If we ever got out we would be free to love again. The bruises and emaciation, the disease and the wounds had gnawed away at the racked bodies, but though they were torn, they would be given another chance. Like a forest that goes on burning after a fire. The soft murmur of the sea at high tide and the waves of the moon would bring other loves and children into those wombs. Under the dome of this horror, we would love. There we would give birth and raise our children. Not on bread but on water. Not on the body but on the scarred soul. This scarred soul of mine opened up to her, longing for her support. But she had already been branded. For the rest of her life she would wander through the Land of Nod. With no brave hunter to go with her. Nothing but her seared spirit.

Softly I asked, since she was the one who knew. 'Will we ever get out of here?' She said: 'They're getting closer. It won't be long before the echoes of the explosions reach us.'

She bent over me and shared her secret. 'I'll be going to Palestine. I have an uncle there, my mother's brother. We used to make fun of him. We said he was crazy going to such a godforsaken place. But here I am now, without any God. I'll join him. He's an important man by now in Palestine.' She uttered the word gently, splitting the name of the country, syllable by euphonious syllable, before her voice dropped to where it became eerie and remote, and terrible.

Clarissa rocked herself as though in a lullaby. She was far away from me by then and we were like moles in a tunnel, except that we hadn't had the welcome sleep those wise animals have. All we had done was to crawl down into the deepest holes where the abomination flowed submissively, begging to pour out to sea. But the sea was thousands of miles away over occupied land. The roots of the burning trees trembled and cowered under the weight of the abomination, demanding to know where the water came from. Every last one of the bridges had been bombed that winter and yet the trains had not stopped crossing the rivers. People had become roots and roots, people. The wise animals listened to the sound of the flowing abomination and wondered when it would let up.

I couldn't go any closer to her. I returned to my cot, as she went on rocking herself, consoling her flesh and her spirit, no longer taking any notice of me.

Winter was digging in around us and we were forgotten.

Heavy rains started to fall it seemed to me that every drop was also carrying a grain of ashes from those consumed by the smoke.

The camp was not bombed, but the approaches were covered in marshy mud, as the trudging of the sticky feet and the sheer fatigue kept beating, like the room of a watchmaker gone berserk. Whenever I turned to look beyond the fences, I saw the treetops swaying in the forest.

It was there that the leaves would fill up with drops of water and the early winter winds loosened off rows of foliage. Some of the leaves blew over the fence and even drifted down into the doorways of the barracks.

These were left untouched. Except by the wind, which, after all, was good to them.

New airplane parts were piled high on the workbenches, and we fitted them together helplessly. The door opened and Clarissa entered, wearing a pair of men's boots. Water dripped off them onto the floor, leaving the tracks of her hurried entrance.

Out of the coat wrapped around her, she took a kerchief and

unfolded it, revealing the shiny redness of forest berries. She opened her mouth and flicked in one berry, then another. The juice oozed down her chin like a festering wound. The meisters, the German mechanics appointed to guard over us during working hours, stopped what they were doing and watched. We all huddled around her as she began stuffing our hands and our mouths with ripe red berries. My mother's jars are filling with red jam, and she lined them up, one by one, on the pantry shelves for all the seasons to come until the following summer.

'Where did you get them?' one woman asked.

'It's a present,' said Clarissa breaking into a raucous laugh and swaying from side to side. 'I'm kept as a lover, didn't you know?'

Then she pressed her head into the empty kerchief and breathed in the lingering fragrance of the fruit. The kerchief covered her, but we could still see the shivers running down her spine. We left her there in her kerchief. Not a single one of us touched her. We went back to our workbenches and clung to them. Even the meisters left her alone, until the door opened again. In the doorway was the officer, some loose strands of golden hair dangling under her hat and falling damply along her neck. She went over to Clarissa, took her by the shoulders and shook her with one powerful jolt. The kerchief dropped to the ground. The red spots had stained it. Then she bent over and picked it up. It was the first time I had seen her bend over. Her spine jutted out under the blouse of her uniform and her breathing came in waves. The sight of her stunned me. A tremendous revelation. Even she, proud as she was, knew how to kneel. The taut cord that had learned how to stretch, never allowing itself to slacken, had loosened ever so briefly. So she was human too.

'*Das ist meine Clarissa*,' she said in a stiff voice. '*Sie ist Mein.*'

'Mine, mine.'

As she straightened up, the kerchief dropped again and she stepped on it. We turned around. Janine was the only one who dared; she took one step forward, shooting out a piercing look. The officer stopped directly across from her.

For a split second their eyes met, a moment that froze in space. The officer turned, let go of Clarissa and Clarissa stumbled. Where is Janine? A Catholic who had coupled her fate with a Jew. Following him eastwards. That's how she wound up with us. Where is Janine now? In some vinegrowers' village near Montpellier not far from the Spanish border, where the grapes are especially juicy, where one can get as drunk on a single bunch of them as on a flask of wine.

I am not yet sixty. I took my granddaughter Hagar to the house from which they took me.

I could not tell the ten-year-old that this was where I had loved another man. There had been a foetus inside me who might have become her father. I told her:

'This is where I once lived. This is where they banged on my door. This is where they dragged us outside and took us to the town square.'

Hagar looked wistfully at the house we had not entered and asked:

'Why don't you knock on the door, Grandmother?'

I said to myself: that door has been slammed shut for good. It can't be reopened. Deep in the recesses of my memory I buried that man who had slept in my bed and was the first to come to me. I don't dream about him anymore. When Hagar's grandfather took me, I cast that chapter of my life aside into a sealed box and threw the key into the depths of the sea. Still it is beyond me how these things seep through and gather in other parts of me, filtering into my children.

The dammed up waters seek new outlets. When I heard them forcing their way, I clasped my head with both hands and ordered: 'Stop!' But they disobeyed. Outsmarting me, they worked their way in between the cracks.

I clasped my granddaughter's hand and felt its fervour. She was standing next to me, so stirred and pure. I said to myself: I'm not trying to get even. I'll be sixty next year, after all. I've brought along my son's daughter, to show the intruders who broke the door down – those masters of the stripes and the whip – that they haven't outdone me.

The foetus died, but here is the child.

Winter was coming and the sun had almost vanished. The rumble of distant explosions blended with the sound of thunder. Nothing but the lightning, slashing the cloud, could keep them apart.

A few weeks before liberation, the meisters began shooting indiscriminately. The factories emptied and the owners vanished. A day before the liberation, we remained all alone in the camp.

We woke up in the chilly dawn and stood in formation waiting, but there were no footsteps to be heard. We ventured out into the gateways of the barracks. Everything was in place. The fences were bolted. In the distance, the tree tops were swaying as though nothing in the forest had changed. Utterly indifferent to us, it had never turned a receptive ear. By noon, the gate had been uprooted. Two dogs still posted to watch over it were shot on the spot, and their carcasses rotted in the alleys.

A Russian division arrived in the camp and our fears gave way to new ones. Fresh from the battles of Stalingrad, they were overcome by cold and lust. But as soon as they saw us, they turned away. Our emaciated bodies were incapable of arousing passion.

We lined up for the last time, facing the row of Russian officers who wished to provide us with the first piece of paper we would need to begin life anew. They gave us back our names. I saw mine but we were strangers to one another.

Janine said it amounted to a baptism, and kept crossing herself. Three Russian officers sat on a desk taken from the camp headquarters. I remembered the fifth chapter. God takes the finest rib, the one that has suffered nightmares, and releases it in the Garden.

Clarissa's icy hand was tugging at mine, the way it did that time when she handed me the medicine.

I turned towards her and she pointed wordlessly at a woman who was working her way into the waiting row. She had taken on our appearance, turned into one of us. Got hold of a striped shirt, hoping to find refuge in our fold as among Jacob's lot. Gone was Brünnhilde's golden hair. She had shaven it all off and her skull bones were showing. All that time, they had been covered by the flowing Brünnhildian mane. The colour was gone from her cheeks, and her anxiety was seeping out, as if through a faulty stopper. I looked and saw her. She had pushed her way into the hush of the women and even from as far away as I was standing, I could see the roundness of her breasts between the stripes. Cut off like us. Now she was hoping for the final Judgement Day. The trumpets of angels.

'Oh, Merciful Christ,' said Janine, stretching out an arm in her direction. Then she spit on the ground and made the sign of the cross.

Thus in the haze of my illness she re-emerges out of the ground in her striped uniform. Her hair falls on her shoulders and the SS insignia is etched in blood on her forehead. Even in my nightmares she bears that same deathly pallor. She leans over me, opens her fist, and shows me some yellow tablets.

I yell: 'I'm not to blame!' She grabs me and forces them into my mouth. I purse my lips, seal them tight, and cry:

'Clarissa, come, help me!'

But it's my husband who shakes me by the shoulder and asks: 'What's wrong? You've been having a nightmare.'

One morning he asked me: 'Who is the Clarissa you keep dreaming about?'

She keeps surfacing. Weaving in and out of the corridors of my memory. Pulling behind the dignity of man and his degradation, his anguish, and his powers of resistance. The eyes of Janine of Gaul harden as she struggles to record what she sees, indelibly, to make sure that she never forgets. Clarissa had said: 'I can't be the one to turn her in.' 'You go,' she told me. 'Go tell the Russians that she's hiding among us.' I froze. My legs wouldn't move. I was unable to shout. I remembered the outstretched palm and the tablets. But Janine had already stepped out of the line and her legs were carrying her unhaltingly, overcome by some secret power. She approached the Russian officers and told them something. Two of them followed her back. Ever so slowly, they approached the line.

Janine stood opposite the Nazi woman and pointed her out with an arched hand. 'That's the one!' The officers dragged her away and the Brünnhilde started screaming and jerking convulsively. But the Russian had a firm grip on her. He made her stand up, as he struck her on her bald pate. That was how I was able to picture her skull lying on the ground after the worms had gnawed at it. He wasted no time, pulling at her shirt, ripping it right off. She began screaming again and covered her nakedness with her hands. But those breasts were not like ours. Full and fleshy they were apparent through the torn material.

He slapped her once across the face and she stopped. Her arms fell to her sides. He raised her arm for all to see. Under her armpit was the mark, carefully etched, as though on a sheet of paper. Furiously he struck her again. She lifted her head and searched over the entire row of women until her eyes rested on Clarissa.

Clarissa turned away, no longer seeing her. Like a madwoman she screeched, her cries rising and falling over our frozen silence. 'Clarissa, help me!' The Russian waited another minute, then dragged her away. She stopped screaming and he pulled her behind him like a tattered sack, behind the first barracks.

A single gunshot, and he was back from the corner. As he stuck his pistol back in its holster as if nothing had happened, he returned to his seat by the desk. I turned to look into the row of women, but no longer saw Clarissa. She had vanished. I shut my eyes. The entire row turned into one long strip, and at the tip of the worm, one after the other, we undressed and put on the clothes provided by the Russians.

Ever since those sinister days, the light for me will forever be flawed.

When I returned home, I found my parents alive. For three days, my ageing father sat with me. Then he packed a small bag. I asked him: 'Why are you leaving now that I've been saved?'

For two months he travelled all over Europe to collect the proof we would need to prove I was widowed and could remarry under Jewish law. 'The only way to find two witnesses,' he explained, 'is to start searching right away. If we wait, they'll scatter all over the world.' My children are grown, and the dead one who dropped out of my womb is over and done with. The ones that followed covered over him with their beauty and brightness.

I once took out a picture of my dead husband to show my

oldest son, but he didn't believe me. The truth, after all, is a great mosaic, with motley pieces forever falling into place. When one piece is missing, sometimes I look for it and sometimes I stop.

Whenever I pass by the roadsigns of our country, I think about her. Maybe she is sitting here, maybe there. Maybe her face is sealed, revealing nothing, except for the wet and oozing sap of berries.

Whenever I dare to lift the stone, I turn it over and over, and things are not the way they were before but rather, the way one sees them in a crooked mirror or through a window on a foggy day. I'm not going to breathe warm mist onto the pane, because I don't really want to see. Clarissa in a golden embrace, and Janine with the vinegrowers of Gaul, and myself in Tel Aviv. Only rarely does my soul wander and turn over, and it no longer reaches back to the way things were at the beginning.

They say: time adds layers of its own and you cannot reach back to the day of Creation without climbing down a great canyon. After passing all seven layers of the earth one moves back a million years, to the Day of Chaos when Creation and Disintegration were one, nesting in a single womb, like Rebecca's irreconcilable twins.

There, a great darkness emerged. They say: it will heal. They say: I will be healed. I am grateful for the sun and for the new light, but on the children's heads, my anguish and and torment will rest like a hat of glass.

Translated by Miriam Shlesinger

13

The Mask Maker

by NURIT ZARCHI

AFTER THE spectators had left the hall, the two of them sat sipping tea on an upturned box, still feeling elated by the presence of an audience. They knew from experience that in a moment this feeling would give way to depression, like the flat expanse exposed after the excitement of the foaming tide. She's about to speak, thought the young man and he threw a narrow, foxy look at Liora, the woman sitting opposite him, in whose workshop he had been working for a while.

'Expert in mending marionettes required' – the notice which had caught Shaul Gottlieb's eye when he returned to the country was near enough, if not an exact description of the craft he had studied during his years abroad.

After completing his army service, a period during which one of the wars had taken place, Shaul Gottlieb had decided to travel to the Far East, a decision which seemed on the surface of things to be dictated by the prevailing fashion. But in fact Shaul felt that this was what he really needed: a mood of detachment and calm, which seemed to him, as indeed to many of his generation, to be personified by the sages of the Far East, wandering in their orange robes amid the mountain mists, where they had retired from the hurly-burly of life and from their own passions, conversing with Master Butterfly and Messieurs Rain and Wind, and quaffing bitter wine in memory of the famous poet who drowned in a river while drunkenly trying to embrace the reflection of the moon.

The road to the culture of the high mountains was apparently too long for Shaul Gottlieb, and the lack of money or enthusiasm caused him to stop half-way. But although his spirit was not strong enough to actually attain his ideal, it was determined enough not to abandon it entirely, and when he was told by the old woman he looked after for a living that there was an old Chinese artist, an expert in making masks, living in the very same house, he did not demur and approached him immediately to ask if he would teach him his craft.

Master Chan, as he was called, did not speak English well, which did not bother Shaul Gottlieb in the least, quite the contrary. From the little he said, Shaul understood that Master Chan was a political exile who had escaped the persecution of his government, a famous actor in his day, who dealt in mask-making. Shaul, in any case, did not discover any signs of his teacher's past in the house, although he searched for them feverishly.

When he arrived at Master Chan's he always found him impeccably dressed, with his sparse white beard neatly combed. He would make a little bow to Shaul, and the two of them would go to the work room. This room was always shrouded in gloom but for the pool of light shed by the lamp on the work table, where everything was arranged in order: the jars of lacquer, the brushes of various sizes, the delicate carving tools, the ivory-handled knives lying side by side like a surgeon's scalpels.

When Master Chan accepted Shaul as a pupil he didn't ask him any questions, apart from his name. The next day he requested permission to examine his hands, and Shaul held them out to him with more than a hint of unease. He had always felt a kind of estrangement from his hands, which were strong, clear, and large, and his long fingers, which seemed to him to have a personality of their own, not at all compatible with his stature, which was not particularly tall, nor the expression on his face, which was rather sly and evasive, and appeared to be trying to hide a shadow of fear. When Master Chan now took his hands and brought them into the lamplight, he felt that he had not lived up to the demands imposed by his own hands. But Master Chan did not seem to hold this against him. And on the same day he began to teach him his craft. That winter and summer Shaul learned to carve dragons, genies, spirits of the sea and land, and the long, hollow-eyed faces of men and women, sometimes smiling their strange mysterious smile, sometimes full of anger or dread.

One day, shortly before he completed his studies, Master Chan looked at one of the masks made by his pupil, holding it closer and farther from the lamp. For a long time he said nothing, and then he turned to Shaul and said in his broken English: 'The face is cold, it has no joy of intimacy, its expression does not stem from any real memory, from love or even from anger.' Then he laid the rebuked mask gently on the table, switched off the lamp, drew the curtain, and took a little ivory box out of his pocket. In the refracted light coming from the street Shaul saw a little face in a picture yellowed with age looking at his gravely. 'Mother, child, wife.' said Master Chan. Shaul could see no resemblance between the picture and any mask carved by Master Chan. This was the only time Master Chan ever commented on his work during the entire course of his studies before they were suddenly interrupted.

One morning Shaul Gottlieb woke up and saw the grey day rising outside the window, so different from the staring, too bright light streaming onto the ficus tree opposite his window in Israel. A light which exposed the existence from which there was no escape: this foreign light steeped in a dark softness which had lapped him up to now in a kind of amorous pampering, suddenly lost all its vitality and left Shaul in a big, empty city bereft of all its mystery. It was as if he had been abruptly cut off from the magnet which up to now had drawn him to the second-hand book stalls, to the midday concerts, when he would slip into a church, drawn by the sounds of the harpsicord or piano bursting into the air through the daytime din and the noise of the buses.

Shaul felt like a puppet manipulated by a hidden hand, cut off from its strings and clattering to the ground. He took advantage of the fact that the woman in whose house he lived had gone away to visit her daughter to avoid saying goodbye in person, and wrote her a note instead.

It was harder to part from Master Chan. He didn't know what to say to his teacher. The fact that he hadn't been doing well in his studies lately made it a little easier for him, and that same day he returned to Israel without saying a word to Master Chan.

For a week he wandered round Tel Aviv without letting any-one from his family know of his return, except for a friend who was doing his army service duty and in whose flat he lived. He felt like someone recovering from a long illness, or from the banishment from the Garden of Eden. If he had been a stranger there, floating high above the ground until he lost the sense of his body, then here, with the familiar people he bumped into in the street, their warm, noisy greetings, and the childhood memories which flooded him, he felt uncomfortably close to the flaming sword.

At the end of the week he plucked up enough courage to open the newspapers. And then he encountered the notice about the marionettes. The next day he went to the address given.

Did she see his silence as an invitation? Shaul sensed that the conversation was inevitable, he noticed her short, fair hair and fixed his eyes on the floor. No, he said to himself, no, no, don't let her start with that, just don't start. He succeeded in shutting his ears and looked obstinately around the room for something on which to fix his eyes. The faces of the puppets which were lying casually on the table seemed to him to be waiting expectantly to catch his eye, seeking an ally with their hard, frozen eyes, as if full of resentment against the life which had been lent them or taken away from them.

All of a sudden he felt frightened. This feeling wasn't new, he admitted to himself, he didn't feel that they were superior to him because of their freedom from the force of gravity, as Kleist felt. He had always feared them, and since he was open to this feeling, for a moment his opacity left him, and Liora's words hit home: 'And they decided,' she said, 'that if they didn't all get out of there alive, the ones left alive, all members of the same party in Israeli society, or in human society in general, I would be ashamed to mention its name, would bring up the children of the other members.'

Shaul's mind refused to yield to the story, like a sheep digging its feet in the ground when you try to grab hold of its fleece in order to move it from its place, and even if Liora noticed this she didn't stop – in any case it is to himself that the story-teller tells his tale, Shaul knew. He felt exposed, like someone caught in the rain, narrowed his shoulders and went on sitting.

'An honourable solution in the circumstances,' said Liora and left behind her the little girl who would bite her hand to prove to herself that she existed, and to the same end would also pass her finger, like other children, through the flame of the candle, and leave it there for one more second, and if she really did exist, who am I?

Shaul moved restlessly in his chair.

'Even though Aunt Sophia and Uncle Leopold, as I called them, never talked about her, I knew that my mother was Jewish. Who am I? I asked Uncle Yona the last time I saw him before he disappeared. At that time you were accustomed to people appearing and disappearing and you never gave it a second thought.

'Near our house was a forest, I used to roam in it and feed the little animals with food I stole from the kitchen. I took Uncle Yona there, in that childhood so full of parents and pretend relatives it seems to me that he was my only real relation, perhaps he was even my mother's brother.

'A sentence he said to me then has remained etched in my memory: People are afraid of ambiguity, he said, a quality they see as a fault, a kind of flaw in thinking, a state which exists before the correct state, which is the one of certain knowledge. But the truth is that ambiguity is the true human quality, only we need patience and strength in order to bear it. The ancients already knew that our world has many aspects and many gods, but modern man refuses to acknowledge it. Think about Bach's contrapunct, and even more sublime polyphony. I'll tell you something, he whispered to me, it's always one more.

'After this I never met him again, as I said – he disappeared.'

Shaul rose to his feet, the scraping of his chair making the sound of an angry gesture in the room.

'You don't agree,' said Liora and her face fell – as Shaul noted with some revulsion, at the bottom of her face, in the corners of her lips, the traces of the sorrow and the pain were evident. He sensed a longing in his hands for the feeling of the masks which he always had to smear with lacquer, and he seemed to feel their smooth cold, gleaming touch on his hands.

'You don't have to go, I can make coffee,' said Liora.

'No need,' said Shaul and sat down again.

The cups were made of porcelain. When Liora poured the coffee Shaul already knew that he wasn't going to leave. He felt limp and helpless, like a fly entangled in a spiderweb. As they drank the coffee they were both silent. The sound of a car driving past came from the street, something optimistic hinting at the possibility of movement penetrated the studio for a moment.

When Liora cleared away the cups it seemed to Shaul that her hands were shaking. When she put the tray down, she slipped her hands into her sleeves. For the first time Shaul measured her with his eyes. The narrowness of her hips gave her a boyish look. The fact that he didn't get up and run for his life filled him with anger.

He tried to guess what she was thinking about, even though he knew how stupid and unimaginative it was to attempt to guess what other people were thinking.

Liora looked at the puppets lying on the table, and they looked back at her with their staring eyes. A dream, that wasn't the term she would have used for the nightmarish sensation, the fear that always accompanied her. Suddenly the puppets would rise from the chairs to hit the table, with their wooden arms – their foreheads made of paper hard as stone and to whisper that whisper and demand that demand, suckle us, suckle us, like in the song which the nuns had taught her at school when she was a little girl –

> Mother of my soul do for me
> What every flesh and blood mother does
> With honey and milk suckle me
> Smooth as a rose on my dry tongue

The next day Shaul found work as a waiter in one of the cafés in the north of the town. He didn't go back to Liora's apartment, and in fact when he had to pass the street where she lived he would make a detour to the next street over. The feeling of nausea that welled up in him whenever he remembered that night gave way to a feeling of weariness and impatience, and a refusal even to discuss it with himself.

As far as Shaul Gottlieb was concerned his interest in masks came to an end together with his interest in puppets, and he dragged his existence out from day to day, no happier to get up in the morning than he was to go to bed at night. Occasionally he felt a fleeting sense of having left the main thing behind him, was it the memory of the tools of his trade which he had brought with him and left in the studio? He laughed bitterly at the thought of what his teacher, Master Chan, would have said about it. The truth was that Shaul preferred them to be where they were; in any case ever since arriving in Tel Aviv he had been unable to imagine the face of the mask which he had it in him to create, and it didn't make any sense for him to carve Chinese masks, dragons and genies, here in Tel Aviv.

He moved into another flat. With his few possessions he had no difficulty in moving into a third flat too when this became necessary, and Tel Aviv seemed to him soft, to the point of rottenness. Living in Tel Aviv, he thought, was like nowhere, and it possessed the lightness of unlimited freedom together with the feeling that you didn't exist.

And thus the winter almost passed, and although the rain continued, making it hard for him to get up in the morning, and equally hard to return to his flat at night, it was possible nevertheless to feel the beginning of summer in the air, and on the bare branches of the trees you could see the shoots sprouting.

One day when he came home from work he was surprised to find a letter under the door. He didn't know that the handwriting was Liora's, because it was the first time he had seen it. He put the letter in his pocket and opened it only on the bus back to Tel Aviv, on his return from the kibbutz, where he had taken part in the Passover Seder with his parents.

For two months it had not occurred to him to go and see Liora, and he had even avoided going anywhere near her flat. But once he decided to go and get the month's salary she owed him, as well as the tools and brushes he had left in her studio, he stood outside in the rain and waited for her to return. He flattened himself to fit under the projecting roof, so as not to get wet, and next to him a stray cat followed his example under the light of the street lamp. The rain pelted down in chains and dived soundlessly onto the wet pavements.

When the taxi approached he knew by the way his heart skipped a beat that it was Liora, and when she got out he noticed that she looked smaller than he remembered her, and perhaps even softer or lost, and Liora who couldn't help showing her excitement at seeing him, welcomed him like the prodigal son, took off his wet coat and his damp socks and seated him opposite the stove, with a blank, worried expression on her face.

Shaul examined her with his eyes: her hair was longer and her face looked less determined than he remembered.

As he sat on the shabby armchair, one hand stroking the cat that had squeezed through the door with him, Shaul felt that there was no need for words. The strange night they had shared, for all its frightening strangeness, had melted some barrier between them. When they got into bed that night Shaul clung to her as if she were a source of warmth in the darkness.

When he got up at dawn and tiptoed to the door, he noticed the puppets (nothing had been said about them the evening before) strewn about in the grey morning light, following him with their staring eyes. He retraced his steps and stood by the bed looking at Liora's face. For a moment he stopped himself from passing his hand over her face. It was very smooth. She lay there still, her eyes closed. For a moment he thought that perhaps she was dead, and in his alarm there was also a tremendous feeling of relief. And with this picture in his mind's eye, he left the house.

Shaul Gottlieb did not return to Liora's house, either that evening or afterwards. He left the café where he was working too. He found work on a farm in the Lachish district. Occasionally he remembered his paintbrushes and tools still lying in Tel Aviv, and he thought it was better this way, because what would he have done with them there, between the milking parlour and the cabbage fields? Unless it was absolutely necessary, he had no contact with anyone.

On one of his days off he went to Tel Aviv. As usual he felt profound relief when he reached the coastal plain, and a feeling of real gaiety seized hold of him when he strolled through the streets. A rotten city, he thought as he crossed Allenby Street in the direction of the sea, and its rottenness is what makes it human, its dimensions are completely human and there's nothing arrogant about it.

'Hey Gottlieb!' someone slapped him on the shoulder from behind. It was the friend in whose flat he had lived when he arrived in the country.

'Where did you disappear to? There's a letter for you lying around somewhere in my flat.'

Shaul felt a surge of resentment. This time it wasn't the paint-brushes, the tools, or the month's salary with which Liora had tried to snare him then, he thought, but a short note: 'Shaul, I'd be grateful if you got in touch with me, Liora.'

That evening Shaul went to her house. If he hadn't been angry, he might have brought her a lily, he thought, as he passed a flower stall.

When he knocked a strange girl opened the door. 'There are no performances,' she said rudely. 'Who are you?'

'Shaul,' he said. 'Why do you ask?'

'Ah,' said the girl, whose aggression vanished when she heard his name, as if something had become clear to her. 'I'm leaving, you can come in if you like.' Shaul looked at her hesitantly.

Liora was sitting in bed reading a book. When she saw Shaul she raised the collar of her dressing gown.

If she hadn't been frightened, thought Shaul, she would have said that she had thought I'd got lost.

'I'm so glad you came,' said Liora and motioned him to sit down on the bed.

'Are you ill?' asked Shaul. 'Flu?'

'I have a thermos of tea here, a friend made it for me,' she said. 'Will you have some?'

The tea tasted as sweet as the tea given at kindergarten.

Shaul was surprised that he felt a need to apologize, but since she did not attack him, he didn't know what to say. He didn't know where to put his hands which now that he was working as a manual labourer, seemed to him heavy and even more detached from him than before. Liora too looked at them. For a moment Shaul thought of putting them in her lap in the blanket, when Liora said: 'Shauli, there's something we should clarify.'

Shauli. A cold shiver ran down his spine, like the time when the children had slipped a frog into his shirt. She didn't say 'must', Shaul noted to himself, and aloud he said, 'I don't know of anything like that.' He looked around for the puppets, which must have been shut up in the cupboard, for not even one of them was visible.

'Yes,' said Liora, 'I would have spared you all this but ...' And after a moment's hesitation she began again.

She doesn't give up, thought Shaul coldly, she must have decided to try a different tack, because Liora said: 'You remember that you were here on the Seder night?'

'Yes', said Shaul, 'but that was a long time ago ...'

'Four months exactly,' said Liora. 'You remember that you were here?'

'I haven't forgotten,' said Shaul.

'No, that's not what I meant.' Liora looked into his face as if asking for help. 'The puppets,' she whispered, 'you remember that they didn't bother us?'

Oh, he thought, we're back on that again. 'Right,' he said aloud, 'you're old enough to know by now that not everything in your head really happens.'

'No,' said Liora, and lowered her head to the pillow.

Shaul noticed the tip of a bandage sticking out of the collar of her dressing gown.

'What happened?' he asked.

'Only the doctors knew, that was the sign,' she said and he sensed that her lips were dry, 'although even before you came I knew too, because I could have breastfed the puppets if I'd wanted to. That's one of the signs, you know, that's how they know it's this disease.'

Now she was crying, she cried quietly, without a sound, ashamed, drying her tears before they appeared.

'It's stupid to speak of love,' she said, 'I need you too little or too much.'

Shaul looked at her. But for the fact that it was his own life at stake he would have known what to say now. But what he said was: 'I'm going now, I have to think, give me time.'

All night long Shaul wandered the streets. There was a little light on downstairs, Liora had left him a note and supper on a tray. If you come back, she wrote, don't let me waste the moment in sleep. Shaul smiled, but he didn't go up to wake her. It was his moment. He absorbed the darkness welling softly from the materials, the cloths, the lightbulbs. Once more the puppets were strewn about, the untidy room looked rich and full of mysterious buried treasures, like Ali Baba's cave.

Despite the late hour Shaul felt a strange lightness in his limbs. He went up to his tools, which were still as he had left them, lined up on the table in the order he had learned from Master Chan. His fingers seemed to work of their own accord, in the dark. When he was finished he brought the face he had created up to the light: it wasn't a man's face, or a child's. It was a face which was in the process of becoming human, the incomplete face of a foetus.

Translated by Dalya Bilu

Contributors

Leah Aini

The Author

Leah Aini was born in 1962 in the south Tel Aviv neighbourhood of her stories. She is an award-winning poet, novel and short-story writer and children's author. She received the 1994 Prime Minister's Prize.

Books Published in Hebrew

Portrait (poetry), Hakibbutz Hameuchad, 1988

The Empress of Imagined Fertility (poetry), Hakibbutz Hameuchad/
Siman Kriah, 1991

*The Sea Horses' Loop (stories and novella), Hakibbutz Hameuchad/Siman
Kriah, 1991

Sand Tide (novel), Hakibbutz Hameuchad/Siman Kriah, 1992

Call Me from Downstairs (youth), Hakibbutz Hameuchad, 1994

Mr Rabbit's Job Hunt (children), Am Oved, 1994

Hi Yuli (youth), Hakibbutz Hameuchad, 1995

Someone Must Be Here (novel), Hakibbutz Hameuchad/Siman Kriah, 1995

Half and Wandercloud/Octopina (children), Hakibbutz Hameuchad, 1996

Works in English Translation

'Shower', *Modern Hebrew Literature* (Spring/Fall 1992), Vols. 8–9, p. 33

'White', *Modern Hebrew Literature* (Fall/Winter 1994), Vol. 13, pp. 14–18

'Until the Entire Guard has Passed', *Jerusalem Post Magazine* (28 July 1995), pp. 20–2

---

*The star indicates in each case the book containing the story which is included in this anthology.

Ruth Almog

The Author

Ruth Almog was born in Petah Tikva in 1936 to an Orthodox family of German descent. After studying literature and philosophy she taught for a number of years. Since 1967 she has been an editor at the literary section of *Ha'aretz*. She is well known in Israel as a novelist, short-story writer and author of children's books. In 1986 she was awarded two prizes for children's literature. *Roots of Light* won the distinguished Brenner Prize in 1989. Some of her works have been published in German, English and Dutch translation.

Books Published in Hebrew

Marguerita's Nightly Charities (stories), Tarmil, 1969

The Exile (novel), Am Oved, 1971

After Tubishvat (stories), Tarmil, 1979

The Stranger and the Foe (novel), Sifriat Poalim, 1980

Death in the Rain (novel), Keter, 1982

Women (stories), Keter, 1986

Gypsies in the Orchard (children), Massada, 1986

The Silver Ball (children), Am Oved, 1986

Roots of Light (novel), Keter, 1987

The Wonder Bird (children), Am Oved, 1991

Rakefet, My First Love (children), Keter, 1992

Invisible Mending (novella and stories), Keter, 1993

A Perfect Lover (novel), with Esther Ettinger, Keter, 1995

Works in English Translation

'The Meeting between Ellsheva Green and Miriam', *Modern Hebrew Literature* (Winter 1981), Vol. 6, Nos. 3/4, pp. 4–16

'The Lucky Flower', *Modern Hebrew Literature* (Spring/Summer 1983), Vol. 8, Nos. 3/4, pp. 53–61

'Dora's Secret', *A Collection of Recent Writing in Israel*, PEN, Tel Aviv, 1991, pp. 62–6

Death in the Rain, Red Crane Books, Santa Fé, 1993

'Shrinking', *Ribcage: Israeli Women's Fiction*, Hadassah, New York, 1994, pp. 93–123

'After Arbor Day', *Stories from Women Writers of Israel*, Star, New Delhi, 1995, pp. 57–63

'Eh-wahwah', *A Collection of Recent Writing in Israel*, PEN, Tel Aviv, 1995, pp. 33–9

Hannah Bat-Shahar

The Author

The name Hannah Bat-Shahar is a pseudonym. Born in Jerusalem in 1944, the short-story writer is an Orthodox Jewish woman who lives in Jerusalem. She graduated from the Open University with a degree in Hebrew literature and history. Her first collection of stories, *Stories of the Cup*, received the Newman Prize for Book of the Year in 1987.

Books Published in Hebrew

Stories of the Cup, Tcherikover, 1985

*Calling the Bats, Keter, 1990

Dance of the Butterfly, Keter, 1993

Works in English Translation

'Among the Geranium Pots', *Modern Hebrew Literature* (Spring/Summer 1991), Vol. 6, pp. 8–14

Orly Castel-Bloom

The Author

Orly Castel-Bloom was born in 1960 in Tel Aviv, where she lives today. She studied film at Tel Aviv University. She is a noted writer and playwright whose works have been published in Dutch, French and German translation. *Where Am I* received the 1990 Tel Aviv Prize for Literature.

Books Published in Hebrew

Not Far From the Centre of Town (stories), Am Oved, 1987

*Hostile Surroundings (stories), Zmora Bitan, 1988

Where Am I (novel), Zmora Bitan, 1990

Dolly City (novel), Zmora Bitan, 1992

Unbidden Stories, Zmora Bitan, 1993

The Mona Lisa (novel), Keter, 1995

Works in English Translation

'How can you Lose your Cool, when the Kinneret is as Calm as a Pool', *Modern Hebrew Literature* (Spring/Summer 1991), Vol. 6, pp. 15–17

'The Woman Who gave Birth to Twins and Disgraced Herself', *The Best of*

Ariel: A Celebration of Contemporary Israeli Prose, Poetry and Art (1993), Vol. 2, pp. 212–14

'The Woman Who Went Looking for a Walkie-Talkie', *The Best of Ariel: A Celebration of Contemporary Israeli Prose, Poetry and Art* (1993), Vol. 2, pp. 215–17

'The Woman Who Wanted to Kill Someone', *The Best of Ariel: A Celebration of Contemporary Israeli Prose, Poetry and Art* (1993), Vol. 2, pp. 218–20

'Ummi fi shurl', *Ribcage: Israeli Women's Fiction*, Hadassah, New York, 1994, pp. 259–61

'High Tide', *Jerusalem Post Magazine* (28 July 1995), pp. 14–15

Haya Esther

The Author

Haya Esther was born in Jerusalem in 1941 to an Orthodox Jewish family. She received her MA from the Hebrew University in Jerusalem. In addition to writing poetry and fiction, Haya Esther is also a painter.

Books Published in Hebrew

Soft Stones (stories), Eked, 1983, 1988

Radiance (stories), Hakibbutz Hameuchad, 1982

A Bird of Hakhaloth (stories), Carmel, 1994

Ha-Shem Interlude – The First Notebook, Carmel, 1994

Works in English Translation

'Liar', *Ribcage: Israeli Women's Fiction*, Hadassah, New York, 1994

Shulamith Hareven

The Author

S hulamith Hareven was born in Poland in 1931 and emigrated to Eretz Israel in 1940. She grew up in Jerusalem, where she lives today. She has published thirteen books in Hebrew, including poetry, novels, stories, essays, a children's book in verse, and a thriller (in pseudonym). She has served as writer-in-residence at the Hebrew University in Jerusalem and was the first (and for twelve years the only) woman member of the Acadamy of the Hebrew Language. Her works have been translated into numerous languages.

Books Published in Hebrew

Predatory Jerusalem (poetry), Sifriat Poalim, 1962

In the Last Month (stories), Daga, 1966

Separate Places (poetry), Sifriat Poalim, 1969

Permission Granted (stories), Massada, 1970

City of Many Days (novel), Am Oved, 1972

I Love to Smell (children), Sifriat Poalim, 1976

*Loneliness (stories), Am Oved, 1980

The Dulcinea Syndrome (essays), Keter, 1981

The Miracle Hater (novella), Dvir, 1983

The Link (novel), Zmora Bitan, 1986

Messiah or Knesset (essays), Dvir, 1987

Prophet (novella), Dvir, 1988

Eyeless in Gaza (essays), Zmora Bitan, 1991

The Balloon that Went Away (children), Dvir, 1994

After Childhood (novella), Dvir, 1994

The Vocabulary of the Peace (essays), Zmora Bitan, 1996

Works in English Translation

'A Conversation with a Cosmopolitan Jew', *Midstream* (Nov. 1968), Vol. 14, No. 9, pp. 21–6

'Accident at Bernina Ross', *Midstream* (May 1969), Vol. 15, No. 5, pp. 61–7

The Miracle Hater, North Point Press, Berkeley, 1988

Prophet, North Point Press, San Francisco, 1992

A Matter of Identity, Mercury House, San Francisco, 1992

My Straw Chairs, Mercury House, San Francisco, 1992

The Emissary, Mercury House, San Francisco, 1992

Twilight and Other Stories, Mercury House, San Francisco, 1992

Two Hours on the Road, Mercury House, San Francisco, 1992

City of Many Days, Mercury House, San Francisco, 1993

'Love by Telephone', *The Best of Ariel: A Celebration of Contemporary Israeli Prose, Poetry and Art* (1993), Vol. 2, pp. 76–88

Loneliness, Hadassah, New York, 1994

The Vocabulary of Peace: Life, Culture and Politics in the Middle East, Mercury House, San Francisco, 1995

'The Witness', *Stories from Women Writers of Israel*, Star, New Delhi, 1995, pp. 67–99

Yehudit Hendel

The Author

Yehudit Hendel was born into a rabbinic family in Warsaw. She emigrated to Eretz Israel as a child in 1938 and grew up in Haifa. Her first novel, The Street of Steps, was staged at the Habima National Theatre. Her second novel, The Yard of Momo the Great (now reissued as The Last Hamsin) was televised. Hendel is the recipient of the Jerusalem Prize.

Books Published in Hebrew

They Are Different (stories), Sifriet Poalim, 1950

The Street of Steps (novel), Am Oved, 1955

The Yard of Momo the Great (novel), Am Oved, 1969 (reissued 1993 as The Last Hamsin)

The Other Power (novel), Hakibbutz Hameuchad/Siman Kriah, 1984

Near Quiet Places (non-fiction), Hakibbutz Hameuchad, 1987

*Small Change (stories), Hakibbutz Hameuchad/Siman Kriah, 1988

The Mountain of Losses (novel), Hakibbutz Hameuchad/Siman Kriah, 1991

The Last Hamsin (novel), Hakibbutz Hameuchad/Siman Kriah, 1993

An Innocent Breakfast (stories), Hakibbutz Hameuchad/Siman Kriah, 1996

Works in English Translation

'Burdened to Weariness', *Israel Speaks* (21 July 1959), Vol. 4, No. 12, p. 12

The Street of Steps, Herzl Press, New York, 1963; Thomas Yoseloff, London, 1964

'Zili and My Friend Shaul', *The New Israeli Writers: Short Stories of the First Generation*, Sabra Books, New York, 1969, pp. 61–76

'A Story with No Address', *Translation: The Journal of Literary Translation* (Spring 1993), Vol. 28, pp. 113–20

'Apples in Honey', *Ribcage: Israeli Women's Fiction*, Hadassah, New York, 1994, pp. 263–72

'Low, Close to the Floor', *A Married Woman and Other Short Stories from Israel*, Star, New Delhi, 1995, pp. 49–52

'The Letter that Came in Time', *Stories from Women Writers of Israel*, Star, New Delhi, 1995, pp. 103–32

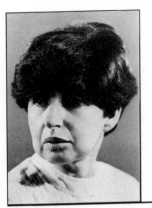

Amalia Kahana-Carmon

The Author

Amalia Kahana-Carmon was born in Kibbutz Ein Harod and raised in Tel Aviv. She studied philology and library sciences at the Hebrew University. Her first collection of stories, *Under One Roof*, appeared in 1966 to great critical acclaim. She has since published three novels, novellas and short stories. She is also an essayist and has lectured widely. She was writer-in-residence at Tel Aviv University and at the Oxford Centre for Post-Graduate Hebrew Studies. She has lived in England, Switzerland and the US and today lives in Tel Aviv. She received the prestigious Brenner Prize in 1985 and the Bialik Prize in 1994.

Books Published in Hebrew

Under One Roof (stories), Hakibbutz Hameuchad, 1966; reissued by Hakibbutz Hameuchad, 1971

And Moon in the Valley of Ayalon (novel), Hakibbutz Hameuchad, 1971

A Piece for the Stage in the Grand Manner (monodrama), Siman Kriah, 1975

*Magnetic Fields (stories), Hakibbutz Hameuchad, 1977

Up in Montifer (stories and novel), Hakibbutz Hameuchad, 1984

With Her on Her Way Home (novel), Siman Kriah/Hakibbutz Hameuchad, 1991

225

Here We'll Live (stories and novellas), Hakibbutz Hameuchad/Siman Kriah, 1996

Works in English Translation

'The House with the Distempered Sky-Blue Stairs', *Adam* (1971), Vol. 36, pp. 10–16

'1948 and After', *Modern Hebrew Literature* (1984), Vol. 10, Nos. 1/2, pp. 8–13

'First Axioms', *Modern Hebrew Literature* (1988), Vol. 13, Nos. 3/4, pp. 4–9

'The Man Who Lives on a Star', *The Best of Ariel: A Celebration of Contemporary Israeli Prose, Poetry and Art* (1993), Vol. 2, pp. 117–33

'I'm not paralyzed, you're not mute', *A Married Woman and Other Short Stories from Israel*, Star, New Delhi, 1995, pp. 35–47

'N'ima Sassoon Writes Poems', *Stories from Women Writers of Israel*, Star, New Delhi, 1995, pp. 31–53

Shulamit Lapid

The Author

S hulamit Lapid was born in 1934 in Tel Aviv. She studied Oriental Studies at the Hebrew University and was chairperson of the Israel Writers' Association. She is the author of short stories, novels, plays and children's books. Some of her books have been published in German, French and Italian translation.

Books Published in Hebrew

Pisces (stories), Eked, 1969

Shpitz (children), Massada, 1971

The Calm of Fools (stories), Massada, 1974

Fever (stories), Yahdav, 1979

Gai Oni (novel), Keter, 1982

As a Broken Vessel (novel), Keter, 1984

Window Poems, Keter, 1988

Girl of Dreams (children), Keter, 1989

Local Paper (novel), Keter, 1989

*What Makes Spiders Happy? (stories), Keter, 1990

New Women's Writing from Israel

Bait (novel), Keter, 1991

The Jewel (novel), Keter, 1992

Works in English Translation

'The Fiancé', Israel Magazine (1972), Vol. 4, No. 3, pp. 58–61

'Myths of the First Aliyah', Jewish Quarterly (1988), Vol. 35, No. 1, pp. 30–3

'The Bed', Lilith (Summer 1989), Vol. 14, No. 3, pp. 19–22

'Thread', PEN Israel 1993: A Collection of Recent Writing in Israel, PEN Israel, Tel Aviv, 1993, pp. 53–5

'Business', A Married Woman and Other Short Stories from Israel, Star, New Delhi, pp. 121–38

Savyon Liebrecht

The Author

Savyon Liebrecht was born in Germany in 1948 and came to Israel as a young child. She studied philosophy and literature at Tel Aviv University. She lives in Tel Aviv. She writes short stories and television scripts. Collections of her stories have been published in Chinese, German and Italian translation.

Books Published in Hebrew

*Apples froam the Desert (stories), Sifriat Poalim, 1986

Horses on the Highway, Sifriat Poalim, 1988

It's All Greek to Me, He Said to Her (stories), Keter, 1992

On Love Stories and Other Stories (stories), Keter, 1995

Works in English Translation

'Hayuta's Engagement Party', *Jewish Spectator* (Fall 1988), Vol. 53, No. 3, pp. 20–4

A Story with No Address, Delos, College Park MD, USA, 1989

'The Influence of the Holocaust on my Work', *Hebrew Literature in the Wake of the Holocaust*, Fairleigh Dickinson University Press, Cranbury NJ, 1993, pp. 125–30

Apples in Honey, Hadassah, New York, 1994

'A Room on the Roof', *Ribcage: Israeli Women's Fiction*, Hadassah, New York, 1994, pp. 231–56

'Apples from the Desert', *Ribcage: Israeli Women's Fiction*, Hadassah, New York, 1994, pp. 71–8

'Excision', *Jerusalem Post Magazine* (18 August 1995), pp. 20–1

'A Married Woman', *A Married Woman and Other Short Stories from Israel*, Star, New Delhi, 1995, pp. 67–73

'Compassion', *PEN Israel 1995: A Collection of Recent Writing in Israel*, PEN Israel, Tel Aviv, 1995, pp. 76–81

Mira Magen

The Author

Mira Magen was born in Kfar Saba, near Tel Aviv and is a practising Orthodox Jew. She studied psychology and sociology before turning to nursing, and today she is a nurse at Hadassa Hospital outside Jerusalem. Her first book, *Well Buttoned-Up*, was honoured by the Israeli Ministry for Science and the Arts as the outstanding first published work of literature of 1994. A collection of her stories will be published in German translation.

Books Published in Hebrew
*Well Buttoned-Up (stories), Keter, 1994

Works in English Translation
'The Red Dress', *Trafika* (Autumn 1995), Vol. 5, pp. 74–80

Nava Semel

The Author

Nava Semel was born in Tel Aviv in 1954. She holds an MA in art history from Tel Aviv University. She is the author of poetry, prose for children and adults, and drama. She is the recipient of several literary prizes, including the American National Jewish Book Award for children's literature.

Books Published in Hebrew

Poems on Pregnancy and Birth, Sifriat Poalim, 1983

*A Hat of Glass (stories), Sifriat Poalim, 1985

The Child Behind the Eyes (monodrama), Modan, 1987

Becoming Gershona (novel), Am Oved, 1988

The Flying Jews or Monsieur Maurice and Hadara (novel), Am Oved, 1990

Night Games (novel), Am Oved, 1993

Bride on Paper (novel), Am Oved, 1996

Works in English Translation

Becoming Gershona, Viking-Penguin, New York, 1991

'A Hat of Glass', *The Best of Ariel: A Celebration of Contemporary Israeli Prose, Poetry and Art* (1993), Vol. 1, pp. 249–63

Flying Lessons, Simon & Schuster, New York, 1995

Povestea Gershonei, Fiat Lux, Bucharest, 1995

Nurit Zarchi

The Author

Nurit Zarchi was born in Jerusalem in 1941. She is one of Israel's most prominent and prolific children's writers and a poet. She has been honoured with every major Israeli award for junior writing, including the prestigious Ze'ev Prize, and has also received an IBBY honour citation twice. *The Mask Maker* is her first work of adult fiction. She lives in Tel Aviv.

Books Published in Hebrew

Nurit Zarchi has published more than 40 children's books of prose and poetry

Wild Plantation (poems), Hakibbutz Hameuchad, 1974

The Unnecessary Thoughts of a Lady (essays), Hakibbutz Hameuchad, 1982

A Woman Brought Woman (poetry), Sifriat Poalim, 1983

The Fish (poetry), Zmora Bitan, 1984

The Garden of the Brain (poetry), Zmora Bitan, 1988

*The Mask Maker (stories), Zmora Bitan, 1993

Village of the Spirits (poetry), Bitan, 1994

Works in English Translation

'Every Night, From the Depths', *Ariel* (1979), No. 49, p. 47

'Ho', *Ariel* (1979), No. 49, p. 46

'The Deer with the Red Lips', *Ariel* (1979), No. 49, p. 49

'Furtively', *Burning Air and a Clear Mind*, Ohio University Press, Athens, 1981

'Wild Orchards', *Burning Air and a Clear Mind*, Ohio University Press, Athens, 1981

'Cliffedge', *Ariel* (1992), Vol. 88, p. 65

'From Three Corners of the Head', *Ariel* (1992), Vol. 88, p. 64

'Weasel', *Ariel* (1992), Vol. 88, pp. 63–4

'Madame Bovary from Neve Zedek', *PEN Israel 1993: A Collection of Recent Writing in Israel*, PEN Israel, Tel Aviv, 1993, pp. 36–9

'And She is Joseph', *Modern Hebrew Literature* (1994), Vol. 12, pp. 20–2